JOHANN ARNDT

A PROPHET OF LUTHERAN PIETISM

JOHANN ARNDT

A PROPHET *OF* LUTHERAN PIETISM

DANIEL VAN VOORHIS, PHD

1517 Publishing

Johann Arndt: A Prophet of Lutheran Pietism
© 2018 Daniel van Voorhis

Published by:
1517 Publishing
PO Box 54032
Irvine, CA 92619-4032

Printed in the United States of America

Publisher's Cataloging-In-Publication Data
(Prepared by The Donohue Group, Inc.)

Names: Van Voorhis, Daniel, 1979–.
Title: Johann Arndt : a prophet of Lutheran pietism / by Dr. Daniel van Voorhis.
Description: Irvine, CA : 1517 Publishing, [2018] | Includes bibliographical
    references.
Identifiers: ISBN 9781945978005 (hardcover) | ISBN 9781945978067 (soft cover) |
    ISBN 9781945500961 (e-book)
Subjects: LCSH: Arndt, Johann, 1555–1621. | Arndt, Johann,
    1555–1621—Correspondence. | Lutheran Church—Clergy—Biography. |
    Prophets—Biography.
Classification: LCC BX8080.A7 V36 2018 (print) | LCC BX8080.A7 (ebook) |
    DDC 284.1092—dc23

To Bruce

Contents

Preface and Acknowledgments

In 2002, I moved to Scotland to study the end of the world. I had been accepted to study at the University of St. Andrews and wanted to investigate the curious nature of a few Lutheran pastors who, in the midst of their work on behalf of the cause, were using alchemy, magic, and astrology to predict and then preach that the end was nigh. While it seemed fascinating to me, my soon-to-be supervisor, Dr. Bruce Gordon, suggested that the field had been well trod over the past few years and had best be left alone. On a drive to a department retreat in the Scottish Highlands, Bruce asked me why I was interested in the apocalyptic works of a few sixteenth-century pastors, and I ended up surmising that it had to do with these men being on the fringe of the movement. I liked outsiders, so we thought out loud of whatever early modern outsiders we could. At one point, Bruce suggested "a man associated with Spener." Spener was Philipp Jakob Spener, father of Lutheran Pietism in the seventeenth century, and "the man" was Johann Arndt. We couldn't remember him as we drove up the steep and windy Scottish roads, but he was on everyone's minds a little less than four hundred years ago. As I argue in this book, his significance is measured in quantitative data such as the fact that his book *True Christianity* was quickly translated into dozens of languages and soon became the Western European second bestseller (behind the Bible, of course) and the first in more than a century to dethrone *The Imitation of Christ*. It may be understandable why when we see the devotional attitude taken in both works. It certainly was not harmful that both books also have very basic titles that indicate that they are the way to "do it right." By merely having the book, you were making a statement about your piety. Eventually, the book that began as the foreword to Arndt's book overtook it. This book, the *Pia Desideria*, or "pious desires," was modeled on the same devotional themes as Arndt, and the author wrote freely of his admiration of Arndt's works. This book examines reasons we no longer read Arndt's work and why we might amid a newfound interest in Pietism. A central question of this book details Arndt's relationship to Pietism and questions earlier orthodoxies.

I was only married for one year when my wife, Beth Anne, agreed to uproot and move with me to the East Neuk of Scotland. As with many marriages, we have early (and especially) fond memories of those fights both silly and strangely serious. I have written elsewhere of this. As always, nothing I do would be possible without her. I love her and the two boys we made: Coert and Raymond. Boys, if you see this because you're checking to make sure all my books thank you, here it is. Don't feel the need to read further. I must thank the Hodels, Brothwells, and Winriches. They have been fonts of wisdom to me and my family as well as places of deep support and encouragement. I have been concurrently writing a piece for publication on the friendship of history, and as baffled as I've been with the research, I am reminded what a friend I have in Jeff Mallinson. Go read everything he writes and watch him on YouTube. A very special thanks to Scott Keith at the 1517 Legacy Project and to all associated acts with whom there have not been fistfights (I'm looking at you, Riley). Steve Byrnes is always a stud with publishing, but not this time. In fact, Steve dropped the ball. Or rather, assigned the ball to his wonderful assistant publisher, Sam Leanza (soon to be Ortiz!). Sam was my TA back when I was impersonating a professor; I knew this job would be great for her and that she would excel with her sharp mind and keen spirit. I do not think I had any aspiration for academics until I was challenged to learn Hebrew and Koine Greek, both with Dr. Mark Brighton. He was a consummate professor and later colleague. Rod Rosenbladt and Steve Mueller hammered the distinctions of Lutheran orthodoxy into my head so well that parts of this book were initially written from memory of old lectures alone. Dr. Bob Kemp taught me that historians can be helpful in conversation, that there can be personal redemption even after a fall, and that it was OK to be both a Christian and a democrat. Dr. Andrew Pettegree terrified me, and I believe reading that would bring him pleasure. We have since become friends, and I am in awe of what he can accomplish with such clarity. He introduced me to the big league of professional historians and painstaking details pertaining to the book trade. Dr. Bridget Heal was always willing to lend an ear over a coffee as I played with ideas. Dr. Peter Maxwell Stuart taught Latin. Dr. Rona Johnston Gordon must have labored hard to get me through all the German courses, and she became second only to her husband in helping me finish my degree. Those whom I toiled with, traveling between Scotland and the continent, became a kind of fun, dysfunctional family in the time I was there. Paul, Disco, and Scotty held it down at the Olde Castle Tavern, Dr. Heather Cova née Huntley was kind enough to let me follow her all the way from Irvine, California, as the older sister of one of my best friends. She was gracious in adopting a brother while doing graduate work in a foreign country. Drs. Michael Springer, Lauren Kim, Alexandra Kess Hall, and Matt Hall welcomed me in as a fresh, wide-eyed twenty-two-year-old. Drs. Sara Barker, Graeme Kemp, and Phillip John braved much of the same with me as long tenured office- and pubmates. There were great times, but very few days did I believe any of it would ever work. I had changed disciplines between undergraduate and graduate studies. Dr. Bruce Gordon came alongside me as a mentor and father figure. Bruce crystallizes thought better than anyone I have ever known. He is widely read and clever, both in person and on the page. But it is his humanity that has forever bound me to him. I was a young scholar but also a man, and he helped train both. His generosity both real and in spirit was some of the brightest light in otherwise dreary times. We finished after a flurry of housing and location changes and ended up either meeting in Irvine or Palm Springs, California. Most tangibly I can thank him for my PhD, but I can thank him in so many other ways. It is to him that I dedicate this book.

Introduction

On May 15, 1621, Johann Arndt was buried at the *Pfarrkirche* in Celle. He had been an ordained Lutheran pastor for thirty-nine years and was sixty-six years old. Fifty-two of those years were unremarkable; in the last fourteen years of his life, however, he had laid the groundwork for becoming the most significant devotional author of the seventeenth century. Copies of his *Vier Bücher von Wahren Christentum* (*True Christianity*) were ubiquitous in the following centuries, whether in the homes of pious Christians or in universities. For the next three hundred and fifty years, his image and his famous book were critiqued, extolled, and, at times, forgotten.

Controversy surrounding Arndt did not die with him in 1621, as books were being written about *True Christianity* at a furious pace. He was regarded as either the most significant Reformer since Luther or an uneducated and dangerous element within the Lutheran church. Based on the sudden drop off of works regarding Arndt in the 1630s, it appeared that his place and his role in the church would remain unresolved. While the occasional biography or analysis of his work appeared in the ensuing centuries, there has been in the last thirty years a resurgence in Arndt research. At the 1988 *Symposion des Vereins für Reformationsgeschichte*, a session was held in which two papers were presented concerning the place of Arndt in the Lutheran church. The lack of any consensus about Arndt's place in post-Reformation Lutheranism was evident in the opposing views of the Reformer offered by Hans Schneider and Wolfgang Sommer, to which we will return. This book explores the complexity of Johann Arndt as a churchman and writer through an examination of his correspondence. The work is based on fifty-two surviving letters, which have been brought together here for the first time. Research in various

German libraries has enabled me to locate letters that were largely
unused by previous scholars. Although this collection of Arndt's letters pales in comparison to other sixteenth-century contemporaries
such as Melanchthon, Calvin, and Bullinger, it provides access to his
voice and a view of his character previously unknown. What emerges
most strongly is Arndt's profound and unshaken belief that he was a
prophet of the church to his age. Repeatedly, he told his correspondents that the Lutheran church desperately required a renewed spirituality if it was to face what he believed to be a distinct crisis of piety.
Arndt, however, was anything but one-dimensional, and what the
letters reveal is that he could speak in different tones. To his various
correspondents with whom he communicated, he revealed different
aspects of himself and his thoughts.

It is important to recognize that Arndt was not a systematic
thinker; although he studied theology, as well as medicine, he was
primarily a pastor who looked to writing as a means of spreading
his message of "true" Christianity. He could be very loose with his
language, and he had little regard for what he referred to as "scholasticism" or "disputational theology," which meant the Lutheran theology of the universities. Much of what has been written and thought
about Johann Arndt has been based on his famous *True Christianity*
(1606–1610). While this book was rightly seen as Arndt's master-
piece, as we shall see, the argument of this book is that it only offers
a partial view of the man. The letters enable us to see him as he
lived, a preacher and writer who was frequently involved in conflict
and forced to respond to controversy. In short, Johann Arndt needs
to be studied in context.

The correspondence of Johann Arndt, this book argues, reveals
the diversity of his character and activities. But to appreciate its full
historical importance, we must consider briefly the nature and character of letter writing in sixteenth-century Europe. In interpreting
surviving correspondence, the historian must be careful to avoid
the pitfalls of naïveté and extreme skepticism. Certainly, it cannot
be assumed that the informal (or formal) letter acts as a key that
unlocks the "true" individual. It does not stand in opposition to the
carefully constructed author of a printed treatise or text. That is a
false distinction. The letter *is* a text that must be read in light of its
context, the relationship between the author and the recipient, and

its content. Susan Fitzmaurice has identified how certain types of letters were regarded as revealing of human character, a view illustrated in the remark by Thomas Sprat that "in (familiar) letters the souls of men should appear undressed."[1] Amanda Gilroy and W. M. Verhoeven, however, have recently suggested that this idea is "the most historically powerful fiction of the letter [that is to suggest that the letter is] the trope of authenticity and intimacy."[2]

This discussion about the extent to which an early modern person reveals himself in correspondence lies at the heart of this book. My approach has been shaped by testing Arndt's letters against the events and circumstances of his life, as well as by examining them in light of his other writings. In applying such critical analysis, I have remained cautious not to create an interpretive grid by which the individual letters themselves are subjected to uniform treatment. I approached each letter individually, and in this I have been influenced by Fitzmaurice's guide to understanding the early modern letter in which she has suggested an "inferential reading": "Meanings that are expressly intended by the author, as well as the meanings that a writer might not intend, but which a reader might infer in any case, but which a reader might infer in any case. In short, inferential meanings are what is meant, never mind what is said."[3]

Fitzmaurice's approach is suggestive and enables us to consider the ways in which Arndt shaped his language to present himself in different ways depending on context and recipient. It also opens some space for us to consider aspects of his character of which he was not conscious. But this must be done carefully, for it carries the danger of unwarranted speculation. In this book, Arndt's letters will be examined inferentially, but only insofar as the context and the relationship between the author and recipient can be known. In many instances, these letters are "halved conversations," and the context of the letter and the individual to whom Arndt is writing make such inferential reading impossible.

How did Arndt's correspondence stand in relation to the dominant style of letter writing in the late sixteenth century? To consider this question, we need to turn to the *ars dictaminis*, developed in Italy at the end of the eleventh century, which served as the basis of the *Dictatores* manuals on epistolary form.[4]

While the *ars dictaminis* remained the preferred medieval form for the growing number of manuals on epistolary style, it suffered from a lack of definition and a number of significant critics. A primary source for this new style was Cicero's *De Inventione*, in which he compared a style of letter suited to plebeians to his own rich style.[5] The *ars dictaminis* was distinguished from classical models by its emphasis on hierarchical relations, in contrast to Cicero, who spoke of letter writing between equals.[6] Because the *ars dictaminis* lacked any fixed principles, it was subject to change and criticism. Petrarch differed from Cicero in that he accepted the notion that a familiar letter could be conversational in tone and change according to the relationship between the author and recipient.[7]

The most influential text on letter writing in the sixteenth century was Erasmus's *De conscribendis epistolis*, which has been described as "the most thorough treatment of the subject hitherto, and it exerted an enormous influence on contemporary and consequent theoreticians."[8] In breaking from the tradition of the *ars dictaminis* to focus on style and form (sometimes) regardless of the recipient, Erasmus wrote the following: "In all of this we must remember there is an important difference between a book and a letter, in that the latter must be adapted as far as possible to the immediate occasion, and to contemporary topics and individuals."[9] Erasmus further insisted that "a letter should adapt itself to every kind of subject and circumstance . . . It will not speak of the same occasions or to all persons alike."[10]

While we lack any evidence that Arndt read the *conscribendis*, there are elements in his correspondence that point directly to the influence of Erasmus's ideas. Arndt had no interest in the Ciceronian style, and his approach to writing letters very much followed Erasmus's advice that they should suit the particular circumstances of the moment. The distinction between book and letter made by Erasmus goes to the heart of the question of how Arndt could appear to say quite different things in different circumstances. It is not only useful to see the influence of Erasmus's approach on Arndt; I believe it is also helpful for the interpreter of early modern letters. While the modern research cited previously is helpful in delineating the two extremes one must avoid, it seems that understanding the Erasmian model for letter writing serves as the best lens for examining Arndt's letters.

The largely literary preoccupations of current research on correspondence do not provide an adequate basis for the interpretation of Johann Arndt.[11] The reason for this, as my research will show, is that his letters cannot be reduced to any particular formula. Arndt, as seen in his published works, wrote with a simple, often repetitive style. He wrote to be clearly understood by the unlearned. And while his correspondents were usually university-educated men, the late medieval and early modern tradition of the *ars dictaminis* was of no concern to Arndt. More significant was the humanist tradition forged by Erasmus in the sixteenth century, but this was largely envisaged for Latin letters, for the vernacular style remained fluid and unfixed. This is what we find in Arndt: elements of established traditions combined with his own distinctive interests and character. A careful reading of the letters enables us to learn much about him both by what is said and by what is left unsaid. The literary approach to the texts has taught us to be sensitive to language and concealed meanings, and we shall find these in Arndt. But the letters must also be read historically for their rich information on events and persons. They are difficult sources, written by a difficult man, and they are anything but formulaic.

Chapter one will examine the small amount of biographical information that is known about Arndt. This will enable us to place Arndt's vision for the church within specific historical contexts. Second, a brief analysis of his enormously popular *True Christianity* will be presented. This was by far his best-known work, and it did the most to establish his public persona across Europe. He wrote it while serving as a pastor, and it contained his proposed remedy for the spiritual malaises of the church as he saw them.

Chapter two will present Arndt's correspondence in the context of Lutheran orthodoxy. While the true meaning of orthodoxy in the Lutheran church can be debated, after the Book of Concord was written and accepted, it became the benchmark for proper Lutheran doctrinal formation. The Book of Concord, especially the *Epitome* of the Formula of Concord, which dealt with the various theological controversies after the death of Martin Luther, will be explicated. The letters reveal Arndt as a concerned and informed Lutheran who wished his writings to be understood in light of the standard of Lutheran orthodoxy.

Chapter three will examine the eclectic and controversial aspects of Arndt's life. His correspondence appears to bear out many of the claims that his detractors held against him. From his appraisal of various medieval and dissenting authors to his own reprinting of the *Theologia Deutsch*, Arndt was an eclectic writer who was sometimes unaware of larger theological issues pertaining to his intended goal of spiritual reform. It is important, and the point will be made throughout this work, that these two seemingly disjointed aspects of Arndt (the orthodox and eclectic) do not amount to an intentionally dissembling character. Whether it was on account of his education or his perception that Lutheran and non-Lutheran sources could feed the regeneration of the church, Arndt created an imaginatively chaotic vision full of contradictions that has been interpreted by his detractors as deceitful.

Chapter four examines Arndt as a prophet. We shall see that his understanding of the prophetic office developed from both the Lutheran and the more spiritualist traditions of the sixteenth century. It was as a prophet that Arndt believed that various elements of his life were unified. Theological and political differences were to be subordinated to the prophetic call for repentance and spiritual renewal. We shall explore the different ways in which he spoke about his prophetic calling to orthodox theologians, friends, and magistrates.

The Arndt who emerges from a contextual examination cannot be easily labeled. He had little doubt about his importance to his age and church. His calling was special, and he believed himself to be unique and did at times compare himself with Moses, David, Paul, Luther, and even Christ. He believed the truth was to be found in the theology of the Lutheran church, but as a prophet, led by the spirit, he felt justified in expressing himself in ways that many of his contemporaries felt unacceptable. Arndt's thought was shaped not only by his studies and contacts with theologians but also by the vicissitudes of his life. The controversies, deprivation, and sadness of his life are deeply reflected in the language with which he expressed his thought.

The Patchy History of Arndt Research

Martin Brecht has observed that Johann Arndt was the "best selling devotional author of the seventeenth century," and the evidence amassed appears to substantiate this statement. Until the Enlightenment in the eighteenth century, the works of Johann Arndt continued to be printed, sold, and read across Europe. Not only were his works read, but also writers continued to debate the nature of his work long after he was put in his grave. Arndt was both praised and vilified.

In the 1620s, there were more books written about Arndt than in any subsequent decade. The number of books written in the 1620s (sixteen) matched the output of works written about Arndt for the rest of the century combined.[12] The most significant work, in terms of the response it created, was Lucas Osiander the Younger's *Theologisches Bedencken Und Christliche Trewhertzige Erinnerung welcher gestalt Johann Arndten genandtes Wahres Christenthum anzusehen und zuachten sey.*[13] Osiander had a reputation as an irascible author who wrote polemical works against Calvinists, Jesuits, Anabaptists, and Schwenckfeldians. It was proposed by some that he "saw the Holy Ghost in the form of a raven, instead of a dove."[14] When Osiander wrote his *Theologisches Bedencken*, he accused Arndt of the errors of the other groups he had criticized. Osiander associated Arndt with Thomas Müntzer, Schwenckfeld, the errors of Flacius, and Enthusiasts, all of whom, in his opinion, believed that God and the true word were to be found by turning inwardly.[15] What was most significant about Osiander's criticism was the names with which he linked Arndt, all of which were intended to demonstrate his heterodoxy. One did not need to be theologically trained to know that Müntzer and Schwenckfeld indicated a different spirit than Luther. Osiander's work inspired ten responses attempting to vindicate Arndt.[16] The most significant of these works were composed by August Varenius, Paulus Egardus, Melchior Breller, and Georg Rostius.

Varenius (1595–1634) was the court preacher for Duke August the Younger of Braunschweig-Wolfenbüttel. He wrote his *Christliche Schrifftmässige wolgegründete Rettunge der Vier Bücher vom wahren Christenthumb* at the behest of the duke in direct response to Osiander's critique of Arndt.[17] That the duke would attempt to protect Arndt from criticism will become more significant as their relationship is examined through the letters Arndt wrote to him near the end of his life. Philipp Jakob Spener would later use Varenius's work in his annotated version of *True Christianity*. Egardus (–1655) wrote a similar defense of Arndt, the *Ehrenrettung Johannis Arndten*.[18] Egardus criticized Osiander for attacking Arndt after he had died and suggested that this criticism was a sign that Arndt wrote from the Holy Spirit.[19] Egardus's work would also be regarded highly by Spener, as he collected the works of Egardus into a three-volume collection between 1679 and 1683.[20] Breller (–1627) was the court physician for Duke August and wrote his *Warhafftiger Glaubwirdiger und gründlicher Bericht von den vier Büchern vom Wahren Christenthumb Herrn Johannis Arndten* in 1625.[21] While Breller's work was important in that it collected a number of Arndt's letters in his defense, Breller was the least theologically qualified to write a work on behalf of Arndt, as he was not trained in theology and was criticized for his affinity for Paracelsus. Georg Rostius (1582–1629) wrote the final printed work of the decade, the *Examin Brevis considerationis Varenii*.[22] Rostius's work was a response to both Varenius's earlier work and a second work by Varenius, which had criticized Rostius's interpretation of Arndt. Rostius was critical of Arndt's spiritualist and Weigelian themes but ultimately believed Arndt to have made these "simple errors" due to his lack of education.[23]

Virtually no works were written about Arndt for forty years, as the Thirty Years' War swept across Germany. While there is evidence that Arndt's works were of great devotional importance for the laity during this time, he would not be taken up by theological authors until Philipp Jakob Spener made wide use of his books and he found popularity among the ascendant Pietist movement.

Arndt and Pietism

In 1674, Spener reprinted a new edition of *True Christianity* with annotations refuting the charges of Osiander and citing passages in the work with parallel statements by Luther.[24] For Spener, Arndt was not merely a spiritual author but a man of great historical importance for the church: "At the time of Hus, in the year 1415, the tree of life took root, at the time of Luther in the year 1517, the tree started to flower; in the year 1618 the harvesters went out to gather in its fruits."[25] Spener's early leadership of the Pietist movement coupled with his view of Arndt as a second Luther made Arndt a most significant author for a movement that began more than half a century after his death. Johannes Wallmann has written that Spener's edition was by far the most read version of *True Christianity* through the eighteenth century, having been published in more than thirty different places.[26] The following year, Spener printed a collection of Arndt's sermons. Spener's introduction would later be expanded into his *Pia Desideria*. According to Wilhelm Koepp, three generations after Arndt had died, he was "beloved by all, every year there was a new biography or a new forward . . . each year there were at least three new editions printed."[27] The affinity that the Pietists had for Arndt has been influential up to the present day. For the next few centuries, Arndt was primarily studied under the rubric of the history of Pietism.

Ernst Valentine Löscher (1673–1749) was a Lutheran during the era of Pietism but did not accept the association of Arndt with the Pietist movement. Löscher has been credited with creating the first religious periodical, the "Unschuldige Nachrichten" (Innocent News), which was created to oppose the writings of the Pietists.[28] Löscher, writing under the assumed name of Timothy Verinus, was among the first to criticize the Pietist movement as something alien to Lutheranism. In one column, he listed the theological loci that he believed to define the Pietists. Among them were the following:

> "the unfounded and general dominion of strange spirits and impulses in religious things," "unlimited love for secret, peculiar, and lofty things. This usually disintegrates into mysticism . . ." "[That] there is only one religion, namely piety; the rest are human trifles," "they rail against the names orthodox and orthodoxy . . . they complain that orthodoxy is too highly regarded," "[that] there are really no external means of grace at all," "Pure doctrine . . . works nothing in spiritual men," "they contrast the external things in the worship service with the inner things in such a way that external things are of no value."[29]

This definition would fit Osiander's earlier critique of Arndt and perhaps justify casting Arndt outside the realm of Lutheran orthodoxy. However, Löscher added a caveat in his dismissal of the Pietists: "For my part, I love the sainted Johann Arndt from my heart as a faithful preacher of righteousness and I believe that his heart was sincere toward God . . . but he had also loved the mystical books [and] took many weaknesses from them, against which he did not guard diligently enough . . . he zealously defended many erroneous and harmful tenants."[30] This recognition of Arndt as not a Pietist and as a well-meaning (but sometimes misguided) Lutheran would become another standard interpretation of Arndt throughout the ensuing centuries.

These opposing viewpoints of Osiander and Löscher in the seventeenth and early eighteenth century saw the continuation of Arndt research as fragmented, with (sometimes) radically opposing viewpoints of Arndt's place within the Lutheran church.

Among the likes of Osiander, Löscher, and Spener, many in the seventeenth century attempted to answer the question of whether Arndt was a follower of the Lutheran confessions, a source of renewal for the church, or an unstable theological influence on the church. The string of responses and counterresponses throughout the seventeenth century produced a polarized image of Arndt that was informed almost exclusively by confessional allegiance. Outside of these works, there were few works of lasting significance. Many were written by devotees of Arndt's spiritualism who attempted to see him in light of the Pietist movement and primarily wrote introductions to the new collections of Arndt's works, hagiographical biographies, and new forewords to *True Christianity*.[31]

Arndt in the Eighteenth Century

In the eighteenth century, there were very few works written on Arndt compared to other centuries. The two types of works that those interested in Arndt worked on were collections of his works and biographies. While the number of books printed pertaining to Arndt was few, there was evidence that he was still widely read.

Johann Andreas Gleich compiled a small booklet of a few of Arndt's letters that revealed him to be concerned with presenting himself as an orthodox Lutheran. This *Trifolium Arndtianum*, printed in 1724, marked the beginning of the collection of Arndt's disparate works and known letters.[32] Gottfried Balthasar Scharff published his *Supplementum historiae litisque Arndianae aliquot inclutorum superioris saeculi theologorum Epistolis constans* in 1727 and added

a few new letters written to Johann Gerhard that established Arndt
as privately upset that he had been maligned and not read in light of
the Lutheran confessions.[33] The largest collection of Arndt's works
appeared in 1736, edited by Johann Jacob Rambach, a Lutheran
pastor and spiritual author. *Johann Arnds Geistreicher Schriften und
Werke I, II, III* contains all Arndt's major works, a large collection of
his correspondence, his two last testaments, and his foreword written for other works.[34] Rambach, who taught at Halle (the eighteenth-
century center of Pietism), similarly studied medicine and became
a professor of theology and eventual church superintendent. His
devotional works reveal him to have been very similar to Arndt in
respect to their affective and internal spirituality. Rambach's collection included hagiography (many *Wundergeschichten* are included)
and a running commentary in his own foreword to Arndt's works.
This work would be the last concerning Arndt printed for the rest of
the century (sixty years) and would coincide with the Enlightenment
and a general distaste for Arndt's supernatural religion within the
theological faculties at German universities. This was not to suggest that Arndt was not read: his works continued to be published
and translated and at least three hundred republications and fourteen translations of *True Christianity* appeared.[35] In 1751, German
immigrants in America requested copies of *True Christianity*, and
a young printer, Benjamin Franklin, ordered copies to be printed,
making Arndt's work the first German book printed in the New
World.[36] Thus while little was being written about Arndt, his popularity among the laity in the eighteenth century is certain.

Arndt in the Nineteenth Century

In the nineteenth century, histories of Pietism became the primary outlet for writing on Arndt. Heinrich Schmid's *Die Geschichte
des Pietismus* (1863) is one significant example. Schmid (1811–1865)
was a Lutheran dogmatician and professor at Erlangen who wrote
specifically on the doctrinal foundation of Lutheran orthodoxy.[37]
He wrote that Pietism was harmful because it split the institutional
church from the individual.[38] He further claimed that Pietism was
not theologically rigid enough and did not distinguish between
the Reformed and Lutheran theologies.[39] Schmid believed that the

Pietists shifted the accent of Lutheran theology from the doctrine of justification to sanctification.[40] Martin Schmidt has suggested that Schmid's work was the closest nineteenth-century counterpart to Löscher.[41] However, Schmid made an important distinction that has proven to be both popular and helpful: he suggested the social phenomenon of the conventicles as the essence of Pietism.[42] Thus while he might have blamed Arndt for "pietistic" thought, the Pietist movement was one with circumscribed dates that placed Arndt outside of the discussion.

Albrecht Ritschl's three-volume *Geschichte des Pietismus* (1880–1886) was a crucial landmark in Arndt scholarship. Much of Ritschl's professional work as a professor at Bonn and Göttingen was opposed to his Pietist contemporaries.[43] Ritschl's theology stressed the action of God in the community of believers as opposed to in the individual.[44] Ritschl's emphasis on community was central to his understanding of Luther and Protestantism. He believed Pietism to be dangerous, as it stressed individual conversion outside of the church without the means of grace. Ritschl opposed the Pietists, as they stressed personal holiness outside of the community of believers. In this sense, Eric Lund was correct in asserting that Ritschl saw Arndt as a "subversive innovator" in the Lutheran church.[45] Ritschl believed that the authentic Lutheran approach to life began to disintegrate with the spread of Arndt's *True Christianity*.[46] Second, Ritschl suggested that Arndt's ethical orientation, and his fractured and incomplete theology, was worse than the theology of the Middle Ages and asceticism.[47] Ritschl devoted a lot of space to Arndt in his *Geschichte* precisely because he saw him as not only a founding father of the movement but also someone who had distorted Luther's message.

Besides the histories of Pietism, Arndt was also the subject of a few simple biographies that presented him as a hero of the faith. John G. Morris and his *Life of John Arndt* (1853) presented the biographical information from Rambach in English. Its significance was primarily as the first work written on Arndt in English as no new biographical information was added.[48] Karl August Wildenhahn wrote *John Arndt: a Historical Life Picture* (1882), a fictionalized account of Arndt's struggles in Braunschweig, which presented a few historical facts but primarily was written to present Arndt as a model of faith and service to the church in light of persecution.[49] While neither of these works was of much significance for a better understanding of Arndt, they showed the growing popular interest of Arndt in the English-speaking world.

Arndt in the Twentieth Century

In 1912, Wilhelm Koepp published *Johann Arndt eine Untersuchung ueber die Mystik im Luthertum*.[50] Koepp's work marked the beginning of modern research on Arndt. Koepp's bibliography of Arndt's works and appendix has become the standard for the past century of Arndt scholars. The scope of his monograph stretched from medieval mysticism through the age of Pietism and Spener. Yet Koepp was clear in asserting that Arndt introduced mysticism into Lutheranism by selecting passages and ideas to insert into his own works. Koepp suggested that Arndt attempted to ground his thought within Lutheranism, yet ultimately mystical theology dominated his books.[51] Koepp wrote that Arndt liberally used the mystics and medieval sources, and this contributed to his "*Sonderreligion*," a peculiar religion that was not quite Lutheran. This was not like the condemnations of those previously mentioned who saw Arndt as a dangerous element in the Lutheran church, but rather depicted Arndt as a preacher whose use of foreign texts put him on the fringe or beyond the pale of orthodoxy. According to Koepp, Arndt energetically tried to fuse orthodoxy and mysticism.[52] While Koepp's work and lengthy appendices led to a renewed interest in Arndt in the following decades, the full flowering of Arndt studies began in the 1960s.

In the 1960s, the question of whether Arndt was a Lutheran or a Pietist was revived in the works of Hans-Joachim Schwager and F. Ernst Stoeffler. Schwager's work was a doctrinal dissertation written in 1961, in which he claimed that Arndt was a true heir of Luther.[53] F. Ernst Stoeffler in his *Rise of Evangelical Pietism* has claimed, "The father of Lutheran Pietism is not Spener, but Johann Arndt."[54] These two conclusions once again raised questions regarding the relationship between Luther, Pietism, and orthodoxy.

1979 was a benchmark year in Arndt studies. *True Christianity* was published and translated into English for the first time in more than one hundred years in the "Classics of Western Spirituality" series, and Heiko Oberman wrote the preface to the new translation. Eric Lund also wrote *Johann Arndt and the Development of a Lutheran Spiritual Tradition*. While the English translation and Oberman's preface brought *True Christianity* back into the English-speaking world, it was Lund's dissertation that attempted to break Arndt out of the molds of being either a Pietist or a mystic. Lund concurred with Schwager in the following assertion: "There is no reason to doubt that Arndt was sincere when he declared his support of Lutheran teachings . . . [he] was not a great systematic thinker, but as a practical minded synthesizer, he addressed the needs and concerns of simple lay people more effectively than most Lutheran theologians."[55] Lund studied Arndt in his context, as a spiritual author and as a devoted Lutheran. While it was not an apology for Arndt's work, it was a scholarly, nontheologically charged attempt to understand Arndt's thought, even as it was often times fractured. Lund's work, which has been quoted in nearly every work written on Arndt since, came at the beginning of the renaissance in Arndt research. Since 1979, eighty monographs and articles have appeared. Prior to 1979, fewer than fifty works had been written on Arndt dating back to 1900. Lund, along with Hans Schneider, Wolfgang Sommer, Christian Braw, and Johannes Wallmann, has been at the forefront of modern Arndt research.

In the 1980s, Johannes Wallmann provided a corrective to earlier models labeling Arndt as a Pietist in his essay, "Johann Arndt und die protestantische Frömmigkeit."[56] Wallmann seemed to avoid labeling Arndt with anachronistic terms. The title of his work, preferring the term *Frömmigkeit* to *Mystik* or *Pietismus*, revealed a careful distinction. The latter two terms have tended to presuppose a particular dating of a movement, while the former implies a form of devoutness without placing Arndt into an epoch or single strain of thought. Wallmann also provided a distinction between Pietism in the broad sense and in the narrow sense: in the former, Arndt could be considered a Pietist; however, the latter required the sociological phenomenon of conventicles.[57]

A significant moment came at the previously mentioned symposium in 1988 when, for the first time, leading theologians and historians came together to discuss Arndt. It was at this meeting that Schneider and Sommer debated whether Arndt was a Lutheran. Schneider argued that gaps in our knowledge of Arndt's life, such as his university studies, make it impossible to answer the question conclusively; however, he remarked that Arndt's interest in Paracelsian, Theosophic, and spiritualist thought "does not engender confidence in Arndt's Lutheranism."[58]

In response to Schneider's paper, Wolfgang Sommer proposed an alternative view in which he agreed that the central question in Arndt research concerned the Reformer's relationship to the Lutheran confessions.[59] However, Sommer wrote that Arndt should not be seen only in his capacity as a devotional author but also in his ecclesiastical position as a preacher and church superintendent.[60] What Sommer proposed was an "Arndtian *Frömmigkeit*," a piety well within the boundaries of the church.[61] Further, Sommer suggested that at the height of confessionalization, Arndt was a confessional Lutheran.[62] The session included a number of leading historians such as Heinz Schilling, Hans Guggisberg, Martin Brecht, and Louise Schorn-Schütte, who were more inclined toward Schneider's view than Sommer's. In 1993, Martin Brecht offered a shrewd assessment of the state of Arndt research: "The image of Arndt is still contested up to the present day, some see him as a representative of spiritualism and mysticism, others assess him as the renovator and reformer of piety in Lutheranism or the father of Pietism."[63]

Recent Studies

Recent work on Arndt has attempted to take the subject in new directions by focusing on particular aspects of his writing. The first significant work was Christian Braw's study of Arndt's prayers as a means of understanding his spirituality.[64] Braw detected those elements of the medieval and Weigelian aspects for which the reformer had been criticized during his life and by subsequent writers but also detected the ways in which Arndt altered these portions to fit with Luther's confessional spirituality.[65]

Following Braw's study came Werner Anetsberger's study of Arndt's sermons.[66] Anetsberger sought to demonstrate that the hundreds of surviving sermons reveal a true portrait of the man. What was innovative about these works was their approach to understanding Arndt. Anetsberger also proposed that these wildly divergent views of Arndt need to be reevaluated and synthesized.[67] They indicated a new way to look at the man and to a shift away from a single focus on *True Christianity* to highlight his public and private life as a pastor.[68]

The approach of this book follows the work of Anetsberger and Braw in examining the contextual world of a thorough examination of a particular collection of Arndt's works. In asking the question, Who was Johann Arndt?, the argument here is that we need to move beyond debating whether he was a Lutheran. Likewise, it is not my primary interest to examine whether Arndt was the forerunner of Pietism; rather, the central question of this book is how we can understand Johann Arndt on his own terms.

CHAPTER 1

Johann Arndt

Hero or Heretic?

The Life of Johann Arndt

One of the goals of this work is to examine Johann Arndt as he saw himself. As mentioned in the introduction, there have been controversies surrounding Arndt for more than four hundred years, and in this chapter we shall examine the key elements of Arndt's life and the debates over his place in late sixteenth-century German Protestant history. The difficulty in this is that we know relatively little about him. Much of the biographical material has been stitched together from fragments and sources that were written with the clear intention of hailing Arndt either as a hero or as a heretic. One of the difficulties appears to be that Arndt kept no record of his own life, and no inventory was collected of his library and correspondence. For this reason, there have been no standard biographical accounts of Arndt's life.[1] Even recent studies have found much of Arndt's life before the publication of *True Christianity* shrouded in mystery and conjecture.[2] To introduce the public Arndt (as opposed to the "private" Arndt of his correspondence), a thematic biography will be presented. The three major motifs in Arndt's life were those of confessional Lutheranism, devotional spirituality, and controversy. Second, we shall conduct a brief analysis of *True Christianity*. As Arndt's circle of contacts was small and local and he rarely traveled, most people would have known of him through his *True Christianity*, which was the one work widely available across the continent. This chapter will tie together much of the substance of the "public" Arndt in service of the following chapters that examine his private correspondence.

Arndt, like most pastors of his age, came from a clerical family. His father, Jakob, was ordained by Johannes Bugenhagen in Wittenberg in 1553. Arndt's mother, Anna Söchtings, had three children, Johann and two younger siblings.[3] Jakob died in 1565 while serving at a parish in Ballenstedt. At the time of his death, he was honored by his congregation as a faithful minister of the gospel.[4] There is no extant information as to what Arndt did until age nineteen, when he went to the newly chartered university at Helmstadt. The university at Helmstadt was a new Lutheran university founded by the Lutheran Duke of Braunschweig-Wolfenbüttel to combat the rise of Calvinism in his duchy. Furthermore, the university curriculum was set up with assistance from Martin Chemnitz and David Chytraeus, two confessional Lutherans responsible for the Book of Concord. Arndt matriculated in 1575 as a student in the philosophical faculty. The subjects for a first-year student included Christian doctrine, Latin and Greek grammar, dialectics, rhetoric, geometry, astronomy, history, and physics.[5] An unsubstantiated story later circulated that during this time, Arndt fell ill and prayed to God for healing; he vowed that if he recovered, he would devote his life to the study of theology.[6]

After a period of two years in Helmstadt, Arndt moved to Strasbourg, where he began his studies in 1577 at the height of the Pappus-Sturm debates.[7] This controversy involved Johannes Sturm, who sought a union of Protestants at Strasbourg but a union not based on the Formula of Concord (particularly on account of the doctrine of the Eucharist). Johann Pappus rejected any overture not based on the Formula due to his belief in the centrality of the Christological doctrine of ubiquity for a proper understanding of the redemptive work of Christ. Ultimately, Pappus's faction won the day as Sturm retired and the university accepted the Formula of Concord. While Arndt was not likely to have been attracted to Sturm's attempt to reconcile Lutheranism and Calvinism (as his work *Ikonographia* would later attest) he was also likely to be critical of Pappus's disputational method. Arndt would be heavily critical in his correspondence of this style of theological debate.

Little is known of Arndt's time at Strasbourg. Schneider has suggested that Arndt may have studied under Johannes Marbach, based on his later knowledge of the Formula of Concord.[8] Schneider's unmatched research into Arndt's studies has uncovered a handwritten note, which claims that Arndt moved to Basel between 1579 and 1582 and studied there under Simon Sulzer and Theodore Zwinger.[9] These two mentors shaped Arndt's later pursuits in both medicine and theology. Sulzer studied at Strasbourg and Basel, was a friend of Jakob Andreae, and had an affinity for the Book of Concord as it was being drafted and published for subscription.[10] While it can be assumed that Arndt studied under Sulzer, no further concrete evidence exists to substantiate this suggestion. It is known, however, that Arndt admired Theodore Zwinger and wrote him a letter in 1579. The letter is of no major significance as Arndt simply introduced himself and wrote of his keen interest in alchemical studies.[11] What was of minor significance, however, is that Arndt signed this letter "Iohannes Aquila/ stud. Med. Saxo."[12] This will be noteworthy later, as some believed him to be a theological amateur. Thus as late as 1579, Arndt continued to consider himself a medical student. Arndt left Basel in 1582 and married Anna Wagner; the couple never had children.[13] Besides being a student of medicine, Arndt had clearly been a student of theology, as in 1583, he was ordained as a pastor in Badeborn (Anhalt).

The charged atmosphere in Badeborn formed the context for Arndt's first confessional test. Duke Johann Georg of Anhalt introduced certain Reformed practices when he forbade the practice of exorcism at baptism, a mark of lay Lutheran identity. During this period of advance for the second Reformation, the situation in Anhalt became more tense as Duke Georg outlawed traditional Lutheran church ornaments. It was against this background that Arndt began work on his first theological tract, *Ikonographia*.[14] Here, against the iconoclasts, Arndt singled out John Calvin and Theodore Beza as the chief propagators of this dangerous doctrine.[15] He categorically rejected Reformed Protestantism and refused to remove the rite of exorcism, with the result that he was barred from his pulpit and forced to move to Quedlinburg in 1590.[16] Quedlinburg served as a temporary respite for the young pastor as he began to hone his own blend of confessional and devotional Lutheran Christianity.

The confessional elements of Lutheranism played a much bigger role in Arndt's life than have been recognized. Nevertheless, it was his constant emphasis on the devotional side of Christianity that was most prominent in his works. The uneasy balance between Arndt's confessional and devotional emphases can be seen in his political and personal battles, and they emerged from the background of his particular training and vocation. Losing his father at an early age and being raised on support from local magistrates and the church likely fostered a sense of the fragility of earthly life as well as a fondness for the church. Furthermore, as Arndt remembered his father as a deeply devotional student of the Bible, it is not surprising that the young man followed in his footsteps. This is not to discount the intellectual and spiritual motivation behind Arndt's devotional fervor, yet it offers some clues as to the origins of the young man's developing spirituality. Much of his devotional theology was expanded in Quedlinburg in the 1590s. Arndt was given relative freedom to publish his *Ikonographia* and produce a new tract entitled *De Antiqua Philosophia*.[17] *De Antiqua* proposed a restructuring of education to stress the practical application of theoretical knowledge. While this work has not survived, fragments give us some insight into the early practical concerns of the pastor.[18] During this period, Arndt's reputation began to grow as many of his parishioners from Anhalt preferred to make the three-hour trip into Quedlinburg to hear Arndt, whom they considered to represent confessional Lutheranism, rather than stay in Anhalt with its Calvinist ministers, who were introduced following the conversion of Duke Georg.[19] In 1595, with the outbreak of the German war against the Turks, Arndt preached a series of sermons on the ten Egyptian plagues, which were published as *Predigten von den zehen ägyptischen Plagen*.[20] In this work, Arndt followed the path set by his earlier confessional brethren, seeing natural signs foretelling the dawn of the end of the age.[21] Yet unlike many of his confessional counterparts, Arndt soon turned his attention from comets and celestial signs to the inner man and related devotional themes.[22]

It was also here that Arndt reprinted and wrote a new foreword to the work that set the tone for his later devotional writings, the *Theologia Deutsch*. Just as Luther had previously reprinted the work with a foreword to suit the theological tenor of the early Reformation, Arndt supplied his age with a new edition and foreword tailored to what he believed was the pressing modern theological dilemma.[23]

Luther had found the anonymous work to be pertinent in its call for a theology of humility and repentance. While these themes were certainly prevalent in Arndt's writings, his own preface stressed the necessity of blending practice and doctrine. These themes had already appeared in *De Antiqua* and later formed the backbone of *True Christianity*. As the Reformation theology of Luther was being defended and consolidated, Arndt believed the medieval devotional tract biblically blended true doctrine with the proper practice of godliness.[24] One notices in this preface, as in Arndt's other writings, a sense of needed reform for the Lutheran church. This was, however, not a call for reform from a distant prophet or enthusiast but rather from one who largely shared the theological stance of his confessional brethren. Arndt never saw himself as a lone rider but as a reformer working within the church and its tradition. He was not a voice crying in the wilderness against confessional Lutheranism, for he accepted most of the religious tenets of his church, but he believed that his church could be enriched by embracing medieval works of spirituality that had been tailored to the Protestant cause. Arndt's devotional works were concerned with presenting an orthodox, affective, and ethically sensitive Lutheranism.

In 1598, Quedlinburg was struck with a plague that killed some three thousand members of the community. On account of the rising death toll, which included Arndt's assistant, the young pastor assumed a greater role in caring for the sick, both medically and spiritually.[25] It was in this context that Arndt began his close relationship with Johann Gerhard, who was then fifteen years old and had been a victim of the plague. As Arndt helped nurse him back to health, he suggested to his young parishioner that, should he survive, he should consider a career in theology. In 1603, after Gerhard had recovered and matriculated at the university at Jena, Arndt wrote him a letter suggesting that he read Bernard of Clairvaux, Macarius, Thomas à Kempis, and other writers not frequently associated with Lutheran orthodoxy.[26] Throughout their lives, they remained close, and as Gerhard became one of the prominent theologians of his era, he often assisted Arndt in the defense of his works against those who charged him with enthusiasm. While Gerhard could suggest that his mentor "thinks better than he speaks," the two remained close, often sharing their works and providing forewords for each other's books.[27] While the two pastors would ultimately distance themselves from one another, there was unmistakably a good deal of mutual influence.

In 1599, after leaving Quedlinburg due to a lack of funding and little enthusiasm for his preaching, Arndt ended up at St. Martin's Church in Braunschweig.[28] The only evidence as to why Arndt was shunned by his congregation in Quedlinburg comes from Arndt's letter to Abbess Anna von Stollberg. Arndt stated that he was despised for preaching repentance, that his payment was often delayed, and that the members of the church were ungrateful for his work during the plague.[29] When Arndt moved to this new church in Braunschweig, he published the first edition of what has been called the "single most influential devotional book in Lutheran history," his *True Christianity*.[30] Arndt was in Braunschweig from 1599 to 1609. During this time, the city had numerous political crises, and Arndt underwent his own pastoral hardships. While he wrote to Gerhard and stated that he was thinking of giving up the pastorate, he undoubtedly used much of the trauma to further develop his devotional themes.

Braunschweig, although not an imperial city, was an important member of the Hanseatic League, and its reputation afforded it a good deal of independence. Yet the city owed its allegiance to the Duke of Braunschweig-Wolfenbüttel, and when Duke Heinrich Julius sought to exercise his control over the city in 1600, a crisis erupted. Duke Julius set up a blockade, cutting off the city from important outside contact. When the people of Braunschweig attempted an armed rebellion, they were reprimanded by the emperor and were offered no support by their Hanseatic neighbors. The city was divided over how to respond to the blockade. This intercity division would continue even after the blockade had ended. The city was further split along social and political lines, the sharpest distinction being between the old ruling patricians and the up-and-coming merchant class.[31] While Arndt favored the more conservative patricians, he disliked the general tenor of social and political upheaval. Ultimately, his support for the patricians would cause Arndt to be distrusted by many in his congregation. Yet Arndt, exercising his pastoral role, began to think about the solution to the deplorable situation. His solution to the turmoil was a deeply spiritual one. What was required from a proud people was true repentance and humility, and this is expressed in the first book of *True Christianity*.

The printing of this first book in 1605 caused immediate trouble for Arndt, as a few pastors, led by Herman Denecke, objected to certain portions of the book that seemed incompatible with Lutheran theology.[32] This controversy, coupled with his support of the patricians during the blockade, eventually led Arndt to entertain the thought of leaving the ministry.[33] While he remained in the pastorate, the rest of Arndt's life was devoted to *True Christianity*. Three additional books of *True Christianity* were written in the following years; two books were added to the work posthumously. These two last books contain letters and brief writings by Arndt attempting to justify his devotional work in the light of Lutheran orthodoxy.

Whatever the opinion of Arndt scholars regarding his confessional and devotional aspects, the controversy surrounding Arndt is essential to our understanding of both his legacy and the nature of the late Lutheran Reformation. Arndt's early years were largely free of controversy, as they were occupied with the development of his confessional and devotional attitudes. During his time in Braunschweig, however, he emerged from relative obscurity as his book was printed across the continent and garnered both praise and criticism. While Arndt had a small community of friends and followers, by the turn of the century and his forty-fifth birthday, he had lived a life of little distinction, causing relatively little commotion with his booklets and reprints. It was in his final years that Arndt's life became enflamed by controversy.

In 1606, only a year after the first printing of book 1 of *True Christianity*, a slightly modified edition was printed in Braunschweig. Despite the initial approval of the work, it began to receive hesitant, mixed reviews. By 1608, Arndt was hoping to publish Books Two through Four, but the suspicion raised by the first book in Braunschweig made this difficult, as the local printer would not print it. Arndt implored his young friend Gerhard to assist him with the printing, and with his help the books were printed a year later in Magdeburg, Jena, and Strasbourg. In the context of this burgeoning controversy over his book, Arndt wrote again to Gerhard that he was despairing of his situation, and due to the venomous nature of the theologians and immorality of his parishioners, he was ready to take up the private life of an author.[34] The very next year, Arndt was offered a position in Eisleben and took the job opportunity. Despite Arndt's own negative summary of his time in Braunschweig, the ministerium (a consortium of local pastors) suggested that his time was less troublesome than he himself had suggested. The ministerium praised his character and work, suggesting that Arndt was prone to a pessimistic appraisal of his work.[35] This sense of pessimism pervaded much of Arndt's own assessments of his work and played into the development of his prophetic persona.

Upon his arrival at Eisleben in 1609, however, Arndt was greeted with suspicion and conflict. The former pastor, Paulus Wolf, attempted to discredit his successor by collecting adverse reactions to *True Christianity*.[36] It was in this context that Polycarp Leyser, a Lutheran pastor, responded, "*Das Buch ist gut, wenn nur der Leser gut ist*" (The book is good, only when the reader is good).[37] This judgment of Arndt was echoed by other Lutheran readers throughout this disagreement over *True Christianity* and with regard to his later works. It was generally held that the book contained some phrases that could be open to misinterpretation but that it was certainly not rank heterodoxy.[38] The acrimony with Wolf did not last long, and when Arndt took the orthodox side of the consistory in a debate concerning predestination, he ingratiated himself among some Lutherans in his region.[39] In 1611, Duke Christian the Elder of Braunschweig-Lüneburg and the local consistory promoted Arndt to general superintendent in Celle. The duke, who sympathized with Arndt, allowed him to work undisturbed to pursue writing and the overseeing of the church and school system in the duchy. It appears that Arndt's move from controversial pastor to general superintendent was abrupt, but having the duke's sympathy and being taken from the office of a full-time preacher appeared to be a viable alternative to quell further troubles. For the first seven years in Celle, Arndt was busy with the work of a superintendent. He preached occasionally at the Marienkirche, prepared a visitation order, and oversaw a curriculum for the schools.[40] It looked for a time as if he would finish his life peacefully and free from strife, yet the final and most trying dispute awaited him.

In 1618, with the Lutheran church still struggling with the encroachment of the Second Reformation and the imminent Thirty

Years' War, a relatively minor situation arose in Danzig with the dis-
covery of a small band of Lutherans reading the works of Valentin
Weigel and Paracelsus, two authors whose spiritualist works were
highly suspect.[41] One of the parishioners was banished and on his
sentencing admitted that next to Weigel and Paracelsus, he was fond
of Arndt's writings. This warranted a new investigation into the
preacher's writings and occasioned the calling of a council to either
vindicate or ban Arndt's devotional works. It was once again Gerhard
who came to his mentor's assistance and persuaded the council to
discontinue further discussion of the matter.[42] Yet Gerhard and the
council were unable to stop the growing sense that Arndt's writings were dubitable and associable with Weigel, Paracelsus, and
Schwenckfeld. In a period of heightened confessional and social tension, suspicion of Arndt swelled among the ranks of Lutheran theologians and pastors.

Since 1616, Arndt had suffered from what is only referred to
as "a sickness." He had written a last testament in that year, but it
proved premature. In 1619, he began to complain more of the sickness. On May 3, 1621, Arndt preached his last sermon. According to
one source, he told his wife, Anna, "I have just preached my funeral
sermon."[43] Arndt died eight days later at home. On his deathbed, he
was said to have told his wife that he had seen the glory of the Lord
and before expiring to have whispered, "Nun habe ich überwunden"
(I have now overcome).[44] Arndt was dead, but the controversy regarding his works and their place in the Lutheran church had just begun.

In 1623, Lucas Osiander, grandson of the famous Andreas,
published what became the standard work of Arndtian criticism.
Osiander's *Theologisches Bedencken* linked Arndt with the destruc-
tive tendencies of Müntzer, Catholic doctrine, and an overzeal-
ousness for good works.[45] Osiander did not believe that Arndt was
malicious, but simply undereducated, and that therefore he should
have refrained from publishing religious texts that could mislead the
pious reader.[46] Osiander's work received full approval from his colleagues at Tübingen and set off a new chain of investigations into
those suspected of being *Schwaermei*, the term first used by Luther
to denounce the fanatics.[47]

While the Thirty Years' War led to increased religious and
political tension, and while some theologians cautiously distanced

themselves from Arndt based on Osiander's criticism, a new wave of Lutheran theologians attempted to vindicate his devotional works. Melchior Breller, Friedrich Dame, and Paulus Egardus published tracts defending the works of Arndt, cautious of his doubtful sayings yet insisting that he be interpreted in the most orthodox sense.[48] During this period, there was also evidence that *True Christianity* was being taught at various universities, most notably at Wittenberg in the latter half of the century by leaders of Lutheran orthodoxy such as Johann Quenstedt and Abraham Calov.[49] Wide recognition of Arndt was finally reached when Philipp Jakob Spener wrote a new foreword for Arndt's *Postills*, a work that praised Arndt and eventually was enlarged to become the *Pia Desideria* in 1675. It was the link with Spener that has created the idea that Arndt was the father of Pietism. Yet his work had only certain similarities to the theology of Pietism. Instead, for a better picture of Arndt's thought in its own right, an evaluation of *True Christianity* will be helpful in discerning Arndt's public devotional theology. So much of what we know about Arndt is tied up with *True Christianity*, as it propelled him to widespread fame and tells us important things about his life and character.

Arndt's *True Christianity*

In 1979, almost half a millennia since the pastor began his small tracts that would become book 1 of *True Christianity*, the work was retranslated into English and placed in a series of the classics of western spirituality.[50] Between the original tracts and the recognition of the book as a classic, the text had undergone a process of being expanded, edited, translated, banned, extolled, and battled over by interpreters. The following is a short history of this evolving devotional work.

Johannes Wallmann has stated that *True Christianity* was initially a work in progress and is therefore difficult to date specifically.[51] We do know that in 1605, *On True Christianity* was published by Jonas Rosen in Frankfurt. However, in the next four years, the text of this devotional tract would undergo editorial treatment by Arndt as the result of criticism and censures from Lutheran theological faculties. In 1606, the text was still composed of the material that we refer to as book 1, yet some editions carried the title of *Four Books on True Christianity*. This is evidence, perhaps, that Arndt was contemplating expanding his work.[52] This second edition, published in Braunschweig, was altered, most likely due to the controversy that surrounded the initial printing, as it was altered theologically to avoid the appearance of heterodoxy. Eric Lund has pointed out three significant changes in the text. The statement that "love should do all in Christ" was altered to "faith should do all in Christ."[53] The notion that the continuous struggle against the old nature "makes" the Christian was altered to read that this struggle merely "proves" the Christian.[54] Lund also notes that the term *rebirth* was replaced with *renewal*, likely to be less suspect to the theological censors.[55] The ministerium at Braunschweig was still unwilling to let Arndt proceed with the printing of his expanded work, but Gerhard persuaded his superintendent to arrange for a publication of Arndt's successive books. In 1609, the first true edition of the *Four Books on True Christianity* was published in Magdeburg by Johann Francke and in Braunschweig by Andreas Duncker. While Arndt was not free from criticism, this arrangement of four books would see eleven different printings (mostly by Franke) in Magdeburg, Strasbourg, Braunschweig, and Mömpelgard by the time Arndt died in 1621. Controversies that followed the book beyond 1621 were handled by defenders of Arndt as they added explanatory and apologetic tracts written by Arndt. These texts would comprise the additional books of *True Christianity*, which was eventually expanded into six books. While theological faculties may have been suspicious of Arndt's work, its popularity among the laity is clear.

Through to the end of the century, the work went through approximately forty editions, being translated into Latin, English, Swedish, Czech, and Dutch.[56] By 1740, the book had more than doubled its number of editions, reaching ninety-five.[57] During this period, at least sixty-five recorded works were published in response to or in defense of Arndt.[58] The translated editions found much success in Sweden, where there were at least thirty printings, and the Latin edition was supposedly a favorite of Spanish Jesuits.[59] Martin Brecht suggests that these data mark Arndt as the most successful devotional author in the Protestant church.[60] Undoubtedly the mystery and notoriety that this small devotional book had among the laity assisted its success, but questions concerning its popularity and enduring success have been a battleground for Arndt scholars. Since

Spener's praise of Arndt, and the proliferation of *True Christianity* in Pietist circles, it has been common to suggest that Arndt's book was a type of protopietistic work.[61] Others, such as Heiko Oberman, have gone in the opposite direction, praising the work for its harvest of medieval sources.[62] Once again, the success of Arndt is predicated on his being transplanted into a different age, into either the pre-Reformation church or the age of Pietism.

The following sections will argue that Arndt's work was a successful adaptation of the late Lutheran Reformation. Arndt's knowledge of the controversies giving rise to the Book of Concord placed him in favor among those who saw his book as orthodox. Ultimately, Arndt's book was not that of a dislocated critic but that of a concerned Lutheran pastor. Yet the printing records suggest that something was different about the book, something that attracted a diverse lot of readers. Perhaps it was merely the controversy, or maybe it was the casting of confessional theology inwardly. In a time of great confessional tumult, perhaps the mere title *True Christianity* attracted the theologically uneducated layman.

An inevitable question relating to the printing of the work is that of the book's audience. According to Arndt, the work was intended for the simple believer.[63] It was not a polemical tract but a guide to practical Christianity. Yet the book took on a life of its own. While it was devoted to the laity, it became a source of intense discord as it found a broad readership in educated circles. Furthermore, the evidence suggests that even among the average reader, the book was more than a manual of instruction. It took on great significance as a symbol of devotion, and even when left unread, it became a mark of confessional, practical Lutheranism. Thus an assessment of the contents of the book does not tell the whole story. Its notoriety would have ensured that it was discussed in public and private settings even among those unfamiliar with the text. These issues ultimately distinguished the book and its author and give us the clearest insight into its reception, both negatively and positively.

The Introduction to *True Christianity*[64]

Arndt began his foreword to the Christian reader with the suggestion that the gospel at the turn of the century had been subject to a scandalous misuse that was apparent from the un-Christian lives of its adherents.[65] This scandal, according to Arndt, was further exhibited in signs of nature. The heaping up of plagues, hunger, flood, pestilence, and imminent war attested to the displeasure of God.[66] What was needed was "true" Christianity. The foreword insisted that this renewal of true Christianity would take place when men internalized the Scriptures, recognized the indwelling of Christ, and produced the active fruits of faith.[67] Arndt's call for an inward, living, and active devotional faith characterized what he called "true" Christianity. Yet this true Christianity was not an amorphous, vague faith: it was the faith of Luther and his confessional forbears. Even in a work devoted to a contemplative and inward-looking Christian faith, Arndt included caveats to assure the reader that he was not suggesting the perfectionist faith of the Enthusiasts. Arndt insisted that this devotional, inward, true Christianity was opposed to the faith of the Papists, Synergists, and Majorists.[68] The Papists, Arndt argued, confused the righteousness of faith with the righteousness of life. The Synergistic controversy surrounded the role of man's will in conversion and was debated between the likes of Flacius and Melanchthon; ultimately, the framers of the Book of Concord decided that the human will had no role in the act of conversion. Arndt insisted that any renewal or change is the work of God alone.[69] Arndt further criticized the Majorists, a defunct party led by the deceased Georg Major that insisted that good works were necessary for salvation.[70] From the outset, Arndt insisted, in strict Lutheran fashion, that his projected devotional renewal must follow on the course set by the confessions. If Arndt was at all critical of his colleagues, it was in the context of the trend to systematize theology and present doctrines in the disputational method.[71] During this period of orthodoxy, the prolegomena to doctrine were becoming increasingly complex.[72] Arndt wrote that theology involved both knowledge and practice (a theme found in the earlier *Philosophia*)— that is, the imitating of Christ in addition to proper doctrinal knowledge. Yet in a foreword distinguished by caveats, Arndt insisted that the present weakness of sin kept perfection from being attainable. The foreword concluded with the standard Lutheran distinction of law and gospel.[73] The proposed renewal could only take place within the context of repentance and humility. Good works are the fruits of faith, and faith was the work of God alone, wrought by the Holy Gospel only when mankind realized its dreadful state of condemnation and eternal death.[74] With this introduction, Arndt proceeded to the main body of the book. He had impressed upon the reader the dreadful state of the world, the present abuse of the gospel, and a solution: "true" Christianity. This is a Christianity that is turned inwardly yet informed by the controversy and confession that defined the Lutheran church.

Book 1: *The Book of Scripture*

The first book of *True Christianity*, the *Liber Scripturae* (*Book of Scripture*), was originally the only one intended for publication, and much of the contents of the later books repeat its central tenets. The *Liber Scripturae*, divided into forty chapters, outlined the Christian faith from the fall of man through conversion, the Christian life, and finally, glorification. This pattern followed the standard *ordo salutis* of the orthodox Lutheran theologians.[75] Yet as Arndt's book was intended as a corrective for the supposed immorality of his age, it focused primarily on the believer's new life in Christ. The beginning of *True Christianity* outlined the standard Lutheran position regarding the initial fall of man. According to this position, man was created in the image of God, but at the fall of Adam and Eve, that image was erased and replaced with the image of Satan.[76] The implications for this in Arndt's writings are threefold. First, by insisting on the complete eradication of the image of God in man, Arndt was distancing himself from the Pelagian view that continued to see the image of God as operating in the soul of the unregenerate. This confessional insistence may have had little effect on the common reader, but in disputation, it could be used as proof of Arndt's confessional fidelity. Second, the argument that man had fallen so completely was an important part of Arndt's devotional schema. The fall into sin was not minor trouble to be worked out with little effort. Due to the complete nature of the fall, man is, by necessity, forced to spend the rest of his life struggling with its effects. The Christian must constantly meditate on the dreadful fall and devote all his efforts to the struggle against it.[77] Third, Arndt referenced the image of Satan throughout the first book, yet carefully distinguished himself from the definition

of Flacius, as the framers of the Book of Concord rejected his interpretation of the image of Satan being the substance of fallen man.[78]
While Arndt did not enter into a discussion of the substance and
accidents of the fallen soul, the matter was diffused, as Arndt sided
with the confession by comparing the soul to a piece of wax that
holds the image of whatever is pressed upon it.[79]

After discussing the fall of man, Arndt moved to the subjects
that pervaded the rest of the first book: repentance and the new life
of faith. Repentance, wrote Arndt, was a wholly internal matter. It is
daily, spiritual, and involving sorrow for sin.[80] Echoing the Formula
of Concord he affirmed that repentance was a daily, purifying, and
spiritual activity.[81] Thus Arndt's doctrine of repentance followed the
orthodox Lutheran teaching. If Arndt is distinguished in any way, it
is in his prolonged treatment of rebirth. It is here a matter of degree
that separates Arndt from confessional Lutheranism. Of the forty
chapters in book 1, thirty-six deal with the issue of internal repentance. The process of loving God and neighbor, the process of rebirth,
and the lifelong struggle between Satan and the regenerate soul are
all based on the internal grasping and regrasping of repentance.[82]

The final chapter of the first book was a recapitulation of its
main points. It is unsurprising that these points revolved around
meditation on the internal aspects of faith and their connected external fruits. Book 1 set itself apart from both the mystics and Pietists
in these respects: carefully distinguished orthodoxy and deep cul-
tivation of a sense of sinfulness. While taken separately, neither of
these aspects is unknown in medieval and early modern Christian
writing, yet the juxtaposition of these two in the first book of *True
Christianity* made it a distinctive devotional handbook.

Book 2: *The Book of the Life of Christ*

Little is known about the origins of the books added to *True
Christianity* in 1609. The second book, the *Liber Vitae Christus* (*Book
of the Life of Christ*), suggests that Arndt had both taken heed of
the debate surrounding the contents of the first book and continued down the path of the confessional, devotional, and controversial
strains that typified his earlier work. The confessional aspects of the
book, those that reiterated the standard Lutheran themes, seemed

to be an attempt at defending the work as confessionally grounded. Yet if the book was written as a mere apology, a number of the sections would make little sense, as Arndt continued to elaborate on the themes of the active, contemplative life. Being unsure of the motivation for the expansion of the book, the simplest suggestion is that Arndt was intent to introduce or expand upon the first book's theme of an inwardly confessional faith. The repetitively confessional arguments need not be seen as empty or feigned, as Arndt had continually shown himself to be concerned with presenting the orthodox Lutheran faith.

In twenty of the fifty-eight chapters in book 2, Arndt dealt with the suffering, faithless, or sinning Christian.[83] One sees in this the traces of Luther. The pervasive sense of the sinful, struggling, and decaying world hardly fits the later Pietists postmillennial expectations. There is no promise of spiritual betterment without the concomitant promise of struggle and failure. Between the confessional introduction and the pervasive sense of Lutheran pessimism, the second book of *True Christianity* presents a strong case for Arndt's confessional identity. Yet the devotional and controversial strains are not at all absent.

In the exposition of the suffering of Christ, the believer's existential identification with Christ began to take form. As Christ suffered, so too does the Christian. As Christ prayed and glorified in God alone, so too must the Christian. These themes were not particularly innovative in Lutheran orthodoxy; Johann Gerhard frequently made use of the believer's identification with Christ in his Postils.[84] Yet Arndt's use of the imitation motif drew some of the strongest criticisms from his detractors.[85] This was perhaps due to the fact that one of Arndt's earliest projects was the reprinting of the medieval devotional classic *The Imitation of Christ* in 1605. Arndt's identification with this devotional work made him an easy target for suspicion of heterodoxy and would set the table for similar controversy surrounding Arndt's devotional emphases. As has been shown, the devotional themes in Arndt's writings, when not explicitly tied to confessional statements, often led to controversy. In the sections in book 2 that relate to prayer, Arndt is known to have borrowed extensively from the medieval nun Angela de Foligno.[86] Gerhard came to Arndt's aid and suggested that the use of a medieval source was not necessarily suspect, as it had been the practice of the older Lutherans to borrow appropriate sections from the suspect authors of antiquity.[87]

Book 2 follows the pattern of Arndt's previous writings. It contained a confessional grounding and a devotional interest that both turns the confessional Lutheranism inward and led Arndt into considerable controversy. One of the central tenets of the Lutheran doctrine of justification was its forensic nature. That is, one is declared righteous and must look for that righteousness outside of oneself in the work of Christ and the declaration of righteousness.[88] Luther defined man's natural sinful nature as wanting to look inside itself rather than to Christ outside of himself. Thus Arndt's internal focus could lead to suspicion of his orthodox intentions. While the eventual consensus was that Arndt's use of medieval and devotional sources in book 2 was sufficiently within the realm of Lutheran orthodoxy, the third book would cause Arndt to be reevaluated.

Book 3: *The Book of Conscience*

Book 3, the *Liber Conscientiae* (*Book of Conscience*), contains the most radically devotional and subsequently controversial material in *True Christianity*. If the first books are characterized by an internal confessionalism, the third is characterized by its internal preoccupation, without tying it back to orthodox doctrine. The theme of the book is the kingdom of God within the soul and the passive contemplation of God as the highest good. The medieval and controversial authors used by Arndt were more apparent in this book, as Arndt acknowledged his use of St. Bernard and Johannes Tauler. Toward the end of the introduction to the book, Arndt approvingly quoted Cyprian as providing the appropriate summation of the book with his call for the contemplation of heavenly things, fleeing from the world, and resting in God.[89] The primary questions for Arndt in book 3 surrounded the Christian's relationship to the present age and the relationship between man's soul and God.

The questions surrounding Arndt and his supposedly world-fleeing piety have dominated modern Arndt research for more than a century. Ritschl accused Arndt of imbibing the pharisaic piety and erotic imagery of the mystics while turning aside from the orthodox

formulations of the early Reformation.[90] The third book has been singled out as the chief culprit, not only by Ritschl, but by even the most
sympathetic of Arndt's contemporaries. While Gerhard did much in
defending and propagating the works of Arndt, he rejected book 3.
What had most alarmed critics of Arndt's world-fleeing piety came in
the tenth chapter of book 3 with the application of Tauler's Sabbath of
the Heart.[91] This inward turn advocated by Tauler developed, as Arndt
suggested, a daily turning inward to the soul and a repeated attack on
the love of anything worldly.[92] Lutheran doctrine did not teach a type
of quietism or ecstatic experience; rather, the Two-Kingdom doctrine
taught that the Christian should be active in the world, as loving your
neighbor was believed to be Christ's work in the Christian.

The second point of controversy for the third book, the issue of
direct, inner communion with God, found itself wrapped in a myr-
iad of medieval sources. The revelation of God in Lutheranism was
often a point of great contention. God was to be revealed in Christ
and mediated through the word of Scripture.[93] Any doctrine of
unmediated communion with God instantly drew attention, as this
was a mark of the Enthusiasts. Arndt's summary of the revelation of
God to the soul began with his approval of Tauler's concept of the
Seelengrund.[94] The Ground of the Soul was for Tauler, and Meister
Eckhart before him, the highest part of the soul that had its origins in
the "uncreatedness" of God.[95] Arndt, in borrowing this concept, bor-
dered on a rejection of the Lutheran doctrine of a complete chasm
between the fallen state of man and God. Furthermore, in this age
of confessional suspicion, quoting from an inappropriate medieval source could cause suspicion. Yet like Luther before him, Arndt
seemed to have appropriated Tauler effectively and remained thor-
oughly evangelical. Eric Lund has dissected the borrowed sections of
Tauler in Arndt and concluded that it was of the utmost importance
for Arndt to distinguish wholly between things human and divine.[96]
Arndt's goals were not pantheistic, but rather he intended to present
a doctrine of union that would be compatible with his ethical concerns. Arndt's works, even the complicated book 3, are not dogmatic
treatises. This work had a single goal of further orientating Lutheran
orthodoxy inwardly. It seems the strongest argument to suggest that
book 3, in its more extreme sections, represents the exception and
not the rule for an interpretation of Arndt's theology.

Book 4: *The Book of Nature*

Book 4 of *True Christianity*, the *Liber Naturae* (*Book of Nature*), represented a return to form after the sprawling third book. The book contained the controversial sources of book 3 but was reinfused with orthodox apologies and possessed a simpler devotional style. The purpose of the fourth book was to draw the same conclusions as the first three books, but rather than using the Scriptures, the life of Christ, or the soul, it utilized signs in nature.

Similar to the first books, Arndt began with an appeal to orthodox Lutheranism. Yet this time, he bypassed any explanation of the concepts and implored his readers directly to judge all his writings and to understand them by the rule set in the symbolic books of the Lutheran church.[97] The final chapter of the book also attempted to place everything firmly within the parameters of orthodox Lutheranism, with Arndt suggesting that his work, while highly ethical in nature, has presupposed the foundation of the orthodox teaching of justification.[98]

Book 4 began with an explanation of the concepts of microcosm and macrocosm, with the soul serving as the microcosm of the universe.[99] While Arndt attributed this theory to the prophet Moses, it was in fact recognizably Paracelsian. One of Gerhard's complaints of Arndt was that "the reading of the books of Paracelsus and Weigel pleased him, for an eye-witness testifies that Arndt brought from them many things into his books on *True Christianity*."[100] Arndt went on to use this model to illuminate the six days of creation from the book of Genesis. Arndt explained each natural occurrence in relation to its significance for the existential Christian experience.[101] This lengthy summary blended devotional insight (i.e., the watering of the earth is an example of Christ's living water that produces spiritual fruit) and orthodox musings on the nature of justification (i.e., the depth of the sea is a representation of both the depth of our sin and the depth of Christ's mercy). While not particularly terse or insightful, the microcosm model served as yet another example of Arndt's blending of both orthodox and esoteric themes.

The second section elaborated on Arndt's conception of God as the highest good. This section distinguished between the love of self, which brings ruin, and the love of God, which brings eternal blessedness. It is in the second section that Arndt combined devotional themes with a unique recasting of Lutheran orthodoxy. With his designations of God as the highest good, and the necessity of turning inwardly to God, much of the Christological focus of Lutheran orthodoxy is left as forgotten or, perhaps, only implied. Arndt's insistence on the double nature of Christian service toward God and neighbor is upheld, as was his stress on humility and the need to avoid worldly entrapments.[102] Book 4 was the recasting of the same argument constant throughout the first three books. Arndt's use of the microcosm and macrocosm were perhaps surprisingly uncontroversial, as orthodox Lutheranism was still in the process of defining its natural theology.[103] The fourth book represented Arndt's ability to present his confessional devotion in diverse methods and under assorted rubrics.

Books 5 and 6

Book 4 was the last planned section for Arndt's magnum opus. The remaining years of Arndt's life would be occupied with added duties as general superintendent and controversy surrounding the four books of *True Christianity*. While working as the general superintendent in Celle, Arndt published a number of tracts that attempted to vindicate his earlier works as well as propel forward his plan for an ethically sensitive and deeply devotional orthodoxy. These were Arndt's last writings, compiled as Books Five and Six, which served as a type of apology for the previous four books. These tracts were added after Arndt's death.

The first appendix in the fifth book was a tract initially written and printed by Arndt in 1620 and was entitled "On True Faith and Holy Life." In this work, written two years after the Danzig controversy, Arndt was exceedingly careful to present an unassailable orthodoxy. Sections such as those on the forgiveness of sins and justification through faith in Christ were wholly confessional, and by his own account were to vindicate his writings that had been misinterpreted.[104] Yet Arndt was not simply writing the tract to gain favor among the orthodox. In the preface to the work, he claimed that Satan attacks three types of men: those who believe they are perfect, those who despise piety (the critics of Arndt's works), and the open sinners (those who have been instructed in an orthodoxy without an ethical impulse).[105]

The second section of Book 5 reproduced another tract by Arndt from the same year, "On the Mystical Union." If the first section was an unabashed statement of faith, this second was a straightforward treatise on the implication of justification and the union with Christ. The treatise was hardly suspect, as Arndt seemed to have learned from the previous controversies to be careful with his wording. God through Christ and the Holy Scriptures, wrote Arndt, enacts the mystical union. This seems to be an attempt to clear up any controversy surrounding his early mystical language.[106] The confessional and devotional aspects of Arndt are blended, as was typical in the first four books, with alternating chapters dealing with the doctrine of the incarnation and the ethical implications of the indwelling of the Spirit, the spiritual wedding of ineffable joy, and its corporeal enactment through Holy Baptism. This second section represented Arndt at the apogee of his confessional and devotional heights.[107] The two themes are blended in such a way that much of the early controversy seemed assuaged.

The final section of Book 5 was a tract, also printed in 1620, entitled "On the Holy Trinity."[108] This third section represents the purely confessional Arndt. The devotional aspects are still present primarily in the discussion on the gifts of the Holy Spirit and the hymn/prayer concluding the section.[109] The tract is divided into brief, numbered affirmations, a device that made the confession readable for the general population and presented a clear case that he was a confessing Lutheran.

Book 6 presented the same pattern of devotion and defense. The first section is a pointed defense of the original books of *True Christianity*, originally dedicated to the mayor and council of Danzig, a fact that attests to the volatile and influential nature of the 1618 controversy.[110] The entire tract was devoted to displaying the proper sense in which the original books are to be understood. Later defenders of Arndtian piety/orthodoxy would employ this same method. If there was to be any question that Arndt perhaps published the first books too quickly and without proper counsel, the second section collected nine assorted letters, sent to prominent theologians, to vindicate the original books. The letters were sent to the likes of

Gerhard, Petrus Piscator, Wolfgang Frantzius, and Duke August of Braunschweig-Wolfenbüttel.[111] If being linked with Paracelsus, Weigel, and Schwenckfeld discredited Arndt, these complimentary letters were intended to associate Arndt with a more respectable community. The letters, while somewhat repetitive, affirmed Arndt's devotion and fidelity to the Lutheran confessions.

The final section of book 6, and the least representative of the final two books, consists of Arndt's two forewords written for the *Theologia Deutsch*.[112] In these two forewords (the first foreword is lengthened in the second), the devotional themes characteristic of Arndt were central once again. The original purpose of the foreword was to commend the book's example of the practice of piety. Against a merely disputational faith, the book presents, according to Arndt, a simple, living faith. The somewhat out-of-place insertion of this into the sixth book may have served a number of purposes. First, the *Theologia Deutsch* was famously reprinted and extolled by Martin Luther and thus associated Arndt with the father of Lutheranism. Second, while the forewords were written in 1597 and 1605, they might have seemed especially relevant as they extolled the virtues of practice over disputation.[113] The fifth and sixth books represented Arndt's commitment to a confessionally devotional faith. Against his detractors, the two books present subtle arguments for the cessation of debate and for the inclusion of Arndt into the confessional community.

Ultimately, the lack of solid biographical information on Arndt has led many to base their judgment of Arndt on their reading or secondhand knowledge of the themes in *True Christianity*. In Arndt's correspondence, many of these same themes are developed more fully in communication with particular individuals. While understanding *True Christianity* is undoubtedly essential for grasping Arndt's thought, his correspondence offers a crucial and different perspective. It is to his letters that we now turn.

CHAPTER 2

Johann Arndt as a Confessional Lutheran

Lutheran Orthodoxy in Early Modern Germany

Was Johann Arndt a Lutheran? Such a question cannot easily be answered, because to do so involves in turn the question of what it meant to be Lutheran at the end of the sixteenth century. When scholars have considered Arndt's relationship to Lutheranism, they have tended to treat his theology as separate from his historical context. The approach here is to place Arndt's theology in this historical context in order to avoid the characterizations of earlier works, which tended to see Arndt in light of either fifteenth-century mysticism or post-Reformation Pietism.[1]

When putting Arndt in his historical context, we must first address the issue of the definition of Lutheran orthodoxy. It was not simply a set of doctrines, but rather a theological movement that developed against the background of the political and economic world of the empire in the second half of the sixteenth century. What makes Arndt's situation difficult to determine is that historians and theologians have tended to pay less attention to the Lutheran church after 1555. Traditionally, the theological world after the Peace of Augsburg has been described in terms of a dry rigidity that contrasted with the liveliness of Luther and Melanchthon.[2] In this chapter, we shall explore the fluid and diverse nature of Lutheran theology after 1555, which we will call the era of Lutheran orthodoxy. This, it will be demonstrated, is a more fruitful way of examining the life and thoughts of Johann Arndt. Especially in his correspondence, Arndt was conscious of his theological and political surroundings, and it was in these contexts that he was able to present his allegiance to the Lutheran church.

In broaching the question of Arndt's relationship to Lutheranism in this period, we must raise the issue of the definition of Lutheran orthodoxy, especially as theologians and historians have taken different views of this term. Robert Preus has claimed, "There is no cleavage between the period of the Reformation and the period of Lutheran orthodoxy."[3] Furthermore, Preus argued that the supposed "dead orthodoxy" label applied by many was false, as the Lutheran church sought to cultivate a piety that was formed by its doctrine.[4] Preus began his study of orthodoxy with the controversies that led to the formation of the Book of Concord (from roughly 1546 to 1577). Robert Kolb has similarly sought "a new, more broadly outlined approach to the Lutheran late Reformation," finding theological continuity as the church expanded into confessions beyond the sole authority of Luther.[5] The more recent and widely variegated "confessionalization" thesis has also had an impact on how confessions and orthodoxy should be treated in the late sixteenth and early seventeenth centuries. Tom Brady suggested that Heinz Schilling (one of the architects of the confessionalization thesis) "has done much to analyze the structure of Lutheran practice and belief, and purports it to be a heuristic . . . comprehensive analyses of society" and stands somewhat squarely on the shoulders of the pioneering social analyses of the Reformation done in the past thirty years.[6] Yet this thesis has been criticized for not addressing seriously the theological content of the confessions and for treating them instead more as tools of social discipline. C. Scott Dixon has questioned the model as an attempt at "[assimilating] so many strands of cause and effect with an analytical tool."[7] Marc Forster similarly questioned the model put forth by Schilling and others, stating that "the historical problem of Confessionalism is then complicated by the different ways the term is used."[8]

Whether a theological approach is taken to defining Lutheran orthodoxy or an approach that seeks to integrate more political and social factors is taken, the most pertinent issue at hand is discerning the context in which Arndt lived and the approach he took to understanding the theological and political issues that concerned him.

The Early Modern German Political Landscape

The significance of the political situation in the empire for the present chapter lies in the hardening of confessional lines, the suspicion of sectarian fringe groups, and the general social malaise that engendered a renewed interest in both confessional and devotional theology. For German Lutherans, 1546 was a deeply troubling year, as they were confronted with the death of Luther. Although Luther's theological positions were well established, his importance as a figure for the Reformation cannot be underestimated. His death deprived the German Protestants of a crucial unifying force, and it was not long before theological disagreements within the church broke into public disputes. All claimed the authority of Luther, but their interpretations of his theology and legacy varied greatly.

The church also faced a reinvigorated Charles V, who, while claiming he was not mounting a religious war, was backed financially by Pope Paul III with intentions to "exterminate all heresy."[9] With the backing of the Lutheran duke Maurice of Saxony, the Schmalkaldic Wars ended with Catholic control of southeast Germany and the Rhineland. Thus left without a leader, and facing a strong Catholic church, the age of Lutheran orthodoxy began in the midst of political turmoil.

Yet the Catholic victory was short lived. Having supported Charles V in return for an electorship, Duke Maurice subsequently turned on the Catholic troops and pushed them back to Innsbruck, ultimately eliminating Catholic control in the Lutheran heartland.[10] The duke's reasons for his change of mind may have been less than theologically pure, but his actions served as a further warning to the emperor that a mix of German nationalism and Lutheranism could be more than a thinly stretched imperial army could handle. The Treaty of Passau, which ended the conflicts in 1552, was extended in the Peace of Augsburg in 1555. This peace was significant in its reserved acceptance of Lutheran magistrates and recognition of the once outlawed faith. Yet it was also significant in the difficult questions it failed to address, primarily the place of other Protestant sects.

The political situation after the Augsburg settlement has been defined as an age both of peace and of polarization.[11] Rather than seeing this era as an inevitable march to war, it is significant that for half a century, there was relative peace in the German lands. On one level, this was due to the abdication of Charles V and the *politique* of his successors Ferdinand I and Maximilian II.[12] Both emperors took into account the usefulness of compliant Lutheran princes and the larger issues looming on the edges of the empire, such as the Dutch Revolt, the French Wars of Religion, and the ever-present Turkish threat.[13] The Peace of Augsburg was successful not in eliminating theological controversy but by channeling it out of the political sphere. Yet this peace, which was genuine for a season, would begin to look illusory due to the emergence of Calvinism, the foundation of sectarian leagues, and the ultimate politicization of religious conflict.

In 1559, four years after the Augsburg settlement, a series of events occurred that would simmer under the newly established religious peace. In this year, the Genevan Academy was founded, John Calvin's final edition of the *Institutes* was first published, and Frederick III of the Palatinate converted to Calvinism.[14] While the Peace of Augsburg allowed for Protestantism congruent with the Augsburg Confession, the emergence of this new Protestant force ultimately led to its undoing. Calvinism saw itself as completing Luther's reform by eliminating supposed papal remnants. This emerging religious force, which had found varying degrees of success in Switzerland, France, and the Low Countries, caused great unease in the empire.[15] On an official level, various Lutheran magistrates and theologians attempted to reconcile the two Protestant groups at the Naumberg Convention of 1561 and the Diet of Augsburg in 1566.[16] Yet these gatherings seemed only to highlight the theological differences between the two parties. The following decades saw the division between the groups on both official and popular levels. The charges of crypto-Calvinism were leveled against a number of prominent Lutheran theologians, most notably Philip Melanchthon, and the confessional struggle intensified. As pastors and magistrates attempted to ban Lutheran liturgical practices, these bans were rejected as undue Calvinist encroachments.[17]

The work of Bodo Nischan has highlighted the role of Calvinist encroachment and Lutheran consolidation in the northeastern German territories. While the Lutheran church was attempting to define itself against the old church, it now had to deal with the Calvinists, who also claimed Luther as an authority in completing the Reformation. Many Lutherans, on both a popular and pastoral level, claimed that the Calvinists were a "dangerous deformation" of the Evangelical church.[18]

A notable controversy ensued when Duke Johann Georg of Anhalt banned the Lutheran rite of baptismal exorcism, hoping to alleviate Calvinist-Lutheran tension in his territories. There were a number of protests, which culminated in the exile of all Lutheran pastors in Anhalt who did not cooperate. Among these pastors was Johann Arndt. These confessional and political issues were often further exacerbated by the growing number of sectarian universities and academic institutions that were training new generations of clergyman and polemicists.

After the success of the Council of Trent, the reinvigorated Catholic church actively supported the academically inclined and especially self-styled "warrior polemicists" of the Society of Jesus founded by Ignatius of Loyola.[19] The church also implemented, at the suggestion of Cardinal Pole, a number of educational reforms with an emphasis on doctrine and missions. This interest in sectarian and polemic academies was mirrored in both Calvinist and Lutheran camps. In southwest Germany, Frederick III attempted to duplicate the Genevan academy in the newly chartered Heidelberg University.[20] The university at Heidelberg flourished as a breeding ground for the Reformed, as its financial security (through princely support) allowed it to attract leading scholars in every field. Furthermore, Frederick and his son Johann Sigismund pushed the university to impose on all professors public oaths to the Reformed faith.[21] As for the Lutheran universities, there were five at which, according to Preus, "the strictest confessionalism and orthodoxy prevailed": Wittenberg, Tübingen, Strasbourg, Leipzig, and Jena.[22]

As the three major confessions took hold in Germany, there was a renewed attempt to form alliances that might prevent the kind of unrest seen elsewhere in Europe. Elector Frederick IV and Christian of Anhalt established the first Protestant Union in Germany in 1609. While past conciliatory measures had been marred by theological tension, this one was weakened by a lack of support from both magistrates and the public.[23] Duke Maximilian of Bavaria attempted to convene a similar union, the Catholic League, in the same year but was also frustrated by lack of support from the emperor and his fellow Catholic leaders.[24]

The growing political and theological tension was compounded by economic stagnation and social unrest. The "little ice age" and the influx of American silver, for example, slowed the German economy.[25] Furthermore, the empire was in transition from an economy based on household production to centralized manufacturing, and unemployment became a lag on society.[26] Alchemists, astrologers, and theologians viewed these signs and others as apocalyptic portents foretelling the coming end of the age.[27] The general tumult, both politically and socially, would culminate in the devastating Thirty Years' War.

There was, amid this tension, a renewed interest in works that were both devotional and confessional in the sense that churchmen were conscious of marking out the physical and spiritual boundaries of their faith. The devotional nature of their works was intended to comfort a hard-pressed and anxious society with reassurance about the coming of Christ and the benefits of heaven.[28] It is in this context that we encounter the writings of Johann Arndt, which, of all the devotional works printed between the Peace of Augsburg and the Thirty Years' War, proved to be among the most popular.

Theological Tension in the Lutheran Church

The theological tension within the Lutheran church became apparent after the imperial troops crushed the Lutherans at Mühlberg and imposed the interim that forbade certain Lutheran practices and incensed many Lutherans as an attempt at re-Catholicization. As we have seen, the victory was short lived and effectively reversed with the signing of the Peace of Augsburg, but the theological tension had repercussions long after the peace was signed in 1555. Most of this tension initially revolved around Melanchthon's role in drafting the Leipzig Interim. The one-time heir apparent to Luther was roundly criticized by many evangelical leaders for his supposed capitulation. Among his detractors were Matthias Flacius and Andrew Osiander, John Calvin, and Johannes Brenz.[29] Yet Melanchthon saw the interim as a temporary solution. In a letter from the Lutheran superintendent of Hamburg, Johann Aepinus, Melanchthon was reminded that "toward you the eyes of many are directed, on your judgement hangs a great part of Christendom, you dare not allow those who place so great a trust in you to remain in doubt and uncertainty." Melanchthon replied, "Since we have greater matters to defend, let us abandon the dissension among non-essentials."[30] Yet what Melanchthon saw as "non-essentials" were things prized more seriously by his opponents. Flacius and Nicolaus von Amsdorf criticized him for abandoning the doctrine of justification by capitulating to Catholic traditions that could confuse the laity and cause a permanent relapse into the old faith. This first controversy surrounding the interim would spawn potentially devastating splits within the Lutheran church, and the ensuing controversies would later be commonly referenced as those between the Philippists and Gnesio (genuine) Lutherans. Robert Kolb has suggested that such party labeling is unhelpful in discerning the true nature of these conflicts, as the parties tended to be fluid, with various antagonists and oftentimes no reference to Melanchthon at all.[31] Therefore, to explore these potentially movement-threatening controversies, we need to give some attention specifically to the major theological schisms that arose during the period: the Adiaphoristic, Majoristic, Synergistic, Flacian, Osiandrian, Antinomistic, and crypto-Calvinist controversies. These debates would shape the form and content of the age of Lutheran orthodoxy.

The Adiaphoristic controversy, at its core, was related to the Leipzig Interim and the restoration of abolished Catholic ceremonies in the Lutheran church. While the interim became a dead letter with the Peace of Augsburg, the question remained: "May Lutherans submit, in good conscience, to Catholic tradition without sanctioning the errors of the old church?" In the two years following the Leipzig Interim, more than twenty publications were printed from both sides of the controversy.[32] At the core of the debate was the future of unionist tendencies in the Lutheran church. The so-called Adiaphorists held that they were following the example of Luther in protecting issues pertaining to the gospel by yielding in minor matters of ceremonies and rites.[33] The opposition led by Flacius accused the Adiaphorists of betraying Luther for political expediency. The broader issue, in both camps, was the place of Luther in the theology and tradition of the post-Reformation Lutheran church. The controversy was finally put to rest in favor of Flacius's group with the tenth article of the Formula of Concord. Yet the question of Luther's authority would become more prevalent in the following controversies.

The Majoristic controversy was named after a student of Melanchthon, Georg Major, who allegedly held the proposition that good works were necessary for salvation. Major was accused of this in a letter from Nicolaus von Amsdorf regarding his appointment as superintendent in Eisleben.[34] Amsdorf countered by suggesting that not only were good works not necessary to salvation, but they were detrimental. This controversy existed on the theological fringe of the church, but those involved attempted to draw both Melanchthon and Flacius into the fray. Neither of them ever responded directly to the question. But the actual content of the controversy was not the primary issue, as the extreme views were never widely held; it was instead the manner in which the church leaders settled the question that was significant. The issue was settled with reference to biblical citations and the Augsburg Confession, not to Luther himself. This controversy placed the battle for the reigns of the Lutheran church not in the realm of Luther's authority but in biblical interpretation and the confessions.

The Syncretistic controversy, pertaining to the freedom of the will in conversion, brought about new questions and attitudes concerning the definition of Lutheran orthodoxy. Rather than cite Luther's famous debate on the issue with Erasmus, the controversy was settled with a disputation, the citing of confessional precedent, and a host of biblical citations. The chief combatants, Victorin Strigel and Flacius, met at Weimar in 1560. The disputing parties agreed to use only "the clear plain text of the Holy Scriptures to weigh more than all the inferences and authorities of interpreters."[35] The dispute was once and for all decided in the 1570s with the declaration that man is unable by use of his natural abilities to effect his regeneration. More significant, however, was the continued trend in relying on disputation, confessions, and a particular philosophical language rather than Luther's words.

The importance of a type of theological language rose to the forefront with the Flacian controversy.[36] This pertained to the nature of original sin and the appropriate language for defining it. Flacius, labeled by later commentators as a Gnesio-Lutheran, was attacked by Strigel at the Weimar disputation for asserting that with original sin the very substance of man was destroyed. Strigel insisted that original sin was an accident in the Aristotelian sense and therefore could

not corrupt the substance of man. The dispute centered on the philosophical question of what in human nature was affected with the Fall
and how this related to justification. In the seven years after the
Weimar disputation, at least twenty publications attempted to define
original sin using the philosophical language of accidental, formal,
and material substance.[37] The Formula of Concord ultimately ended
the debate by positing a middle way, affirming both the real depth
of sin and the dignity of humankind. Yet the new nature of Lutheran
dispute was becoming clear. Theological codification, philosophical language, and a lack of explicit reliance on Luther would set the
course for the post-Reformation Lutheran church.

These various disputes over central questions of the faith revealed
the extent to which the theology of the Lutheran church was something of a mixed bag. What was widely recognized was the need for
some form of remedy to restore harmony. In an age of religious wars,
discordant theological voices were extremely unwelcome. Therefore,
in light of the disputational and confessional manner of discourse
within the church, it was acknowledged that an official theological document to define the new course of Lutheran orthodoxy was
required. The initial attempts to restore unity by the princes, such as
the efforts by Otto Henry of the Palatinate and Augustus of Saxony,
were unsuccessful. Their "Frankfurt Recess" proved futile in its
attempt to assemble a unified Lutheran front, most likely because it
did not address the increasingly complicated theological tensions.[38]
Rather, it was the efforts of established Lutheran pastors, led by
Jakob Andreae and Martin Chemnitz, that established the theological framework of Lutheranism after Luther. Andreae and Chemnitz,
with the help of David Chytraeus, enlisted a group of pastors to com-
pose a document entitled the Swabian-Saxon Concordia to address
the theological controversies and submit it to a council of pastors for
approval.[39] Elector August of Saxony criticized the document, as did
others, for its technical Latin terms and lack of citations from Luther.
However, it established the new standard for pursuing theological
peace. Elector August subsequently appointed a group of pastors,
including the respected Lucas Osiander, to submit a new document that might build on the limited success of the Swabian-Saxon
Concordia.[40] This Maulbronn Formula (named after the cloister in
which it was composed) was, however, deemed incomplete and was

therefore augmented by Andreae, Chemnitz, and others at Torgau in 1576.[41] The elector rejected this larger confession, the *Torgau Book*, though it was later accepted in a condensed version as the Formula of Concord. The Formula of Concord was accepted by a majority of pastors in northeastern Germany and found further success in the rest of Germany and in Scandinavia. The substantial degree of theological agreement led to the announcement of a jubilee year in 1580 and the compiling of an official compendium of Lutheran confessions, the Book of Concord. The Book of Concord included, most notably, the Augsburg Confession, Luther's catechisms, and the Formula of Concord.

It would seem naïve to expect that this codification of Lutheran doctrine would be a panacea eliminating further theological debate. Yet the Book of Concord, and especially its Formula, set forth an official document defining Lutheran orthodoxy. The question, What did it mean to be a Lutheran? could be answered definitively, based on this theological standard.

Thus the age of Lutheran orthodoxy, beginning in strife, witnessed relative political peace with the Peace of Augsburg and theological definition with the reception of the Book of Concord. While political and theological tensions continued to exist, the basic framework of the age of orthodoxy was set. To be a Lutheran in this age of orthodoxy no longer meant adherence to the theology of Luther but rather to a theological standard as summarized in the Formula of Concord. It was the Formula of Concord by which Arndt established his orthodoxy; therefore, we will now turn to a more detailed analysis of this crucial text.

Toward a Doctrine of Lutheran Orthodoxy

The following doctrines were expounded and explained in the Formula of Concord: original sin; free will; the righteousness of faith before God; good works; law and gospel; the third function of the law; the holy supper of Christ; the person of Christ; Christ's descent into hell; church usages called adiaphora, or indifferent things; God's eternal foreknowledge and election; and other factions and sects. While the Formula expounded twelve distinct doctrines, it is essential to see each of these as supporting the chief article of the Lutheran church: justification. In the debates leading up to the production of the Book of Concord and in the controversy surrounding Arndt, this is the one doctrine that provided the framework for the discussion of all other doctrines.

Original Sin

The themes of the depth of sin and the corruption of human nature were hallmarks of the Lutheran Reformation. Original sin was defined as the stain on every soul inherited from the Fall and was perceived to be the theological bedrock on which the Lutheran theological structure rested.[42] If it was not taken seriously enough, the theologians claimed, the magnitude of grace could not be comprehended. However, if it was misunderstood and taken to logical extremes, the essence of humanity could be seen as inherently sinful, thus creating theological issues pertaining to God as the creator of evil and the philosophical impossibility of the incarnation of Christ. The authors of the Formula thus sought to present the affirmative theses and antitheses that carved out the accepted teaching regarding the depth of sin but safeguarded against positing God as the author of evil. The Formula presented three affirmative theses. First, it was proposed that although sin had damaged mankind's relationship to its creator, it had not *essentially* damaged it. That is, God's handiwork in creating mankind is still noticeable, and any self-inflicted stain did not corrupt what was initially and essentially a work of God. The second thesis furthered this idea and upheld the necessity of the distinction: If the essence of humanity were sinful, then the incarnation of Christ as truly man, yet without sin, would be impossible. The final thesis buttressed the previous statements by affirming that sin is not a "slight corruption of human nature, but that it is so deep a corruption that nothing sound or uncorrupted has survived in man's body or soul, in his inward or outward powers."[43]

The negative theses listed the rejected doctrines that were believed to be the fruits of a skewed understanding of original sin. The nine theses reject the Pelagian error of asserting that after the Fall, man retained his spiritual powers in good form and the Manichean errors that failed to distinguish between nature and essence. The antitheses rejected any idea of sin being a mere impediment and stressed the depth of man's fallen nature.

The most obvious feature of the Formula's explication of original sin was its insistence on tying together the doctrines of sin and redemption. The doctrines of sin in the Formula are presented in such a manner that they protect the essential doctrines of Christ's substitutionary atonement. In a pattern that was repeated for the remaining doctrines, all the caveats, corrections, theses, and antitheses were put in place to protect the doctrine of justification.

Free Will

In the first century of the Lutheran church, there was perhaps no more contentious and commonly misunderstood doctrine than that of free will. This was, after all, the issue that helped catapult Luther to broader fame by means of his debate with Erasmus. In the Erasmus debate, Luther proposed the extreme bondage of the will, unable to do anything pertaining to either its salvation or its damnation. Yet as the Lutheran dogmaticians set themselves up against the emerging Calvinist party and its doctrines of double predestination (God actively selects some for heaven and others for hell), the questions pertaining to the freedom and bondage of the will required clarification. The issue of free will had also seriously divided Calvin from Melanchthon.

This second article, like the first, presented three positive theses regarding the freedom of the will. First, it was posited that in regards to spiritual matters, man is blind and incapable of understanding spiritual things. Second, man's will is not only blind but completely turned against the things of God. This thesis is posited, in the words of the Formula, such that "we are not of ourselves sufficient to claim anything as coming from us; our sufficiency is from God."[44] The final thesis prevented the doctrine of the freedom of the will from lapsing into any kind of determinism by arguing that although God alone can effect conversion; He does so through the use of the ordinary means of the Word and Sacrament.

The antitheses attacked particular groups, by name, with the charge that they either downplayed the bondage of the will or took the doctrine to an extreme and suggested that man is so completely passive in his own conversion and that God elects and converts without any external means. The Stoics and Manicheans are presented as members of the latter group, as they were condemned as teaching a type of fatalism. The Pelagian and semi-Pelagian groups were condemned for their belief in fallen man's own ability to comprehend and accept the gospel message. Those in the third group criticized were labeled *Enthusiasts*, and this was explained as "the term for people who expect the Spirit's heavenly illumination without the preaching of God's word."[45]

The overarching theme in this section of the Formula of Concord is the avoidance of the extremes of exaggeration, either Stoic or Pelagian. The doctrines were set forth in such a manner as to augment the teaching of the gospel, the office of the Word, and justification. The theological endeavor of the Formula thus far presented doctrines not in isolation but in the practical service of the foundational doctrines of redemption.

The Righteousness of Faith, Good Works, Law, and Gospel

The next three doctrines treated were presented in relation to the previous two and highlighted the theological foundation of the Lutheran church. The question of the righteousness of faith arose as two Lutheran theologians debated the nature of Christ's imputed righteousness. A debate between Andrew Osiander and Francis Stancaro as to whether Christ's righteousness was according to his humanity or divinity was limited in scope, yet it broached the topic of the nature of justification and led to a confessional clarification: "Accordingly we believe, teach, and confess that our righteousness before God consists in this, that God forgives us our sins purely by his grace, without any preceding, present, or subsequent work, merit, or worthiness, and reckons to us the righteousness of Christ's obedience, on account of which righteousness we are accepted by God into grace and are regarded as righteous."[46] This standard formulation, while hardly challenged within the Lutheran church, had led some to assert conflicting understandings of the concomitant doctrines of good works and of the distinction between the law and the gospel.

The disagreement over the place of good works arose when Major and Amsdorf posited their opposing opinions as to the place of good works in the Christian life. The Formula denied both formulations and presented a doctrine of good works that attempted to not only protect justification from the encroachment of works but also present a practical and feasible doctrine of the Christian life.

The affirmative theses hung on the use of the words "necessary," "ought," and "must." According to the Formula, these words must be used "correctly and in a Christian way applied to the regenerated and they are in no way contrary to the pattern of sound words and terminology."[47] Having set up a safety net with the explanation of the use of these words, the Formula affirmed the old Lutheran tension between obedience and sin and stressed that good works are not coerced or compelled from the believer but rather come naturally to the renewed individual. While this article fell in line with the past confessional documents in the Lutheran church, the claim that formulations must follow a certain pattern of sound words and terminology marks an ambiguity in the confessional standard. The tension lay in whether it was the form or content of the doctrine that was important. The insistence on a particular language would fuel later controversies in Arndt's day. While one such as Arndt would claim fidelity to a confessed doctrine, his use of language other than confessional language would cause concern. While the Formula's vocabulary may have been rigid, the content echoed the other doctrines in attempting to protect the doctrine of justification.

The second doctrine in this section dealing with the application of the gospel and the tension between obedience and sin pertained to the central Lutheran practice of dividing the law and the gospel. This article provided the practical crux of the entire Formula. The distinction of the law and the gospel organized the doctrines of sin and justification to protect and provide a framework for the teaching of the gospel.

The question at hand was whether the preaching of the gospel was "strictly speaking only a preaching of grace which proclaims the forgiveness of sins, or [was] it also a preaching of repentance and reproof?"[48] The controversy arose as two factions in the Lutheran church sought to understand the preaching of the passion of Christ and its function as either a terrifying or comforting event.

The affirmative theses stated that this distinction between law and gospel was "an especially glorious light that is to be maintained with great diligence in the church so that . . . the Word of God may be divided rightly."[49] Essentially, the law was any preaching or admonition that condemned that which was sinful. The gospel, on the other hand, was any preaching or teaching that taught that man had fallen short of the demands made by the law and taught that Christ had paid for all the guilt and obtained for him the forgiveness of sins. While it was acknowledged that the term *gospel* had various functions in the Bible, it was affirmed that when the teaching of the gospel was juxtaposed with the teaching of the law, when Christ was pitted against Moses, the gospel referred only to that which consoled. Once again, a desire for strict adherence to narrowly defined terms would stir up controversy with Arndt in his correspondence. While the protection of the doctrine of justification is still the primary theme of the Formula, an insistence on a particular language is also evident.

The Third Function of the Law

The explanation of the doctrine of the third function of the law, along with the teaching of the doctrine of good works, served as a type of corrective against those who would take the doctrines of gospel and turn them into a type of Lutheran antinomianism. The Formula initially presented the first two functions of the law, which had been covered in other doctrines. First, the law served as a type of external curb against unruly and disobedient men. The moral law was a type of universal conscience that served to keep fallen humanity from sinking to its basest level.[50] The second function of the law was that which served to terrify and condemn the unbeliever such that they would turn to the gospel. This function was that intended in the previous doctrine of the distinction between the law and the gospel. The third function of the law was to give Christians "a definite rule according to which they should pattern and regulate their entire life."[51] The question at hand was whether this third function of the law should be urged upon Christians in sermons and devotional writings. The Formula asserted that this law was to be "diligently applied not only to unbelievers and the impenitent but also to people who genuinely believe."[52] Yet the Formula made a distinction based on what it designated as "works of the law and fruits of the Spirit."[53] Accordingly, that which was coerced from fear of punishment was a work of the law, while that which came spontaneously from a regenerate heart was designated a fruit of the Spirit. This distinction between works of the law and the fruits of the Spirit attempted to keep the law applicable to the regenerate while safeguarding any type of legalism that employed coercion and fear in the service of sanctification. Having made this distinction, the Formula condemned the idea that this third function of the law was useless to the believer and therefore not to be urged. This fine distinction, while doctrinally tenable, would serve to cause some confusion in later controversies surrounding Arndt. If one was seen as overemphasizing the third function of the law, one could be condemned as subverting the doctrines of the gospel. Yet as is seen in this explication, the Formula taught that an urging of the law upon believers was in agreement with confessional Lutheranism.

The Holy Supper of Christ and the Person of Christ

The previous doctrines had been set forth to finally establish the Lutheran teaching of sin and justification in the face of conflicting doctrines within the Lutheran church. The following two doctrines, the Holy Supper of Christ and the person of Christ, arose as the church sought to establish itself in the face of the encroaching second Reformation. As some within the Lutheran church had supposedly fallen prey to the opinions of the Swiss and French Reformers, these two contested doctrines received more space than the previous doctrines. While those had pertained to the depth of sin and the preaching and practicing of the doctrine of justification, the following delved into theological questions regarding the person of Christ and his presence in the Holy Supper.

The first contested question was whether the actual, physical body of Christ was present in the Sacrament of the Altar and whether he was received by both the believing and unbelieving alike. The document further explained the two methods by which the so-called Sacramentarians had supposedly altered the received Lutheran doctrine. The first of the deceiving groups was labeled "crass" Sacramentarians, as they set forth "in clear German words what they believe in their hearts, namely, that in the Holy Supper only bread and wine are received."[54] Others, however, were judged to be less forthright and "crafty" Sacramentarians. These individuals allegedly "in part talk [the Lutheran's] language very plausibly and claim to believe a true presence . . . but assert that this takes place spiritually by faith."[55] Having made reference to the subtleties of the debate, the affirmative theses were presented. The Formula asserted that Christ is indeed truly and essentially present on account of the words of institution. Furthermore, as per the Formula, Christ is able to be present insofar as He is truly God, and therefore omnipresent, and that God is capable of various modes of presence. Finally, the Formula affirmed the teaching of the Augsburg Confession in asserting that Christ is received by believers and unbelievers alike (the former to salvation and the latter to judgment) and that the eating of Christ was not "Capernaitic"—that is, in the normal manner that other food and drink is consumed. The antitheses reaffirmed the true body and blood as present and condemned both the Reformed understanding of "spiritual" eating and the Catholic doctrine of transubstantiation.

What seems a scholarly debate regarding modes of being and eating took on a surprisingly totemic role within the Lutheran community. Far from being an academic dispute, it became a popular marker of Lutheran identity and confessional fidelity.[56] While the argument was largely semantic, the Lutherans believed the Reformed to be "over-reforming" and robbing the laity of a great comfort, focusing on the preparedness and worthiness of the partaker rather than on the merits of Christ.

The second doctrine dealing with the theological encroachment of the Reformed dealt more specifically with the doctrine of the person of Christ. This doctrine, also a seemingly academic dispute, took up the largest portion of the Formula. The question in dispute regarded the sharing of the divine and human properties in the person of Christ. According to the Formula, the Sacramentarians (Calvinists) "declare boldly that the personal union makes merely the names common."[57] The affirmative theses claimed that the two natures are so united as to form a single individual that is, in reality, both God and man. The Formula went back to the fourth-century debate regarding the person of Christ to claim for Mary the title of *Theotokos* (mother of God) and not merely mother of the man Jesus. The Formula further asserted that the claim that Christ is "at the right hand of God" does not refer to a spatial location but rather a position of esteem and power. The antitheses denied all doctrines that separated or confused the divine and human attributes of Christ, denied Christ's ability to be omnipresent physically, and confused the states of Christ's humiliation and glory. The purpose of this doctrine was not only to affirm the previous doctrine regarding the Sacrament but also to protect the divine and omnipotent qualities of the person of Christ.

As will be established later, these were far from tangential issues for a devotional author such as Arndt. Rather, in ascertaining the legitimacy of one's confessional credibility, these doctrines were among the most contested and fiercely guarded. Likewise, these doctrines can be seen as bolstering the major argument of the Formula, that of the safeguarding of the teaching of justification. The confusion of the two natures clouded Christ's redemptive suffering and His ability to forgive sins in the present. As was the case with the previous doctrines, all the safeguarding and qualifying was in the service of establishing a particular understanding of the Lutheran doctrine of salvation by grace through faith. These doctrines were not presented as mere semantic exercise or only pertaining to confessional subscription but rather of the nature of the entire Lutheran doctrinal enterprise.

Christ's Descent into Hell

The question at issue regarding Christ's descent into hell seems the least pertinent to safeguarding the essential Lutheran doctrines. Despite being seemingly peripheral, the doctrine of Christ's descent into hell can be seen in light of the greater concern of the Formula to protect the essential doctrines of the gospel. The issue at hand was when and how Christ descended into hell, whether this happened before or after his death, in what manner he descended, and whether this doctrine belonged in the category of Christ's suffering or glorification. While the question was disputed among confessing Lutherans, the Formula paid little attention to the individual arguments and stated the following: "It is enough to know that Christ went to hell, destroyed hell for all believers, and has redeemed them from the power of death, of the devil, and of the eternal damnation of hellish jaws. How this took place is something that we should postpone until the other world."[58]

The Formula argued that this doctrine of Christ's descent cannot be comprehended with the senses or reason and must be accepted by faith alone. Furthermore, it is stated, disputation regarding this article should not be engaged. The two benefits that this summation provides to the greater theological framework are an acceptance of apparently difficult or conflicting doctrines and a greater weight being placed on the good news of the gospel rather than theological subtlety. It was, to the authors of the Lutheran confessions, acceptable to give some biblical statements more weight in the service of Lutheran doctrine than others. Accordingly, if a particular passage seemed to contradict accepted teachings regarding the doctrine of justification, it could be left aside for understanding in the afterlife. The doctrine of Christ's descent into hell questioned the place and time of the work of redemption and thus confused Christ's redemptive suffering and his glorification. Rather than raise doubt among simple believers, the question of the descent was sidestepped. The Formula also affirmed that the point to this, or any other theological query, was to comfort the believers in the certainty of their forgiveness. Questions of suffering versus glorification, as well as the mode of Christ's descent, are left unanswered, and the believer is instead assured that the power of death has been defeated in Christ's redemptive work, regardless of opinion concerning the place and reason for the descent. The pertinent theme was that of distaste for theological subtlety. Arndt would repeatedly voice his distaste for speculative or seemingly obtuse theological discourse.

Church Usages Called Adiaphora

The article discussing church usages and those things called adiaphora related directly back to initial controversies raised with the disputes concerning Melanchthon and the Leipzig Interim. Accordingly, the Formula attempted to chart the proper course, avoiding both the strict exclusion of indifferent religious ceremonies and their exploitation in times of controversy.

The Formula began by setting up the doctrine of things indifferent. The affirmative theses confirmed that there existed ceremonies and church usages that were neither commanded nor forbidden in the word of God. Second, these ceremonies had changed throughout the centuries of the church, as they were most profitable to the community. Opposing the Calvinist doctrine of church rites, whereby all that was not commanded was forbidden, the Formula suggested that while some rites may be conducive to the general welfare of the church, they do not constitute divine worship. The motivation to uphold these rites was certainly theological, but it also had a social dimension so as not to disturb the consciences of the simple believers and their attachments to the old church rites.

The antitheses attempted to safeguard against the perceived Philippist tendency toward undue concession to the emperor. The principle in use with such controversial but indifferent matters would be that of *In Statu Confessionis*, the principle that in matters of confessional fidelity or in times of controversy, there were no indifferent matters.[59] For example, if the elevation and breaking of the Host was being treated as an essential rite in one church body, it would be necessary to refuse the practice so as not to give the impression that the church was bound by one particular practice. The underlying theme in this principle was that in a time of persecution one should not make concessions to the "enemies of the Holy Gospel."[60]

This article, while fundamentally an attempt to safeguard Lutheran confessional fidelity, marked an interesting aspect to the quantification of orthodoxy. A gray area of intention is once again introduced whereby that which is confessional is based on circumstance and context. Granted, those doctrines that were previously set up in the Formula as essential could not be altered. Yet in some matters of church practice, the definition of what was considered confessional was not completely prescribed. The importance of context was employed by Arndt, as he suggested that his era required an alteration of theological discourse and special attention paid to the spiritual issues that he believed plagued his church.

God's Eternal Foreknowledge and Election

The penultimate article in the Formula dealt with an issue that had not, at the time, developed into a public debate. The debate concerning God's eternal foreknowledge and election had been a minor issue in the Lutheran church, but with the Calvinist churches in Germany and the "crypto-Calvinistic" controversy, there was a need for doctrinal clarification. The Formula also stated that the doctrine should be addressed as "it is such a comforting article when it is correctly treated."[61]

The affirmative theses centered on a distinction between foreknowledge and eternal election and on the person of Christ. Accordingly, it was taught that this doctrine was not to be investigated in the secret counsel of God but rather in the word of God, which leads the reader to Christ, who is the elect of God. Second, God's foreknowledge, while extending over good and evil, is not to be seen as the cause of evil but merely a control to the limits of evil. The affirmative theses taught that election was to give the believer assurance and was not directed to those who would perish.

The antitheses attacked those who taught the doctrine of predestination in such a way that it was not presented as gospel. The Formula rejected those who taught that God's ostensible desire to save all men was disingenuous. The Formula rejected the teaching that God has predestined some to perdition, regardless of their sin, in His secret counsel before the foundation of the world. The Formula also rejected as blasphemous the teaching that God's election was caused by any work or disposition in the elect.

The exposition of this doctrine shows once again the desire to tie all doctrines back to the teaching of justification. Unlike the Calvinist teaching of double predestination, the Lutheran doctrine of foreknowledge and predestination was only to be taught to engender comfort and consolation. While other speculative doctrines were not covered in the Formula, this section set a precedent for other such theoretical doctrines.

Other Factions and Sects

The final section in the Formula dealt with other factions and sects that had not committed themselves to the Augsburg Confession. These groups were singled out by name as the Anabaptists, Schwenckfelders, new Arians, and anti-Trinitarians.[62] The Anabaptists were attacked for holding the most damaging doctrines regarding both the church and the state. The doctrines the Anabaptists were charged with holding concerned the person of Christ, the baptism of children, Christians serving in government, taking oaths, and the possession of private property. While the latter doctrines dealt with civil order, the former sought to protect those doctrines that had been previously treated and expounded to protect the doctrine of justification.

The errors of the Schwenckfelders were similarly rejected, as they were denounced for denying the person of Christ to be fully God and fully man.[63] They were also criticized for denying the efficacy of baptism and the Sacrament of the Altar as well as for pinning the efficacy of these rites to the holiness of the minister. The so-called new Arians were condemned for denying Christ the properties of God the Father, and the anti-Trinitarians were condemned for either separating the Godhead into three distinct divine essences or confusing the three distinct persons and associating only certain attributes with each.[64]

The significance of this final article lies in its choice of condemnations. There were certainly many groups that would have fallen into the category "other factions and sects which have not committed themselves to the Augsburg Confession." Yet the choice of the radical reformers revealed the awareness that it was not only the established bodies of Calvinists and Papists that were to be defended against. While the Lutheran church had always condemned the more extreme reformers' sectarian positions, their inclusion in this brief, streamlined confessional statement gives them a certain status as particularly dangerous enemies of the church. It will be noted later that these terms (Schwenckfelders, Anabaptists, etc.) would become watchwords for heresy in the following decades. Even someone such as Arndt, who held little to nothing in common with these groups, could be condemned with the charge and name of the aforementioned groups. It is also significant that for the matters for which these groups were attacked, there were doctrines that had already been treated in the Formula and tied to the church's mission of protecting and promoting the doctrine of justification. These condemned beliefs of the enthusiasts were not seen as tangential to the authors of the Formula but related directly back to the central core of the Lutheran church.

In twelve articles, ranging from sin to the person of Christ to the sects, every doctrine was presented in a manner in which the doctrine of justification was protected and made central. Despite a few loopholes, and areas where contextualization may have been made possible, the theme of the Formula is protection of the doctrine of justification as the core of the gospel. If there is any distinctive emphasis that can be gleaned from the document with which we might quantify orthodoxy in the following decades, it is the centrality of the doctrine of justification. This central emphasis will be seen in the letters of Arndt, where he sought to justify himself as a genuine Lutheran; he used the language, doctrines, and overall motif of this, the most recent and relevant, confession by which Lutheran orthodoxy was judged.

Orthodoxy in Arndt's Correspondence

We shall now turn to the question of how the doctrines of the Formula of Concord were treated in the correspondence of Arndt. Our way of proceeding will be to look at the central loci of the Formula and how these key theological themes were handled by Arndt when writing to friends and colleagues. As we have made clear, these doctrines were never conceived as disparate loci. These twelve doctrines were intertwined with the goal of upholding the basic thrust of the Lutheran Reformation: the safeguarding of the doctrine of justification by grace through faith alone. The overlapping of these doctrines can produce redundancy, yet each of the doctrines also had a distinct history, controversy, and particular language. Finally, the locus-by-locus treatments of the doctrines in the Formula of Concord were composed after the standard theological method of the late sixteenth century. Johann Arndt's correspondence was not. Naturally, Arndt's correspondence was never intended as systematic theology. Yet in his letters, he could address precise doctrinal questions, and the relationship between theology and context is what interests us here.

Original Sin

The first doctrine of the Formula of Concord, original sin, was a favorite of Arndt's in his presentation of himself as a Lutheran. When explaining his situation, the teaching on the depth of human sin served various personal and prophetic causes and was consciously confessional. The most notable occurrence of such a confessional use is found in his correspondence with Wolfgang Frantzius in 1620.

Arndt wrote to the confessionally conservative Frantzius, describing the foundation of his work as a great struggle against evil. Arndt explained, "The abyss of all evil, which is original sin, must be recognised."[65] He explained that this sin is so embedded in the heart of natural man that no one of their own volition will fight against it, and this deep stain calls down the wrath of God.[66] Yet in keeping with the confessional balance in the Formula of Concord, Arndt stated that despite the blemish, the law of God is still engraved on the heart of man, as witnessed to by the prophet Jeremiah.[67] Rather than follow Flacius in ascribing original sin to the actual substance of mankind, Arndt portrays this sin as something accidental. Arndt stated that the foundation of his theology is "the fall of man, the lost image of God and the new creature."[68] The language of the "lost image" with reference to the fall of man follows the exact language of the Formula.[69] To a supporter of the confessions such as Frantzius, Arndt had explained the centrality and depth of original sin and did so using the exact language of the Formula, thus avoiding the contention that led to the initial, pre-Formula controversy.

A second letter in which Arndt exhibited a consciously confessional approach to the doctrine of original sin was that written to Balthasar Mentzer in May 1620. In explaining the fundamental points of his theology, Arndt claimed to have combated the errors of the Enthusiasts and their teaching that it is possible to perfectly obey the law. Arndt claimed to have defended the confessional position by asserting the doctrine of the lost image of God and the concomitant teaching of the powerlessness of man to do any spiritual good. Arndt wrote, "[Regarding] the lost image of God and the intrinsically corrupt human nature I have spoken clearly with much care and diligence."[70] Arndt claimed particular confessional allegiance to the teaching of the Formula of Concord in this matter, presumably as it was the one confessional document that treated the errors of both the Flacians and the Enthusiasts. Arndt went on to expound his understanding of confessional Lutheranism and did so by highlighting the knowledge of original sin and the corruption of human nature. Arndt claimed that without a proper understanding of original sin, all the other doctrines pertaining to the gospel were impossible to grasp.[71] Arndt thus followed the confessional standard in proposing to teach not only proper doctrine but also all doctrines as subservient to justification. Arndt's conscious adherence to both the content and form of the Formula of Concord illustrated his desire to be understood as a representative of conservative Lutheran theology.

In a letter to Petrus Piscator from January 1607, Arndt once again mentioned his specific reliance on the Formula of Concord and the necessity of understanding the corrupt age as one affected by the consequences of original sin.[72] This letter is not a theological apology but still references the Formula and the necessity of understanding original sin. Similarly, in a letter to Johann Gerhard in 1608, Arndt wrote that the first goal of teaching should be to turn men inwardly. While this inward turn would be a hallmark of Arndt's own spirituality, Arndt stated in confessional terms that "man should turn inwardly to see the abyss of his misery, and then turn to Jesus Christ, the treasure of all blessings."[73] Arndt's brief explanation of the doctrine and the confessional turn of language support the argument for Arndt's consciously confessional self-representation.

Arndt has in these letters presented the doctrine of original sin, made explicit reference to the Formula of Concord as his own standard, and tailored his language to fit his confessional correspondence and to avoid the positions of either Strigel or Flacius.

Free Will

The doctrine of free will and the charges of synergism were particularly vexing for Arndt. In his letters, he referred on numerous occasions to adversaries who had slandered him, forced foreign meaning into his words, and misunderstood his teaching concerning the freedom and bondage of the will. Within the Lutheran church, from Melanchthon's *variata* to the synergist controversy, there was a heightened sensitivity to teaching on the doctrines pertaining to the human will. On various occasions, Arndt argued for the necessity of human volition in moral improvement and the responsibility of the individual to devote himself to the imitation of Christ. Yet in a few letters to his confessional brethren, Arndt attempted to distinguish between himself and those who taught the necessity of human responsibility in conversion. Arndt claimed dependence on the confessional understanding of free will by denying it in a spiritual sense to unbelievers, restricting it to the converted only, and relating it back to the doctrine of justification.

In a letter to Johann Gerhard in February 1607, Arndt reported that he had been slandered as a synergist.[74] To protect his reputation and counter the claim that he had mishandled the doctrine of free will, Arndt declared that in his writings, he had removed all references to human ability, both before and after conversion. Arndt further claimed that he had done all this in order to safeguard reliance on the mercy and grace of God in Christ.[75] The inclusion of "and after conversion" would go beyond the confessions, which attributed a degree of free will in spiritual matters to the converted. Yet the context of both the situation and the letter show Arndt attempting to take drastic measures in order to protect himself from the claim that he had mishandled the doctrine. A second letter to Gerhard, written six months later, revealed Arndt's continued frustration with the claims of synergism and took a modified approach in presenting his understanding of the doctrine.[76] Arndt had recently received a censure from the theological faculty at Jena regarding *True Christianity*, and he claimed that the faculty had read too much into his work and had thus labeled him a synergist.[77] Arndt clarified his position on free will by claiming that it is the natural man who struggles against God and is powerless to use his will to effect conversion.[78] Arndt modified his position from his letter to Gerhard six months prior; it is now only the natural, unconverted man who is bereft of free will. His earlier inclusion of the clause "and after conversion" is absent. Once again, Arndt buttressed the argument by tying his doctrine of free will to the core of justification.[79] While it is clear that in both letters, Arndt's goal was to clear himself of the charges of heterodoxy, this second letter shows heavier reliance on the Formula, as it was careful to distinguish between the will in mankind's four states: pre-Fall, post-Fall, postconversion, and in glory.

The final letter to Gerhard regarding free will and synergism, written the following year, reveals Arndt's clearest presentation of his confessional representation regarding the charges of synergism. Arndt stated in this letter that there is in fact a free will, but it is only made free with the anointing of the Holy Spirit.[80] He reversed his earlier judgment that removed all power from mankind both before and after conversion. Arndt further clarified that his writings may seem synergistic, but that is only if one does not understand that he does not write to the unconverted heathen but to Christians who have the means to renew themselves and make progress in the Christian life.[81] Regarding any further claims of synergism and details pertaining to free will, Arndt deferred to the writing of Martin Chemnitz, chief author of the Formula. In three letters over the space of a year Arndt had clarified and presented his case for orthodoxy regarding free will and the charge of synergism.

As Arndt was writing to Gerhard about the censure he received from the theological faculty at Jena, Arndt also wrote to a member of that faculty, Petrus Piscator. Against the charge that he had mis-handled the doctrine of free will, Arndt presented a threefold case for his confessional fidelity. First, Arndt claimed, "I have pointed out in over twenty places from the text of my book where my thoughts are clear and opposed to synergism."[82] Second, Arndt claimed that while his understanding of the issues may have been clouded by his particular manner of speech, the wider context of his work bore out his confessional claim. Arndt further agreed to make any necessary changes in the future additions.[83] Last, Arndt affirmed his belief in the absence of a free will prior to conversion and stated that he had denied the role of human volition in conversion.[84] Arndt concluded his argument by reaffirming the necessity of tying this doctrine back to the doctrines of God's grace and forgiveness, finally concluding with the apostolic maxim, "Not I, but the grace of God in me."[85]

In these four letters, Arndt consciously defended his works and reputation against the accusations of synergism or heterodox views on free will. His tone varied, showing vehemence in his letters to Gerhard while striking a more conciliatory note in his letter to Piscator. What united the letters was a desire to follow the Formula with reference to the doctrine of free will.

The Righteousness of Faith before God

The central doctrine of the Lutheran church, the righteousness of God imputed to the believer by means of faith, has been seen to be central to all other doctrines. Thus in this analysis of the confes-sional Arndt, the doctrines pertaining to justification (shorthand for the righteousness of God imputed to the believer by means of faith) are rarely seen in isolation. The few instances of Arndt's refer-ences to justification will be examined, but the bulk of the analysis is best done when tied to the following doctrines of good works and the distinction between the law and the gospel. It will be seen that the confessional Arndt was very adept at following the confessional model of tying all doctrines back to a Lutheran understanding of justification.

One such instance of Arndt professing the confessional doctrine of justification occurred in his letter of April 20, 1621, to Duke August of Braunschweig.[86] In a previous letter, the duke wrote to Arndt regarding a theological censure written by Matthias Lauterwald concerning Arndt's extensive use of Johannes Tauler. While Arndt maintained his defense of selectively using the fifteenth-century mystic, he also was careful to present himself as faithful to Lutheran orthodoxy. Arndt began the letter by praising what he claimed to be the kernel of Lauterwald's censure. Arndt wrote that the censure has, to its benefit, properly and carefully distinguished between justification by faith drawn from Scripture and justification by works.[87] Arndt affirmed that this was the very essence of Christianity.[88] In a letter that at times contained strains of the eclectic Arndt, the author is careful to present himself in accordance with the chief article of the Lutheran church.

A second, lengthier discussion on the doctrine of justification occurred in a letter written to Gerhard Colemannus, a friend of Johann Gerhard. The letter suggests that Colemannus had written to Arndt to discuss the finer points of his theology. Arndt responded by condemning idle speculation and directed his correspondent to the foundation of the faith. Arndt contended that the essence of Lutheranism is faith, which leads to the application, imputation, and apprehension of Christ to the remission of sins and the consolation of Christ.[89] This language of imputation and remission was uncommon in the scope of Arndt's works and was most certainly employed to stress his own confessional reliance. In Arndt's published works, he would typically move from faith back to the disposition of the individual, yet he here redirects the reader to the author of the faith. Arndt wrote, "Doesn't God produce this all through faith?"[90] Additionally, Arndt decried the state of many in the church who debate justification rather than simply accepting it as the foundation of the church.[91] While Arndt was chiefly defending justification, he used the doctrine as a foundation by which Colemannus might also better understand the doctrine of good works. Arndt moved from the substance of faith to its fruits. Arndt wrote of the very clear effects of faith and suggested, as did Luther, whether a barren faith produces such qualities.[92] Following the Formula, Arndt was careful with his language in neither commanding nor coercing but proposing that good works are of the very nature of faith. While the Majoristic controversy heightened sensitivity to the language concerning good works, Arndt sidestepped the controversy by referring to works as the effects of faith, rather than to their necessity. While Arndt wrote that these good works are expected, as good fruits from a good tree, the context of the entire letter made clear his orthodox intentions.[93]

The Law and the Gospel

One of the more straightforward defenses of Arndt's confessional adherence occurred in a letter to Piscator from 1607.[94] Throughout Arndt's *True Christianity*, there existed pleas to contemplate the passion of Christ, something undoubtedly inherited from his preferred fifteenth-century mystics. During the initial period of censure from various theological faculties, a letter from Piscator questioned whether this contemplation confused the doctrine of the law and the gospel by portraying the sufferings of Christ as good news rather than as the wrath of God against sin. The essential question, which was a controversial point before the drafting of the Formula, was whether the crucifixion was a terrifying or comforting event. Arndt very deftly qualified his statements by affirming, "The death of Christ, insofar as it testifies to the wrath of God and sin is in itself the preaching of the law which brings about penitence and sorrow."[95] Arndt tempered himself slightly by writing that if the death of Christ worked remorsefulness and sadness, it can only be classified as the work of the law, yet the distinction between law and gospel can be difficult to ascertain in an issue such as this.[96] Arndt composed his response to Piscator in light of the Formula and acknowledged his dependence on the Formula and its distinction between the law and the gospel. While he ultimately did not abandon his views as expressed in *True Christianity*, he had attempted in this letter to placate Piscator's complaint with a clear reference to established orthodox teaching.

The Third Function of the Law

The presence of the third use of the law in the writings of Arndt is understandably ubiquitous. As a moral and devotional author concerned with the renewal of the Christian life, he would stress the law's third use to such a degree that no one would suggest that he repudiated the Formula's insistence that the law be "diligently applied not only to unbelievers and the impenitent but also to people who are genuinely believing."[97]

As has already been noted, the third use of the law (the didactic use) was appropriate only insofar as it was taught that good works flow freely from the converted individual. Second, regarding the controversial words "necessary," "ought," and "must," the Formula asserted that the language used to teach this aspect of the law must "in no way be contrary to the pattern of sound words and terminology."[98] In a letter to Duke August, Arndt made it clear that he believed that good works were necessary and essential to the practice of true faith.[99] While in this letter Arndt had stressed the necessity of good works (in the manor of Major), he reaffirmed that he is in no way repudiating the Lutheran interpretation of justification and has not turned Christ into a mere example as he claimed the monks had.[100]

In the letter from January 14, 1607, to Petrus Piscator, Arndt wrote once again that he believed that the third function of the law was necessary to teach. Arndt pointed Piscator to his *True Christianity* and claimed that a confessional approach to the third use of the law was at the very heart of his most popular work. Arndt claimed that it was his particular calling to show believers the proper use of the law after their conversion.[101] Similarly to the previous example, Arndt cushioned his insistence on pressing the third use of the law by testifying that this should not be taught as anything other than the nature of faith. Thus while the law must be taught to believers, any compliance with the law was, in the words of Arndt, "Not I, but the grace of God in me."[102]

The Person of Christ and the Lord's Supper

While Arndt never did explicitly address the theological contours of the person of Christ or the Lord's Supper, there exist in his correspondence particular references to his desire to be understood in light of the Formula of Concord. In the letter from 1620 to Frantzius, Arndt criticized those who would teach that Christ was spatially located at the right hand of God. Arndt disavowed the Calvinist (and sometime Melanchthonian) approach to the person of Christ that held that his glorified physical body was incapable of existing corporally on earth. Using the Lutheran argument that was employed against those who taught that Christ's glorified body was spatially located in heaven and thus could not be present in the Sacrament, Arndt condemned those who "think that Christ is placed at the right hand of God and therefore no longer on earth . . ."[103]

In a letter from the same year to Balthasar Mentzer, Arndt was made aware that some had accused him of following the heterodox teachings of Valentin Weigel with regard to the person of Christ and the Lord's Supper. Arndt stressed that he derived his teaching concerning the person of Christ and the Sacraments from the Augsburg Confession and the Formula of Concord.[104] Later in this letter, Arndt claimed once again to follow the standard of the Formula of Concord in his teachings regarding the personal nature of Christ: "I have hotly defended the pure teaching of the person of Christ, after the example of the Formula of Concord."[105] While Arndt's correspondence does not treat these subjects with any type of systematic detail, he was cognizant of the pertinent issues: the intermingling of Christ's human and divine natures, the corporal presence of Christ in the Sacrament, and the confessional importance of the Formula of Concord in addressing these issues.

Adiaphora

Arndt's confessional approach to the matter of church rites became evident early in his career. In his first known letter to Duke Georg of Anhalt, Arndt wrote that he would not discontinue the rite of baptismal exorcism. Baptismal exorcism was not a confessional issue but a common Lutheran rite. Luther had published an order of baptism in 1523, which followed closely an older Catholic order. While baptismal exorcism was not uniformly popular, it was never condemned as heterodox. While this would become a contentious point with the Calvinists, Duke Georg seemed to have been proactive in his desire to quell inter-Protestant feuding. Yet Arndt laid out a confessional approach to rejecting the duke's request. Arndt followed the Formula of Concord in presenting the rite as a tradition that had a lengthy precedent and was not forbidden. Arndt wrote that the faithful church fathers had established exorcism as part of holy baptism thirteen hundred years earlier, that it had become a general ceremony of the true church drawn from the meaning and true interpretation of Scripture, and that it was not an offensive ceremony.[106] The confessional model for things adiaphora stated that rites that are neither forbidden nor commanded should only be abolished if they made undue theological concessions to Rome. Nothing was written of concessions to the Calvinists. But Arndt, whose early work was directed against the encroaching second Reformation, took a confessional stand. This confessional platform and his banishment from Anhalt on account of it would serve as his most frequently advertised badge of confessional fidelity.

Election

In Arndt's correspondence, there was little discussion of the doctrine of predestination. As was seen in the Formula of Concord, the doctrine was presented only to distinguish their understanding of predestination against the Calvinist teaching. The Formula taught that predestination was a gospel comfort, and Arndt would make known his distaste for the Reformed teachings of predestination as a cornerstone of theology. Arndt seemed, as in other doctrinal discussions, more willing to defer to the theologians on the matter of election. In 1608, Arndt wrote that concerning the various nuances of election and predestination, he would assent to the work of Chemnitz.[107] Arndt never treated the doctrine of election directly, yet he distanced himself from the erring parties and knew the proper authorities to whom he could appeal. It would seem unlikely that the nature of Arndt's theology would attract any kind of controversy surrounding predestination as the thrust of his major works centered on sanctification. Yet the controversy surrounding the so-called crypto-Calvinists, and the prevalent practice of attacking theologians by affixing maligned sects to their work, was well known to Arndt.

Other Sects

An integral part of theological culture during the Reformation was the use of pejorative names. These names carried with them particular meanings and were not simply insults. They pointed to specific theological issues, and that is why they must be taken seriously in Arndt's correspondence. Much could be said of an opponent with a single designation, whether crypto-Calvinist, Schwenckfeldian, Weigelian, or Philippist. The constant references in Arndt's correspondence to those who slandered him by affixing names to his thought reveal sensitivity to the confessional issue of other sects.

Arndt either wrote of the other sects in general terms as *schwaermer* and *enthusiasteri* or mentioned particular sects by name, particularly those of Weigel and Schwenckfeld. While the Formula expressed its particular concerns with the teachings of the other sects, it was for Arndt enough to write that he had no interest in their errors. Arndt's most sweeping disavowal of the new sects came in a letter to Frantzius, when he condemned the practice of affixing the names of sects to the unlearned and simple preachers of repentance. It was, Arndt wrote, unfair to charge the simple with adhering to particular theological errors.[108] Arndt wrote that he shared the contempt for the newer sects that the Formula presented. And while there is little theological detail, Arndt condemned those names that were fastened to him.

Conclusion

To be a Lutheran in the age of orthodoxy was to conform to the theological content of the accepted Lutheran confessions. While this might seem simplistic, the political and theological atmosphere demanded such a confessional approach. For the purposes of answering the question, Was Johann Arndt a Lutheran? the standards of his day must be invoked. The Formula of Concord was the ideal benchmark for its relative brevity and contemporary context. It is evident in Arndt's correspondence to his confessional brethren that he believed the Formula to be the preeminent reference by which he could establish his claims to orthodoxy. Johann Arndt undoubtedly knew the Formula well, and he presented his beliefs in light of it. Was

Johann Arndt a Lutheran? According to a selection of his correspondence to select individuals, and by the standard they themselves set, it clearly appears that Arndt was concerned to present, and capable of presenting, his thought within the boundaries of the confessional church.

It must, however, be noted that the Formula was just that, a formula. It was not a precise code that encapsulated all the duties of a pastor or spiritual author. There are two mistakes that must be avoided in reviewing Arndt's confessional fidelity: reductionism and cynicism. The reductionist error would ignore the particular charismatic elements in an author and pastor such as Arndt. It would reduce Arndt's writings to a mere parroting of the Lutheran confessions. It is obvious in his spiritual works, and in other parts of his correspondence, that Arndt was interested in extraconfessional spirituality. The second error of cynicism would suggest that Arndt simply repeated the words of the confession to save his reputation without actually believing in them. Giving the historical figure the benefit of the doubt, we should see Arndt as a sincere Lutheran. Yet with his specific spiritual concerns and lack of systematic writing, we should not suggest perfect erudition in regards to confessional theology. Yet as the Formula exhibited, the core doctrine was that of justification, and thus, as Arndt made clear his orthodoxy in regards to that doctrine, he can be partly excused for errors in peripheral doctrines.

The following chapter will examine the spiritual aspect of Arndt in his correspondence as he strayed beyond the confessional boundaries set by the Formula and cast an eye widely over the history of Christian spirituality.

CHAPTER 3

The Eclectic Arndt

Introduction

As demonstrated in the previous chapter, confessional fidelity was an important issue for Arndt. He was conversant with the language of the Formula of Concord and consistently expressed his desire that his writing be interpreted within the context of the Lutheran church. Yet confessional Lutheranism was not the totality of Arndt or his thought. There existed a fluid definition of theology largely defined by a focus on the Spirit and the renewal of the inner man. For these purposes, Arndt drew from a wide range of Christian authors and traditions. This spiritual eclecticism is present throughout his correspondence as well as in the works he chose to reprint. Furthermore, it is this particular emphasis in Arndt's works that has gained him notoriety, whether as the father of Pietism, a dissenter within the church, or as a herald of true Christianity. Ultimately, the significance of Arndt's spirituality lies in his attempt to reinvigorate the Lutheran church with an appreciation for what he termed "true spirituality."

The passages from Arndt's correspondence that deal with this spirituality should not be interpreted as evidence of a conscious rejection of the confessional material in the previous chapter. Arndt believed that his theology of spiritual renewal did not contradict confessional allegiance. He saw his theology as a unified, confessional whole, even if many of his contemporaries did not. In a letter from Johann Gerhard to Nicolaus Hunnius, Gerhard suggested that Arndt's fragmented theology was well intentioned but suffered from two major problems: "First, he was given to the study of medicine in the academies and had not yet shaped his judgment about theological controversies by listening to lectures and holding discussions;

but the second, that the reading of the books of Paracelsus and Weigel pleased him, for an eye-witness testifies that Arndt brought from them many things into his books *de vero Christianismo*. In the meantime, I am sure of this: that he feels more correctly than he speaks."[1] The notion that Arndt was simply too uneducated to expound clearly correct doctrine is an idea that has been brought up in current literature, as well as in his own lifetime, by both his friends and adversaries.[2] The problem with this supposition, how-ever, is twofold. First, Arndt was certainly educated, having studied medicine, being Latinate, and studying under Pappus and Sturm at Strasbourg. Second, the information regarding Arndt's exact course of study at various universities is unclear. He did study medicine and theology, but to what extent remains unknown. Arndt was hardly ignorant, but to what extent his university training formed his thought is unclear.[3] Nevertheless, it is not insignificant that it was Gerhard who would suggest this interpretation of his former pastor. While Gerhard remained sympathetic to Arndt, he kept a safe dis-tance from Arndt's spirituality, despite numerous letters urging him to borrow from a wide range of Christian authors.

Arndt Defines the "Spiritual Author"

That Arndt was willing to cast a broad eye over the whole spectrum of Christian spirituality is most clearly seen in a letter to Gerhard from March 15, 1603.[4] This letter, often referred to as "De Studio" in the literature, reveals his affinity for spiritual authors well beyond the range of Lutheran orthodoxy. Composed as Arndt's young protégé was twenty-one years old and preparing to study for his master's degree at the University of Jena, "De Studio" represents Arndt's clear-est ideas on the pious and learned Christian scholar/pastor.[5] From the contents of Arndt's reply, it seems that Gerhard had written to his former pastor to elicit advice on how to build a personal theological library.[6] In his brief letter, Arndt advised Gerhard on the traits that make a worthy theological book and provided a list of authors and works. The authors and works recommended were the following: the Vatable Bible; a Hebrew Lexicon (either Johann Habermann's or Pagninus's);[7] the works of Bernard, à Kempis, Jean de L'Espine, Louis of Granada, and Augustine; Seneca (for philosophy); the biblical commentaries of Rudolf Gwalther and Benedictus Aretius; the ecclesiastical history of Lucas Osiander; and the *Harmony of the Psalms* by Elias Hutter. Of the fourteen authors recommended, only three were Lutherans. An examination of a few of the lesser-known names reveals Arndt's attempt to build for Gerhard a theological library with a distinct irenic and mystic strain.

The first work recommended, the Vatable Bible, was named for François Vatable (1495–1547) and had a curious and significant history. Vatable, who was appointed a professor of Hebrew at the Royal College of Paris by Francis I, had little to do with the work that carried his name, however.[8] Vatable never published anything but rather lived into posterity through the notes of his students at the Royal College. The author/compiler of the Vatable Bible was instead Robert Estienne (Stephanus), a student of Vatable and later professor at the Sorbonne. As Estienne worked on the Bible using Vatable's notes, he fell under suspicion by the faculty of the Sorbonne. Estienne fled to Geneva, where he became a close friend of Calvin and a publisher of his works. He wrote against the Sorbonne, and Catholicism in general, and played a part in the execution of Michael Servetus.[9] In Geneva, Estienne made use of the translations of Leo Jud and the Zurich Bible for the Old Testament as well as Theodore Beza's New Testament. The finished product was a Bible/commentary with strong Swiss/Reformed tones. Before his death in 1547, Vatable in fact repudiated the work as reeking of "new opinions."[10] Why would Arndt have recommended this Bible, as opposed to translations and commentaries done by theologians within his own church? The argument could be made that Vatable's Bible was simply the most reliable text and that academic concerns would trump confessional fidelity. However, the tenor of this letter and the other authors recommended reveal ambivalence, if not distaste, for some authors within his own church.

Arndt next recommended that Gerhard purchase a Hebrew Lexicon, either Johann Habermann's or Pagninus's. The choice of Habermann makes sense for two reasons: he was a professor of Old Testament at Wittenberg and would likely have been Gerhard's instructor; he and Arndt were like-minded in their affinity for devotional literature. Habermann not only worked as a professor but was also a printer and author of devotional literature; he eventually published a *Gebetbuchlein* that found criticism among his Lutheran peers.[11] Pagninus's *Biblia Universa* was a widely used work (parts of it were used in Vatable's Bible and Olivétan's French Bible).[12] Wolfgang Frantzius, a correspondent of Arndt, believed Pagninus's work to be on par with Luther's Bible. This was not uncommon as Lutherans in the sixteenth century continued to use editions of the Vulgate. The *Biblia Universa* was commonly used at Lutheran universities.[13]

Arndt wrote that for a book to animate and penetrate the soul, it must be written in the Spirit. He did not, however, provide any test for determining whether a work had a true spiritual character. He chose rather to list a number of authors whom he believed to have written truly "spiritual" works. The list includes the following: St. Bernard, à Kempis, Macarius, Jean de L'Espine, Louis of Granada, and St. Augustine.

Arndt continued on to recommend biblical commentaries. He admitted a lack of knowledge of commentaries, a telling admission for a pastor with his own unique theological interpretations.[14] And indeed, Arndt's two suggestions are curious: Rudolf Gwalther and Benedictus Aretius. Both were Swiss theologians with ties to the Zwinglian tradition (Gwalther was Zwingli's son-in-law). Arndt would likely have had an interest in Aretius, as both were trained in the sciences and showed an interest in *Naturtheologie*. Gwalther would eventually become the successor to Heinrich Bullinger in Zurich and wrote widely as he also traveled throughout Europe. Arndt's failure to mention any Lutheran commentaries (of which there were many) bolsters the argument that Arndt was not particularly concerned with only Lutheran literature. Perhaps he felt that Gerhard would get enough instruction in Lutheran literature through his education, so he saw himself as expanding on that curriculum. A single revealing sentence interrupts the list of recommended literature: "avoid disputational theology."[15] As has been seen in Arndt's other letters, the terms *disputational* as well as *scholastic* were general watchwords for theology that he saw as dangerous and wrongheaded.

This brief letter is among the most straightforward in this collection. Arndt was obviously attempting to mold the young Gerhard into his own spiritual likeness. While he may have assumed some knowledge of Lutheran authors and commentators, he made no reference to any work firmly within his own confessional context. Nowhere did he recommend the writings of Luther. He can be seen as implicitly condemning his own church for a lack of truly spiritual works as well as suggesting to Gerhard that he himself felt comfortable reading outside of his own denominational lines. The date of this letter then seems especially significant, as it would coincide with Arndt's own disenchantment with his pastoral situation at Braunschweig and the beginning stages of his composition of book 1 of *True Christianity*.

Two years later, Arndt would write another letter to Gerhard in order to advocate two other devotional works that defined Arndt's own brand of eclectic spirituality. Arndt began with an apology and stated that some may disapprove of his selections but that he would remain steadfast in his approval of the works he had held dear. Arndt continued by reminding Gerhard that his charge was now, through his sermons, to penetrate and cultivate the inner life of his parish and to bring about renewal.[16] All of this, Arndt wrote, was not for anything superficial, or for pride, but in imitation of the humility of the Savior. Arndt then commended to Gerhard the *Theologia Deutsch* and the *Imitation of Christ*.

Arndt wrote to Gerhard that it was not any kind of mystical theology but rather that particularly practical theology derivative of the *Theologia Deutsch* that he wished him to cultivate.[17] Arndt reminded Gerhard that Luther rediscovered this little book almost a century earlier and recommended Luther's own edition.

The second book recommended by Arndt was the *Imitation of Christ*. This was a work that Arndt had similarly recommended in the "De Studio" letter two years previously. Similarly to his recommendation of a particular edition of the *Theologia Deutsch*, Arndt mentioned that he had heard of a version with "very few errors in it" edited by Henricius Harphii.[18] Raidel, the editor of a collection of letters that includes this one, perceptively suggests in a footnote that Arndt was being very careful in recommending this book, prudentially mentioning that he had "only heard" of this work.[19] Arndt later had a new edition of the *Imitation of Christ* printed, but he did not add any foreword to it, and his theology was more molded after the idea of imitation than it would be affected by any particular theological aspect of à Kempis's work.

While much of this letter concerned Arndt's own experiences during the concurrent siege at Braunschweig, Arndt wrote plainly that even though Gerhard had graduated, he wanted to further influence his study of theology. From these early letters to Gerhard it appears that Arndt believed the work that best summed up his approach to spirituality was the *Theologia Deutsch*.

The *Theologia Deutsch*

Steven Ozment has highlighted the special relationship between mysticism and various theological parties in the sixteenth century, with particular attention paid to the *Theologia Deutsch*.[20] While he has referenced the work with regard to Luther, Hans Denck, and Sebastian Castellio, among others, the work also had a lasting influence into Arndt's day, even being reprinted with a new foreword by Arndt himself.[21] This enigmatic work blended individual piety and theological emphases that many found congruent with Protestantism.

From Luther's first reprint in 1516 through significant editions and translations up to Arndt's reprint in 1621, this small devotional tract often found a place within varying theological circles. That this small booklet would be read and recommended among parties that were otherwise in opposition to each another suggests the book had not only broad significance but also the malleability of mystical Christianity.

The *Theologia Deutsch* is composed of fifty-four short chapters that attempt to encapsulate the totality of the Christian faith. While the work is generally associated with medieval mysticism, it is dogmatically simplistic in both its tone and its style. The outline of the book centers around four questions: What is man? Who is God? How is a union between the two affected? And what effect does this have in the life of man? The primary themes in the book are those of the poverty of the human spirit, *Gelassenheit* (peaceful resignation), *Vollkommenheit* (completeness or perfection), and *Vergottung* (partaking in the divine nature). While generally "mystical," it is not so in the pattern of Meister Eckhart and the scholastic mystics but rather in a type of earthy, crude mysticism devoid of transcendental speculation. It appears that the malleability of the work stems from its lack of specificity. Man is sinful, God is the highest good, and there is a paradox in God drawing man to Himself and man's willful submission. The effects of the union are both internal and ethical. This rather commonplace theological content left much room for interpretation.

Nevertheless, the *Theologia Deutsch*, in order to be appropriated by the reformers, had to be selectively interpreted, and the various forewords and addenda shaped and highlighted an agenda different from that of its original context. This had begun with Luther in the years surrounding the dramatic events of 1517. Both the 1516 and 1518 Luther editions of the *Theologia Deutsch* reflect Luther's early thought. Luther ignored the deeper ontological questions of man's ability to fashion himself in God's image. Rather, Luther, in the very title given his reprint, focused on how Adam must die and Christ lives in the believer, the passivity of the process of salvation, and the true locus of wisdom.[22] The sinfulness of man was a cornerstone of every Christian theology of the sixteenth century. By stressing this point, Luther could be read in conformity with any particular system. Luther emphasized the depth of sin and repentance as the cornerstones of Christianity. The seed of Luther's belief that one is *Simul Justus et Peccator* is already present in this early work. With this foundation, Luther can be seen to have interpreted the *Gelassenheit* of the *Theologia Deutsch* in light of his maturing views on justification. *Gelassenheit*, or resignation, is not then a disposition of the soul but an acceptance of God's election and salvation through faith in Christ. This resignation is an early form of solafideism. Last, Luther's emphasis on the mystical terms of the *Theologia Deutsch* is seen in his railing against spiritual pride. This, according to Luther, was the chief downfall of the Roman church. Humility was then found, not in the pomp of ceremony or in good works but in the base and demeaned. Wisdom came from the hidden things and out of the mouths of babes (*ex ore infantum*).

In the ten years before the next edition of the *Theologia Deutsch*, a significant amount of Luther's theological understanding had changed. Luther had evolved from the outcast rebel to a spiritual leader. His movement was on its way to becoming an institution, and with such a new institution came a new wave of theologians who would interpret the work differently. These Spiritualists and Anabaptists rejected the Roman church but also many of Luther's primary tenets. The small booklet that helped articulate Luther's ideas would subsequently be used to counter his movement. The 1528 edition of the *Theologia Deutsch* was printed by the anti-Trinitarian Ludwig Haetzer. The text itself underwent almost no change, with one significant exception. Steven Ozment has pointed out that Haetzer reordered a passage on authority that read "Scripture, faith, and truth" to "truth, faith, and Scripture."[23] The reordering seems an obvious inversion and attempt to existentialize authority as per Schoeffer's contention that truth is found in oneself and is not subservient to someone else's definition of faith or interpretation of Scripture.[24] In the brief foreword by Schoeffer, the purpose of the *Theologia Deutsch* was made clear: the essence of true Christianity was the personal experience of the Holy Spirit. According to Schoeffer, all truth was to be found in the internal appropriation of the Spirit. Denck's *Hauptreden* served a similar purpose in positing the need for freedom and the necessity of union with God.[25] This union with the creator was neither doctrinal nor sacramental but ontological. Unity was not found in an ecclesiastical institution, or in irenic overtures, but by absorption into the Godhead. Furthermore, *Gelassenheit* was not simple passivity in the Cistercian or Franciscan model, or in the abandonment of good works, but rather in the primacy of the Holy Spirit effecting unity with the Godhead.[26]

The 1542 edition, with an extended preface by Sebastian Franck, built on elements from the previous editions with an added anti-institutional bent.[27] The themes of Franck's preface were the primacy of experience over knowledge and the hidden nature of truth. A primary theme in the *Theologia Deutsch* itself was the hidden nature of truth, and Franck found the antithesis of this hidden truth in the scholasticism and dogmatism prevalent in the universities of his day. Franck echoes Luther in placing wisdom *ex ore infantum,* yet these babes are inspired directly by the Spirit and outside any form of an institutionalized church.

Sebastian Castellio's Latin translation of the *Theologia Deutsch* in 1557 highlighted particular themes seen elsewhere in his works and used the malleable mysticism of the *Theologia Deutsch* against the Protestantism of the budding confessional age.[28] Castellio's preface highlighted God's transcendence but without the spiritualism of the earlier editors. Rather, for Castellio, God's transcendence was seen in the simple piety of doubt, rebirth, and the practice of godliness.[29]

Bengt Hägglund has suggested that, of the more than two hundred editors of the work during the Reformation century, Valentin Weigel was "perhaps the one who used the *Theologia* the most."[30] Georg Baring has pointed out that the *Theologia Deutsch* is the fundamental work for understanding Weigel.[31] This is unsurprising, as Weigel's own person was as amorphous as the work he reprinted in 1571. Weigel's edition appeared at a crossroads in both his own life and the life of the Lutheran church. Weigel was still an ordained pastor in the Lutheran church, yet he was undoubtedly dealing in pansophism and reading Paracelsus with approval.[32] The church was also undergoing its first major movement toward confessionalization, yet the *Theologia Deutsch* was still accepted as a fruitful devotional work on the basis of Luther's approval. Weigel was not only interested in the book insofar as Lutheran theology could appropriate it. He saw in the work the totality of the Christian faith, highlighted by its insistence on the liberal and transcendent gift of the Holy Spirit, the new authority that it presented, and the complete internalizing of the faith.[33] Weigel praised both Eckhart and Paracelsus in his foreword and emphasized the internal nature of faith with little reference to the external highest good. He challenged the older authorities in placing the onus for right thinking and action inside the self rather than in submission to an institution.

In 1597, more than seventy years after Luther's editions of the *Theologia Deutsch*, Arndt prepared a new edition of the spiritual manifesto.[34] While this edition would not include any foreword by Arndt himself, his fascination with the work led to a new edition in 1605 to which he added a foreword and a collection of thoughts concerning the importance of the work. Arndt surprisingly claimed to have rescued this book from obscurity, suggesting that it had been hidden in the dust and comparing it to the biblical patriarch Joseph thrown into the pharaoh's dungeon.[35] While the lengthy printing record of this book has been established, undermining Arndt's contention to have recovered it from the dust, he was greatly influenced by the anonymous author of the *Theologia Deutsch*. The significance of Arndt's edition is threefold. First, he included the *Hauptreden* of Denck's version; second, he openly published his own *Bedencken*, which would be reprinted late in his career; and third, he expanded on the definition of spirituality found in his correspondence.

The addition of Denck's *Hauptreden* was a red flag for any confessional Lutheran. Denck's interpretation of *Gelassenheit* as an ontological unity with the Godhead would contradict any Lutheran dogma concerning theology proper and especially theological anthropology. It is also significant that this work would be reprinted late in Arndt's life, only one year prior to his death. This puts to rest any suggestion that Arndt's seemingly fractured theology was a product of his early writings. Arndt did not publish this work under a pseudonym or with a lengthy apology. He claimed the highest status for this work and offered that his *True Christianity* was a parallel work for anyone interested in delving deeper into the themes found in it.[36] In his *Bedencken*, roughly twenty-eight theses on the *Theologia Deutsch*, Arndt expanded on the broad definition of spirituality seen in the correspondence spanning his entire career in the church. The pertinent themes are his animosity toward disputational theology, a call for a third marker of the true church (beyond the gospel and Sacraments), and distinctions between the inner and outer man and between works and words. Arndt wrote that the Tower of Babel was an important image in the New Testament and that it was particularly apt for the present spiritual milieu. Arndt wrote that the Tower of Babel was a powerful prefigurement for the New Testament and refers to the clerical estate. He also mocked those clergy who sought to build with books their own towers to heaven; such towers, Arndt remarked, were made of books and numerous disputations.[37] Arndt had also recalled the words of St. Paul to Titus to avoid disputes about the law, for they are unprofitable and worthless.[38] He went on to suggest that, as a Christian, one did not need many books other than the Bible (certainly an odd approach in a preface to a theological treatise).[39] Arndt further claimed that, because Christ alone is the truth, the need for more books and guides has passed.[40] Arndt also claimed that the church had made a great error in assuming that the pure teaching is preserved alone in the schools and churches by writings and disputations, while the Christian life is forgotten.[41]

A consistent theme in Arndt's *Bedencken*, and his work in general, was a distinction between true and false Christianity. As Arndt wrote, he would pit "true" Christian authors against false prophets and true piety against "chin-wagging." This was a recurring distinction for Arndt, as it distinguished between "mere" words and works. Arndt believed that the author of the *Theologia Deutsch* made this

same proper distinction. Arndt suggested that his own day was particularly in need of this message, as the church had focused too much
attention on doctrines and not enough on leading people to acts of
repentance and the imitation of Christ.[42] He further claimed that the
book rejected the bickering, redundant, and clamorous speech of his
age in favor of a focus on true love, a longing for the highest good,
a rejection of the vain world, the crucifixion of one's own flesh, and a
transformation into the likeness of Christ.[43] Arndt likewise appealed to
St. Paul's injunction to the Corinthian church, which he claimed was
also overly concerned with doctrine, and called on the church to
express itself instead in acts of love.[44] This emphasis on life as opposed
to teaching is expressed in some manner in each of Arndt's twenty-
eight *Bedencken*. Arndt never dismissed teaching but placed it alongside proper living in the imitation of Christ.[45] It is unsurprising, then,
that Arndt would suggest that the church was in need of a third mark
in addition to the gospel and the Sacraments. Due to the number of
false Christians, Arndt wrote, this third mark must be love.[46] Arndt
was thus able to mold the *Theologia Deutsch* in the image of his own
brand of spirituality. The work is careful to remember the importance
of teaching, he claimed, but it criticized disputation and argued for the
supremacy of Christian charity in distinguishing the "true" Christian.

Arndt's Spirituality

In 1979, Eric Lund proposed that Arndt's significance lay in his
development of a Lutheran spiritual tradition.[47] This thesis presupposed two important ideas: first, that there was no defined "spiritual
tradition" within the Lutheran church during its first century, and
second, that spirituality was something distinct from theology. Both
of these assumptions must be questioned, however. In Luther and
the Lutheran confessions. spirituality and doctrine were connected.
Spirituality (usually denoting personal piety, prayer, good works,
etc.) was a by-product of faith in Christ. Luther's small catechism provides an example of this; after each doctrine was presented, he wrote,
"What does this mean?" and tied the doctrine to one's daily activities.
From Luther to Johann Quenstedt, there existed a firm belief that
doctrine informed action.[48] Yet there exists a strain of commentators
who have referred to the period between 1555 and the rise of Pietism

as a time of "dead orthodoxy" and as a battle between theology and piety.[49] This portrait of late sixteenth-century Lutheranism is evident even in the modern English translation of *True Christianity*. Two forewords are included; the first, by the translator, Peter Erb, suggests that Arndt was combating a church bereft of true spirituality.[50] The second, however, written by Heiko Oberman, insists that this "dead orthodoxy" label was merely a bogeyman exploited by pastors and authors of devotional tracts.[51] The question of orthodoxy and spirituality seems largely a case of equivocation with regard to the term *spirituality*. If they were one and the same, then a high period of interest in orthodoxy would necessarily entail spirituality. Yet as will be seen, Arndt's spirituality and his "spiritual tradition" are divorced from specifically Lutheran doctrine. It was not antithetical to doctrine, but it took a broader view of the Christian life. Such was Arndt's definition of spirituality, and this is evident in his correspondence. Rather than using the established confessional guidelines for proper practice, Arndt defined his spirituality with two distinctions: the spirit versus the flesh and works opposed to mere words.

An illuminating insight into Arndt's own definition of spirituality is found in his letter to Gerhard from March 15, 1603. As he wrote to his friend on choosing books to begin a theological library (see earlier section of this chapter), he added a brief aside: too many theological works are written from the flesh; the key to discerning true spirituality was to find those authors who wrote with the aid of the Holy Spirit.[52] This sentence, wedged into a list of recommended authors, informed much of Arndt's spiritual thought. An author, Arndt suggested, was not to be judged by confessional fidelity when it came to matters of spirituality. For Arndt, spirituality was broader than confessional boundaries. This dichotomy affirmed the larger split in Arndt's writings between the confessional and spiritual. This understanding of Arndt's spirituality begs two questions, however: how does spirituality differ from doctrine, and what (or who) is the final arbiter in judging the source of one's writings? Doctrine was defined as an affirmation of theological loci, while spirituality was a matter deeper than assent and belief. It was defined as something practical, internal, and spiritual.

In the same letter to Gerhard, Arndt made another distinction central to his own definition of the true Christian life, the internal versus the external. He was at the time also responding to criticism from his parishioners in Braunschweig. Arndt had been attacked from his own pulpit by his fellow pastor Herman Denecke, and many members in his church were critical of his preaching style. He stated that his preaching was not scholastic but intended to promote godly living through an active faith. If he was being attacked on doctrinal grounds, he turned the argument back by suggesting that what he was doing was something different from and beyond theology. Arndt wrote that the crux of what he was doing was distinguishing between the inner life and the external world.[53] As Arndt was expanding on this definition, he was also in the process of writing *True Christianity*. This distinction between the inner and outer man was central to that work. Such distinctions, however, did little to deter the complaints of those in his congregation. On account of the suspicion that he raised, he would soon leave his church in Braunschweig.

Despite Arndt's inability to convince his Braunschweig parishioners of the central importance of distinguishing between the inner and outer man, it was precisely this distinction that appears in another letter to Gerhard, this one offering counsel on how Gerhard himself should approach his pastoral duties. In a letter of January 10, 1605, Arndt wrote to Gerhard to commend him on the completion of his studies and to express his desire to further influence his study of theology.[54] Arndt suggested that now that Gerhard was entering the pastorate, he had to keep in mind his calling as a minister of the gospel. He wrote that the true theologian/pastor is not simply one who cultivates speech and theory, and stands upright during sermons, but is one whose job it is to penetrate and cultivate the inner man and stir up restoration among his flock.[55] Once again, there is no direct attack on the church that Gerhard served or a rejection of its theology; rather, Arndt stressed that there was something else beyond mere external theology. Arndt further wrote that this spirituality would "penetrate the soul" of the hearer.[56]

As Arndt's magnum opus, *True Christianity*, was in its final stages of completion, he took care that it would not be rejected among the theologians of the Lutheran church. Through his friends Piscator and Gerhard, Arndt sent copies to their respective universities to be examined.[57] In every known instance of these examinations, the work came back with censures to which Arndt would respond with an explanation of his intentions. Such a censure and response came from Arndt to Gerhard on November 27, 1606.[58] Arndt accepted that some changes could be made and that future editions would contain rewordings and deletions as the University of Jena suggested.[59] But while Arndt was willing to make doctrinal concessions, he was unwilling to alter that which pertained to the "*Theologia Practicum*."[60] Arndt argued that Christianity had always been something more than words; it consisted also of works.[61] This would hardly be controversial after the Majoristic controversy of the 1570s, but Arndt did not reference the ultimate decision of the church as expressed in the Formula of Concord; rather, Arndt added an addendum to this argument: "thus said Arnobius."[62] A reference to a fourth-century monk rather than his own confession sheds some small light on Arndt's frame of mind; he was not attempting to argue for confessional fidelity, but rather for true spirituality.

When Arndt subsequently wrote to Gerhard on August 3, 1607, the first book of *True Christianity* had been published. As he would throughout his life, Arndt would write to Gerhard as both mentor and apologist. Considering Gerhard's stature in the church when this letter was composed, however, Arndt wrote less as a mentor and more as one seeking advice and defending his cause. Claiming that the natural man could not understand his writings, Arndt wrote that his writings were not intended for the unconverted.[63] Arndt instead contended that he wrote of the practice, or the course, of conversion with the grace of God in Christ Jesus.[64]

Arndt addressed spiritual issues not only with the theologian, Gerhard, but also with those of important political stature. The first letter to Duke August of Braunschweig from Arndt was written on April 20, 1620.[65] Arndt wrote to the duke in reference to a controversy with another Lutheran pastor, Daniel Cramer, who had criticized Arndt's work and his citation of Luther's words claiming that Christ was given to us as a norm and example to follow.[66] According to Arndt, Cramer was attempting to cast aspersion on his theology and his use of Tauler. Arndt stressed an understanding of "a revelation of the kingdom of God within us."[67] He claimed that he had confirmed his belief in the confessions and was trying to point out the depth to which spiritual gifts could enhance the life of the believer.[68] Arndt claimed that this internal revelation was a gift and that it was the foundation of all piety, blessedness, and spiritual wisdom.[69] Arndt here continued his insistence on those things that were internal and existential as opposed to external. While Arndt continued to argue that he was not teaching heresy, he insisted on self-denial and renunciation.[70] This once again stressed the need to internalize one's faith. It was not enough merely to affirm the correct doctrine and thus be saved, but it was necessary to draw near to God spiritually through the practice of self-denial.

According to Arndt in this same letter, the Lutheran church had relied too heavily on the learning of doctrine and had not properly explored the application of the spiritual disciplines.[71] This had led Arndt to accuse the church of fostering dead faith.[72] According to the Formula of Concord, faith by its very definition was something active and living: one either had faith or did not. Arndt did not see faith as binary but rather as a spectrum upon which one could find oneself. This is yet another small example of Arndt's spiritual concerns overtaking doctrinal issues and his stressing the internal state of one's soul rather than the external confession of one's mouth.

In another letter to Duke August in response to the Cramer controversy dated January 28, 1621, Arndt continued to defend his proposal that he was not anticonfessional but was rather attempting to renew the spiritual life of the church.[73] The idea that true knowledge of Christ was found in the imitation of Christ was perhaps the defining idea behind Arndt's eclectic spirituality.[74] Less than one year after Arndt wrote this letter, he was buried, and upon his headstone was engraved, "Christus hat viele Diener, aber wenig Nachfolger" (Christ has many servants, but few imitators). This epitaph encapsulated the notion that there is both a visible and invisible church (an idea foreign to Lutheranism). Thus true believers had to examine their works and test the sincerity of their faith in order to discover whether they were truly believers. This ideal of works and internal investigation was the hallmark of Arndt's spirituality.

The Significance of Arndt's Spirituality for the Lutheran Church in the Seventeenth Century: Arndt's Popular Appeal

Thus far, through some of his correspondence, a picture has been painted of Arndt as a pastor and author who in both roles borrowed from a variety of sources, creating a theology that was not opposed to, but also not confined by, the Lutheran confessions. From his broad interpretation of spirituality, Arndt created a distinctly internal piety that focused on the distinctions between the heart and the mind and the flesh and the spirit. An evaluation of the effect of this spirituality further highlights the significance of Arndt's person and body of work. First, the popular image of Arndt will be examined through various popular tales surrounding the author after his death. Similarly, to strengthen the argument for his particular place in the history of the Lutheran church, the printing record of his most popular works will be examined. Second, uproar caused by Arndt's broad spirituality will be examined through an investigation of those on whom he had an immediate impact. The focus will especially be on those who defended him after his death and on their brief but intense dialogue with those who believed Arndt to be beyond the pale of Lutheran orthodoxy. Finally, a brief comment will be made on the lasting impact Arndt's work had for Pietism, arguably the most significant movement within the Lutheran church since the beginning stages of the Reformation.

An aspect of Arndt's popularity can be seen in the sixteenth- and seventeenth-century tradition of *Wundergeschicten*. These miracle stories would be passed on by devotees of Arndt's work in order to justify the special calling of their controversial hero. Throughout most of the literature on Arndt, the most retold story involved a pious Lutheran family gathered together for morning devotions.[75] As the family gathered together, a group of Catholic soldiers burst through the door and burned the family library, including their Bible and works of Luther. As the soldiers left and the family sifted through the ashes of the burned books, they discovered that one remained perfectly untouched by the fire: Arndt's *True Christianity*. With an obvious reference to the biblical account of the prophet Daniel's three friends saved from death in a furnace, this story represents the esteem bestowed upon Arndt by his admirers. Similar stories were told concerning Luther during the early years of the Reformation.[76] Another story circulated in various forms concerning a young man walking through the forest, where he was confronted by the devil. Through some type of Faustian bargain (the details of which have not been uncovered in any surviving accounts), the devil banned the young man from reading two books: the Bible and *True Christianity*. A final, less miraculous story circulated regarding a man visiting a Jesuit library in Madrid. When the man asked the librarian for the best devotional book he had, he was handed a copy of *True Christianity* with the cover torn off and only the name "Randtius" on the title page. Whether this was meant to be an indictment of Catholic devotional literature or a demonstration of the broad appeal of Arndt's works, the same message of Arndt's special status is clear.[77]

If these stories are anecdotal in portraying Arndt as a popular figure in seventeenth-century Europe, the printing record of Arndt's works displays a more concrete basis on which to illustrate the popularity of Arndt, despite his detractors. What is significant about these records is that they reflect the version of *True Christianity*, which had been enlarged by two books shortly after Arndt's death. The fifth and sixth books included a number of smaller works by Arndt as well as a selected and edited batch of Arndt's correspondence. The letters chosen and edited were primarily those that painted Arndt as a persecuted and faithful Christian. In total, Arndt's works were printed in the following locations: Frankfurt, Braunschweig, Jena, Magdeburg, Strasbourg, Prague, Montbéliard, Goslar, Lüneburg, Leipzig, Riga, Nordhausen, Wernigerode, Giessen, Sonderhausen, Stade, Lemgo, Halle, Regensburg, Nuremberg, Halberstadt, Berlin, Stuttgart, Schleusingen, and Gotha.[78] In the hundred years after Arndt's death in 1621, there were at least 141 editions of his work translated into Dutch, Latin, English, Swedish, Danish, Bohemian, Hungarian, French, Yiddish, Old Church Slavonic, Russian, Turkish, Wendish, Talmudic, Hebrew, Warungian, and Malabrese.[79]

There were at least four different Dutch versions, as well as a remarkable thirty-seven editions printed in Swedish. In a study of estate inventories done for the years between 1660 and 1821, 12,593 collections yielded 1,340 copies of Arndt's writings. That is one-fourth the number of Bibles that were recorded and double the number of copies of the next most popular devotional book, the *Imitation of Christ*, which was recorded 682 times.[80]

J. V. Andreae, Spiritual Eclecticism, and the Emergence of Pietism

It has been common in scholarship to gauge the influence of Arndt's spirituality by looking later in the seventeenth century to Spener and the Pietist movement.[81] Yet such a leap (in both time and ideology) is not easily justified. There were, however, important links between the controversial and internal spirituality of Arndt and the socially conscious pietism of Spener. It was Johann Valentin Andreae who bridged the gap and was the most significant supporter of Arndt in the early to mid-seventeenth century. After the initial Arndt controversies, Richard van Dülmen has suggested, in some parts of Germany, the Lutheran church was divided between those who supported Arndt and those who opposed him, with Andreae being the fiercest of his supporters.[82] Another biographer of Andreae, John Warwick Montgomery, has claimed that Andreae was "one of the most influential and worthy theological luminaries [of the seventeenth century]."[83]

In 1618, Andreae drew up a list for his *Societas Christianae*, a group that included various Lutherans for the promotion of church reform. This list included the likes of Gerhard, Matthias Hafenreffer, and Johannes Kepler, and was headed by Arndt. Later in his career, in a letter to Duke August (who knew Arndt well), Andreae wrote of "six blessed athletes and faithful shepherds of God's flock: Arndt, Luther, Brenz, Jakob Andreae, Hafenreffer, and Gerhard."[84] While Andreae would certainly have been aware of the differences between Arndt, Luther, and his own grandfather, he included Arndt as an important link in the sustaining of the Lutheran church.

Andreae's most famous work, *Christianopolis*, a utopian work in the vein of Thomas More and Thomas Campanella, blended the internal piety of Arndt and social concerns for the Lutheran church in Germany. Andreae dedicated the building of this city to Arndt: "Thou most holy and worthy man Johann Arndt, Rev. Father in Christ, this our new state recognizes and respects thee, for inasmuch as it has its source in that Jerusalem which thou didst build with a mighty spirit against the sophists, it is impossible not to refer all things to thee, to give thee thanks for the institutions and laws."[85] After Arndt's death, his circle of influence grew as a wider number of supporters were recruited through the contacts of Andreae and Christoph Besold.[86] Andreae went as far as to promote his spiritual father as a new Elijah and reformer of the church.[87] Duke August suggested that Andreae was nothing more than an "Arndischen Theologian."[88] Based on the duke's later support of Arndt, this would not seem to be a derogatory label.

Arndt's influence on Andreae can be especially seen in his distaste for scholastic theology, a desire to meld doctrine and praxis, and his broad appreciation of authors outside the conventional Lutheran mold. Andreae employed Arndt's modern application of the tower of Babel in writing that "this new scholastic theology will soon entangle our brains and tongues that we will no more be able to understand one another than were the builders of the tower of Babel."[89] In his autobiography, Andreae summed up the problem with the church by mirroring Arndt's claim that Lutheranism had become morally polluted due to the over-emphasis on doctrine.[90] Van Dülmen has also noted that Andreae stood with Arndt in decrying the gap between teaching and life.[91]

Another similarity can be found in Andreae's appropriation of a wide variety of Christian authors. His *Rei Christianae et Literaria Subsidia*, a work in which Andreae celebrated the masters in various theological and scientific fields, included, for example, Melanchthon, Paracelsus, Johann Kepler, Marsilio Ficino, Juan Luis Vives, Theodore Zwinger, Sebastian Münster, and Johannes Sleidan.[92] This work, dedicated to Duke August, represented Andreae's breadth of reading and his appreciation for a broad spectrum of authors.

While Andreae represented the most ardent and notewor-thy of Arndt's supporters, these two figures ultimately illuminate one another as part of an active strain of a new spirituality within the Lutheran church between the Peace of Augsburg and the rise of Pietism. Recognizing this helps dispel the opinion shared by Drummond and others, who saw the seventeenth century as an arid and monolithic era in the church. It is also not surprising that both Arndt and his new posthumous protégé would ultimately be polarized in posterity as either faithful servants of the church or dangerous elements undermining Lutheran orthodoxy.[93] In reality, they both represent (with Arndt leading the way) what might best be described as an eclectic Lutheran spirituality.[94] Arndt was not the founder of Pietism, as this later movement included a social aspect absent from his own work. But his spirituality, taken up by Andreae as an addition to his social thought and then assumed by Spener, would form the beginnings of that highly controversial and signifi-cant movement at the end of the seventeenth century.

The picture thus emerging of the eclectic Arndt is that of a spiri-tual pastor/author who sought to discover and define true spirituality through a number of distinctions (spirit versus flesh, inner versus outer, doctrine versus practice, etc.) and a variety of texts beyond the Lutheran tradition. This served as the most polarizing feature of Arndt and has informed the portrait of the man up to the present day. Once again, however, it is important to note that Arndt never explicitly condemned the church's confession; he rather saw himself as a type of reformer for the church in the new century. The thesis of this chapter does not contradict the previous chapter, nor is it sufficient to present Arndt as consciously dissembling. Arndt was not somehow unaware of what he was doing. Much of his spiritual theology caused him great distress, and his confessional understanding has been established. As both his friend (Gerhard) and his enemy (Osiander) suggested, Arndt often found himself in trouble only when he assembled a patchwork theology of divergent texts, but we must assume this was intentional, not based on a lack of education. Second, and perhaps most importantly, the picture emerging of Arndt is that of one who saw himself above the perceived arid scholasticism of the church and as one who was called to be a prophet of true spirituality. The following chapter examines this crucial aspect of Arndt's self-appraisal and self-representation.

CHAPTER 4

Johann Arndt and the Prophetic Voice

Introduction

Johann Arndt believed himself to be a prophet to his particular age, which he viewed to be exceptionally degenerate and deserving of the wrath of God. The only solution to this crisis of piety, as Arndt saw it, was spiritual renewal. It was in this context, at the beginning of the seventeenth century, that Arndt came to see himself as a prophet leading an invigorated movement within the church through the preaching office and the dissemination of his *True Christianity*. Arndt, unlike others who would utilize a prophetic voice in the sixteenth century, did not believe his prophetic voice to be outside the church, for he called for the revitalization of the Lutheran church. Arndt's essential prophetic proclamation was that there was something more to Christianity beyond mere affirmation of doctrine. He wrote that this renewal came about through spiritual exercises and daily, active self-examination and repentance. It is in this prophetic voice that we see the confessional and eclectic elements of Arndt's correspondence come together.

Arndt's notion that he was a particular prophet for his age was based not only on theological or moral observation and speculation; it was also existential. Arndt's life of suffering and rejection, coupled with his propensity toward embellishment, created the prophetic voice found so clearly in his correspondence. This prophetic voice, however, was not without precedent. The Reformation was fertile ground for a wide variety of prophetic examples. Arndt borrowed from these various strains: Luther, the more conservative Lutheran confessions, and the radical line from Müntzer and Weigel (about whose thought Arndt was known to be ambivalent).

Prophets and prophecy in general have not been overlooked in early modern German historiography. The literature concerning both the confessional and the dissenting groups has identified the role of the prophet as an essential locus for interpreting those particular voices calling for social and moral reform. Luther's role as a prophet inveighing against the Catholic church and as the prominent voice of the reform movement has been examined in monographs and general biographies.[1] That this prophetic voice was transferred into the Lutheran confessions and into the office of the preacher has also been suggested.[2]

The dissenting and more radical prophetic voices have understandably received more attention. The early prophets of the Reformation era, with the Zwickau prophets and Müntzer, have been established as figures crying out against the established churches on all sides of the Reformation debate. Secondary sources have also documented how, as the sixteenth century moved forward and the warring parties became more militant, the eschatological and esoteric aspects of these self-proclaimed prophets became more dominant.[3] The dominant prophetic emphases in most secondary literature pertain to the more radical and apocalyptic elements.[4]

Those controversial and esoteric aspects of the prophet have been discussed to the extent that one might assume that these elements constitute the whole of the prophetic picture. Yet given the example of the biblical prophets, from Moses to St. Paul, there were certainly other common prophetic aspects evident to the early modern Bible reader; however, most approaches to the broad prophetic voice have been suggestive rather than analytical.[5]

Suffering and the imitation of the martyrdom of Christ and the lesser biblical prophets were central to the early modern prophetic self-representation. The fact that early modern preachers presented themselves as beleaguered and persecuted has been noted in recent literature, broadening our understanding of their self-perception.[6] The presenting of oneself as beset by enemies may have appealed to certain social or psychological needs and perceptions, but it is more pervasively tied to the established theme of imitation. The biblical prophet was verified not only by prophecy and a direct (or indirect) calling but also through personal hardship. Particularly in the Lutheran understanding of the *theologia crucis*, suffering served a double purpose: it could both strengthen the faith of the individual and vindicate the individual's vocation.

Another, less obvious, prophetic connotation, applicable to both the confessing and dissenting groups, was that of association. It was often levied as an attack on new religious movements in the sixteenth century that their innovation was in fact heresy. In associating themselves with biblical models, innovators sought to establish a link to the "pure religion" of the Scriptures. There would always be a precedent needed, and the prophetic model—the isolated man of God preaching against a corrupt generation—seems to have been the appropriate example.

With regard to the particular prophetic voice of both the Lutherans and more radical groups, much attention has been paid to the dynamic categories of predictive prophecy. Yet it was also the central role of the prophet to preach received doctrine and exhort to obedience. Much of the writings of the biblical prophets and their self-assumed inheritors simply recast established doctrine and preached spiritual and moral renewal.[7]

The categories of prophet, preacher, and martyr then can be linked in such a way as to broaden the prophetic persona. Such an expansion of the prophetic persona enables a large section of Arndt's own correspondence to be seen as properly prophetic. Arndt borrowed from a varied tradition as he created a particular prophetic tone that included strains of both the radical and Lutheran traditions. An appropriate starting point in the discussion of the prophetic persona is Martin Luther. Arndt's connection to Luther was made explicit when he reprinted the *Theologia Deutsch* in 1597 as a call for a new reformation within the Lutheran church.

Luther as Confessional Prophet

Luther's ideas concerning the prophetic role are most clearly expressed in a letter to Philip Melanchthon of January 13, 1522. Luther wrote from his exile at the Wartburg Castle concerning the radicals in Wittenberg. He referred to these new radicals as "so-called prophets" and requested that Melanchthon deal with them severely and according to their folly. As the role of prophet was self-proclaimed, Luther suggested two methods for discerning whether they were legitimate: the mode and means of the prophetic call and the experience of suffering. Luther first quoted the counsel of St. John that spirits are to be tested.[8] Luther submitted that the testing of the prophets can take two forms, either by men or by signs.[9] As the age of miracles had passed, Luther argued that the prophet was made legitimate through the calling of men in the office of public teaching.[10] Thus the office of the prophet, for Luther, was not separate from the office of the preacher: the modern-day prophet was not a para-church critic but rather its called and assigned leader.

Luther then proceeded to elaborate on the critical mark of a prophet—one's life of suffering: "In order to explore their individual spirit, too, you should inquire whether they have experienced spiritual distress and the divine birth, death, and hell. If you should hear that all [their experiences] are pleasant, quiet, devout (as they say), and spiritual, then don't approve of them, even if they should say they were caught up in the third heaven. The sign of the Son of Man is missing, which is the only touchstone."[11] In dealing directly with the issue of what validated a prophet, the issue of predictive prophecy is noticeably absent. Rather, Luther's understanding of the prophet seems more mundane and tied to the external issues of ecclesiastical calling and persecution.

Ten years later, Luther would echo this in his commentary on the book of Galatians; commenting on the types of callings, Luther wrote, "God calls in two ways, either by means or without means. Today he calls all of us into the ministry of the Word by a mediated call . . . nevertheless it is divine."[12] Later, Luther would boast of his own divine call. "I do [act in the particular office] as one who has a command and a call. For the voice of the Lord has come to me, not in some corner, as the sectarians boast, but through the mouth of a man."[13] Luther thus established the normal office of the prophet as one who has been called by a mediated voice and has suffered on account of this call. These two foundations would become the basis of the prophetic office in the Lutheran church through the confessional age and up into Arndt's time.[14] While Arndt would use the themes of Luther's prophetic voice, he would also borrow from a tradition developed by one of Luther's chief combatants, Thomas Müntzer.

It is unclear whether Arndt would have read Müntzer, although he would certainly have been aware of him, as he was a student of theology. More significantly, Müntzer's more radical prophetic style would be inherited by later reformers with whom Arndt definitely did have contact with, such as Valentin Weigel and Adam von Bodenstein.

Müntzer as Radical Prophet

The dissenting counterpart to Luther in the early Reformation was the leader of the early radical reformation, Thomas Müntzer. At one time, he was a defender and ally of Luther, yet his radical understanding of his own prophetic role would eventually lead him into direct opposition to Luther and the Lutheran movement. As Müntzer eventually came to attack the established Lutheranism, his prophetic self-representation took its clearest form.[15] It is worth noting for the section that follows that Müntzer would not greatly deviate from Luther's understanding of the office of the prophet; the essential elements of the call and suffering were both present. Yet it is the nuance of Müntzer's prophetic qualifications and voice that set the stage for the emerging differences that occurred in the following generations of self-styled prophets. Müntzer's clearest exposition of the radical concept of the office occurs in his *Vindication and Refutation*, a letter sent to Luther defending his own prophetic integrity.[16]

Müntzer wrote to Luther in 1525 while banned from his post in Allstedt. The twofold nature of the prophetic understanding comes into focus as Müntzer attacked Luther's prophetic position and asserted his own. While this letter was written in direct opposition to Luther, it shared a few assumptions on the nature of the prophetic office. Müntzer painted himself in the light of the biblical prophets, presented suffering as the prophetic trademark, and suggested that something beyond a mere internal call was needed to justify the prophetic voice.

Müntzer's prophetic voice began with the first line of the letter, in which he described his station as "the cave of Elijah," praying for deliverance from the "calumnies of man" and the "wiles of the evil-doers."[17] Müntzer acknowledged that he had been the object of slander and scorn, and by referring to the cave of Elijah, he made it clear with whom he associated himself. Müntzer continued to qualify himself in light of biblical and prophetic references, comparing himself to Noah's dove (as opposed to Luther's black crow) and to Jacob rightly usurping authority from Esau (i.e., Luther).[18] Müntzer later compared himself to David, using Luther as a foil to represent both Goliath and Saul.[19] Müntzer's strongest assertions of his prophetic pedigree came with direct comparison to Christ. Müntzer claimed, "The Jews wanted to see Christ insulted and humiliated on every occasion just as Luther now tries to treat me."[20] He moved on to a brief exposition of John 8, comparing Luther and his followers to the Pharisees who tried to dispute with Christ using subtle, misleading arguments.[21]

The second prophetic aspect employed by Müntzer was the means by which he credited himself with prophetic endowment. Unlike some medieval prophetic forebears, Müntzer did not rely on an immediate internal calling, nor did he rely on the mediate call into the preaching office (as did Luther). Müntzer stated, "Whatever I declare to the people comes through the testimony of God from the Holy Scripture . . . I will gladly suffer correction by God and His dear friends and be subject to them."[22] In doing so, he claimed both an objective and subjective basis for his prophetic qualification. The subjective "correction by God and His dear friends" leaves Müntzer with room to maneuver, as he can judge both the means of God's correction and the definition of his "dear friends."[23] Müntzer located the prophetic power of the keys (as he would later the power of the sword) in the whole community rather than in a particular office.

Müntzer also took issue with Luther and affixed names to him such as "doctor liar," "doctor lampooner," "the godless flesh," "Father pussyfoot," "arch-heathen," and "arch-wretch." The language is harsh and derisive, as one would expect from a self-styled prophet, reflecting not only the biblical counterparts but Luther as well. As Müntzer and Luther argued, their prophetic imagery and allusions, in many ways, concurred. Yet Müntzer's assertion of a subjective qualification for a prophet would be his lasting legacy. As the Reformation century progressed, it transformed from a focus on the charismatic leader to the consolidation of movements and theologies. The prophetic strains still existed, but especially for the Lutheran church, the individual prophet gave way to the definition of an office.

Confessional Lutheranism and "Prophecy"

Confessional Lutherans were ambivalent about the early sixteenth-century apocalyptic fervor. Unsurprisingly, they followed Luther's own sometimes-discordant approach to prophets, prophecy, and the end of days. Robin Bruce Barnes, in his study of apocalypticism in the late Lutheran Reformation, has noted this ambivalence in stating that for Luther's confessional heirs, "prophecy is most commonly understood as the prediction of future things; more generally and more properly it refers to any spiritually inspired preaching or warning."[24] Barnes's monograph traces the fantastic and apocalyptic strains in confessional prophetic thought but recognized that this "does not represent the entire prophetic persona."[25]

A recent contribution to the importance of the prophetic role and the office of the called minister in the confessional Lutheran documents is Scott Murray's essay, "What It Meant to Be Lutheran among the Orthodox Fathers."[26] Murray studied the confessional Lutheran documents to demonstrate that doctrines of the prophet and prophecy fit within the context of the office of the ministry. The only genuine prophetic voice was held to exist within the particular, mediated calling. Article V of the Augsburg Confession, for example, stated, "That we may obtain this faith, the Ministry of Teaching the Gospel and administering the Sacraments was instituted. For through the Word and Sacraments, as through instruments, the Holy Ghost is given."[27] While not seemingly prophetic in the foretelling sense, the added condemnation makes it clear that the office of the ministry was set up to qualify the proper prophetic voice as opposed to the fanatics: the document declared, "[We] condemn the Anabaptists and others who think that the Holy Ghost comes to men without the external Word, through their own preparations and works."[28] Article XIV further read, "Of Ecclesiastical Order [we] teach that no one should publicly teach in the Church or administer the Sacraments unless he be regularly called."[29] Johann Gerhard, Arndt's confessional confidant, similarly claimed that the proper and called prophetic office differed from "the confusion of the Anabaptists, who snatch for themselves a slice of the ecclesiastical ministry without a call. We refer to those places in the New Testament where the characteristics of the false prophets and false teachers are stated."[30] Further, in his commentary, Gerhard stated the following: "We propose this general rule: that the public office of teaching in the church is never rightly administered in either the Old or New Testaments, except where there was a divine call to that office . . . Also today he gives pastors and teachers, no longer without means, of course, but by a legitimate call, which must not be understood as less divine than the immediate call."[31] Another established voice of the confessional period, Johannes Quenstedt, added to the distinction between the called prophet and the false prophet: "The call rightly to carry out the ecclesiastical ministry is not arbitrary but especially necessary: because God absolutely detests those who presume to teach publicly without a call . . . the Lord has shown his detestation for prophets who are not sent but go away with the words of Jeremiah 23. Those who go and are not called, who come and are not requested are false prophets and false apostles against whom Christ has warned in Mt. 7:15 and the apostle in 2 Cor. 11:12ff."[32] The Lutheran idea of the prophet was tied directly to the doctrine of the call. Thus the prophet must adhere to the office of the ministry, and the voice of the prophet would therefore be one that proclaimed Lutheran doctrine. While this does not necessarily mean that this ideal was always upheld, it established the confessional standard.[33] While other strains existed, and the prophetic voice was larger in scope and in practice, one would expect to see this line of thought in Arndt's claim to be a confessional prophetic voice. While the Lutheran church was consolidated upon its confessions, the tradition of Müntzer survived primarily through individuals. One of the most significant models for Arndt's context was Valentin Weigel, whom Arndt was known to have read; indeed, he borrowed sections of his work for his *True Christianity*.[34]

Valentin Weigel: The Dissenting Prophet[35]

Valentin Weigel (1533–1588), while initially a Lutheran pastor, attacked the established church through his anonymous and post-humously printed works.[36] Weigel's prophetic calling did not come from his mediated call or office but rather from his self-styled ability to discern the Scriptures without confessional aid and to see the crisis of his age. According to Weigel, "All knowledge of divine things comes from man himself and not from books, if only the universities and wise men of the world could grasp this 'handle' and brief rule."[37] Weigel further presented the dire state of established Christendom by stating, "Many thousands know nothing of the inner word. Such blindness and ignorance come from the false teachers who wrongly interpret Scripture and have power through the assistance of the government."[38] Weigel was unmistakably referring to the established Lutheran church. He continued to speak against that confessional calling, claiming, "Preachers should be angels of the Lord taught and sent by God and not men. Should one among us really desire to preach from the Bible, he would not be permitted to do so."[39] Weigel demoted the office as the official prophetic marker and made the word immediately available in the individual. He then moved on to attack the established theological faculties. "All the universities know about as much about Christ as the Jews, who said that he was the natural son of Joseph."[40]

Weigel's strong words against the established church, and his claim to have the correct interpretation of the Scriptures, placed him in the subjective prophetic scheme seen in Müntzer's work. Weigel's idea of the prophet stressed the immediate call and a particular anti-establishment program of reform. This pattern seen in Müntzer and carried on in Weigel was also revealed in some of Arndt's letters.

From Luther and the Lutheran confessions to Müntzer and Weigel there existed a tentatively established idea of the prophet that shared similar elements but was also contradictory. The office of the prophet was not simply one of prediction and foretelling but of forthtelling in one's immediate context. It was a prophetic voice that was tied to a position both inside and outside of the established church, based on identification and suffering. Arndt inherited this varied prophetic form as he suited his own distinct prophetic voice to his range of correspondents.

The Idea of the Prophet in Arndt's Correspondence

Arndt's perception of his prophetic calling dominates his letters, and references to the prophetic mantle are found through almost all his correspondence. Yet his prophetic tone was not monolithic: the different people to whom he wrote reflected different aspects of his thought. While he blended the various prophetic strains throughout his correspondence, there were distinctive aspects that revealed themselves to correspondents with whom Arndt had differing relationships. There were, however, certain aspects that colored all his prophetic writings—namely, his exile from Anhalt and his certainty that his age was mired in a crisis of piety. These common themes will be examined before we see the confessional, personal, and political aspects of his letters.

Perhaps the career-making event in Arndt's life was his exile from his homeland of Anhalt. This early experience in Arndt's pastoral career, while undoubtedly tragic, provided him with the intimate understanding of the prophet without honor in his own homeland. Arndt recounted the beginning of his career of hardship to Petrus Piscator in his letter from January 14, 1607, in which he wrote the following: "I have served the community of Christ for twenty-four years, and since I was a youth have been educated in our true religion, but I have experienced much misery, and I have tolerated great affliction and persecution from those dissidents against me in my fatherland, the duchy of Anhalt . . . [it was there] that I wrote concerning the iconoclastic controversy and was thus exiled from my church."[41] To Balthasar Mentzer, he wrote of being exiled from the duchy of Anhalt because of his unwillingness to agree with those with whom he was in dispute over their teaching of faith.[42] To the Braunschweig Council, Arndt wrote that he was still mistreated and received "thankless pay, because I am an exile, as I was driven out of Anhalt by the Calvinists."[43] To Statius Kahlen, Arndt wrote that he was still caused grief on account of "the persecution and repudiation by my beloved Fatherland."[44] These excerpts do not reveal Arndt as simply using his exile for sympathy but as genuinely heartbroken that his homeland, where his father was a preacher before him, had rejected him. While he spent the final thirty years of his life in four different pastorates, he was generally unhappy that he was unable to finish his career where it had begun. But this sadness was also his point of comparison with the prophets and to Jesus, whose ministry was marked by the absence of honor in their homelands.

Arndt was also consistent throughout his letters in claiming that his age was one of great evil and suffering from a lack of godliness. He wrote to Wolfgang Frantzius, "This evil was so great that the noise has risen to heaven," and he expected calamity similar to "the fire of Sodom and the famine of Samaria."[45] Arndt was obviously juxtaposing his own time with the wickedness of the antediluvian era and himself with Noah and the remnant that survived God's wrath. He also wrote to Frantzius noting the refusal to accept such writings, particularly among the young, who lacked sufficient grounding to distinguish between good and evil.[46] Arndt would thus be the one who would proclaim the true word of God that might open the eyes of the blind. To Piscator, Arndt wrote of the "dire evil of our corrupt age" and "innate corruption of the heart of man."[47] To Gerhard, to whom Arndt was often most forthcoming, he simply wrote, "The world is entirely sinful."[48] While this pessimism would certainly cause Arndt grief, it also underpinned his mission of reviving true Christianity.

The themes of the exiled prophet and the evil age were common among all strains of the prophetic voice in the sixteenth century. Luther and Calvin, Müntzer, Schwenckfeld, and others would all experience a period of exile, and none was convinced that there were better days to come.[49] But Arndt, like many pastors of his day, accepted the calling to imitate the prophets, apostles, and Jesus in proclaiming true theology to save mankind, in either this world or the next.

While these themes were common in Arndt's letters (as well as in *True Christianity*) there were distinct aspects of the prophetic calling in particular letters that show Arndt to be both sincere and savvy. He recognized his audience and, based on his relationship to them, would tailor his prophetic voice and mission to ingratiate himself or further his cause. These distinct themes are found as Arndt wrote to influential theologians within the Lutheran church but with whom he had little contact, to his friends whom he believed to have similar beliefs, and to various magistrates with whom he had professional contact.

We shall begin by looking at Arndt's letters to Mentzer and Frantzius. Both were theology professors at Lutheran universities in the 1620s and were aware of the controversy that surrounded Arndt in 1618 and the ensuing years. Both letters reflect the prophetic voice that fitted within the boundaries of the Lutheran confessions. However, they are not mere facsimiles of each other. To Mentzer, the strictly confessional prophetic role was presented, while in the letter to Frantzius, we shall see a slight development of Arndt's more enigmatic and prophetic personality.

Letter to Balthasar Mentzer, October 29, 1620[50]

Balthasar Mentzer (1565–1627) was a professor of theology and then general superintendent at Giessen between 1607 and 1625. As no other surviving correspondence exists between these two figures, we are forced to look at this letter as an isolated text. However, the context in which it was written helps us understand its meaning. There is no direct evidence that Arndt and Mentzer knew each other personally, yet it was perhaps his knowledge of Mentzer's theological interests that allowed Arndt to consider him a possible ally. First, Mentzer had written strongly against the Calvinists and iconoclasm, with particular reference to their abolition of the rite of exorcism at baptism.[51] As a professor at Giessen, he may have been involved in the feud between his university and the university at Tübingen. As Lucas Osiander and the Tübingen faculty had been critical of *True Christianity*, Arndt may have seen Mentzer as an orthodox ally. As a fellow superintendent, Arndt may have sent this letter as a general introduction or as a letter to assure Mentzer that his works were not heterodox, as the Tübingen faculty suggested with their ban.

This letter provides us a picture of Arndt, writing in a turbulent time in his career, asserting his firm belief in a spiritual renewal. However, we can see in this letter Arndt stressing his prophetic credibility by employing the standards of the Lutheran confessions. Arndt made clear to Mentzer that he believed that "God was [found] in his word, and works through his word."[52] Arndt further claimed that his renewal of the church was founded on "the revealed word of God, by means of the merit and example of Christ, the work of the Holy Spirit and the illuminating faith and justification."[53] While Arndt went on to stress "true repentance" as the need for the church (something that suggested there existed a false repentance and therefore might be read as criticism of the church), he had couched everything within the confessional understanding of the prophet: true doctrine based on external means. Arndt furthermore reminded Mentzer of his service to the church within the office of the pastor and his faithfulness: "From my youth to my old age . . . I have not been shown to have erred in my teaching concerning the Augsburg Confession and the Formula of Concord."[54] This letter represents Arndt's sincere attempt to provide Mentzer with reason to support his call for a spiritual theology that would result in true repentance and a theology that was both doctrinal and affective. Arndt had thus written to a confessional Lutheran regarding his prophetic plan for renewal but within the understood model of the prophet as established by the Lutheran confessions. In the following letter, written in the same year to a comparable advocate of confessional Lutheranism, we will see Arndt using similar confessional approaches to his prophetic calling but with a slight hint of his more enigmatic approach to his particular calling.

Letter to Wolfgang Frantzius, March 29, 1620[55]

The letter to Wolfgang Frantzius shares certain commonalities with the one to Mentzer. It was written in 1620, after Arndt's name and reputation had been established and called into question, and was written to someone with whom we have no indication that Arndt had personal contact. Frantzius was a Lutheran professor and pastor in Wittenberg, teaching history and theology at the university and preaching at the Schlosskirche.[56] Frantzius was also a successful printer.[57] Due to Wittenberg's early censure of Arndt's work, and the possibility that he might persuade Frantzius of his orthodox intentions, this letter is another attempt to promote his message and special calling within the confines of the Lutheran confessions. Most interesting about this letter is that it was written with the intention that it should be printed and circulated. Arndt began the letter by writing, "I have answered this in the German language, so that everyone can read this, my apology."[58] So while Arndt was writing to a supporter of the Lutheran confessions, he would also have intended a wider audience. Arndt claimed that his work was not one of fanaticism but was tied to "the glorious means, the word of God."[59] While Arndt was writing an apology for his work, attempting to vindicate his reputation and to speak to the church, he had begun to elaborate on his special calling. Arndt began to identify himself with the prophetic model of the suffering servant. He claimed to have suffered "noxious slander," and he wrote, "I have endured many such storms and let these pass with great patience."[60] Arndt's most explicit prophetic identification came in this letter as he explained that he suffered, because through his work "the old serpent has his head tread upon."[61] This was an obvious illusion to Genesis 3:15 and Romans 16:20 and the prophecy well known to the Lutheran church that Christ would crush the head of the serpent.[62] Arndt had thus compared himself and his work to the greatest of all biblical prophets. Against the charges that were circulating from Danzig that Arndt was an enthusiast, Arndt claimed that he was happy with the label, at least under certain terms as "were then the Prophets and Apostles enthusiasts as they were filled with God and filled with the Spirit?"[63] While Arndt would normally disassociate himself from the *enthusiast* tag, he accepted the term on the basis of its association with the biblical prophets. In a piece of allegorical prose, Arndt laid claim to the prophet office: "Where is the broken heart? Where is the impassioned weeping? Where is the solitary little bird sitting on the roof that keeps watch and sighs? Where is someone to stand at the rupture and form a wall against the wrath of God?"[64] Arndt was the little bird keeping watch and the man whose plan for spiritual renewal would keep the wrath of God from bringing disaster. He finished the letter by explicitly assuring his reader that what they would find in his book was a statement of true Christianity, and he detailed its essential components such as the Fall, the lost image of God, the new creation, the life of Christ in faith, the struggle against the flesh, and the imitation of Christ.[65]

These two letters stand together as they were both written in the same year, amid the controversy surrounding Arndt and the Thirty Years' War. They were both written to orthodox Lutherans with whom Arndt was attempting to ingratiate himself, with the goal of leading the church to a fuller understanding of the Lutheran faith. Both letters were written cautiously with confessional caveats; however, the letter to Frantzius is a clearer example of the more unfettered Arndt, as he presented himself in stronger imagery. This more explicit picture of his self-understanding as a prophet of the Lutheran church is evident in the following letters, where Arndt wrote to his friends.

Letter to Petrus Piscator, January 14, 1607[66]

On January 14, 1607, Arndt wrote to Petrus Piscator (1571–1611), professor of theology and Hebrew at the University of Jena. Piscator remains an elusive character in the history of the late Lutheran Reformation.[67] The available sources for discerning Piscator's confessional leanings come from his position at Jena, a handful of publications, and the letters from Arndt. Based on his teaching at the University of Jena, it would seem likely that he fell into a more confessionally conservative camp.[68] Likewise, Piscator's few publications included commentaries on the various Lutheran confessions and disputational tracts in defense of confessional Lutheranism.[69] Arndt's letters to Piscator suggest he was a Lutheran for whom confessional fidelity was important. Yet Arndt's letters also reveal a friendship, as he wrote more freely and with a less apologetic tone. Arndt wrote more forcefully to Piscator concerning the necessity of reforming the church and his particular calling to guide the church to a more spiritually affective theology. As seen previously, Arndt had written to Piscator concerning his suffering and his fidelity to the confessions. Arndt's language was a blend of both confessional and spiritual theology, and he claimed that his particular rhetorical style was modeled on Luther. "I can call Luther as a witness, who spoke differently when he was disputing or when he was chastising blasphemers, and in some places in his Church Postils where he writes of good works and of election and uses these in order to urge repentence and improvement of life."[70] Arndt also claimed fidelity to Luther in teaching the importance of sanctification. This marks the only place in Arndt's correspondence that he referred to Luther. The point has been made previously that by the late sixteenth and early seventeenth centuries, Luther was no longer seen as the standard for Lutheran orthodoxy, as the confessions consolidated some of his writings and other doctrines. Arndt was not referring to Luther for theological reasons but rather as a symbol of prophetic status. Although the confessions supplanted Luther doctrinally, he was still regarded as the great prophet of the early Reformation. Thus it was understandable that Arndt would select Luther as an example in this letter in which he was establishing his own prophetic standing.

Another characteristic that is particular in this letter was Arndt's designation of the audience he was attempting to reform. Echoing the first chapter of *True Christianity*, Arndt wrote that he did not write for those who were not yet converted but rather for those who have recognized Christ in faith but continue to live as nonbelievers.[71] This is one of the major indications that Arndt saw himself as a prophet; he was not called to be an apostle to the unbeliever but as the prophet warning God's people of the wrath to come if they do not repent and return to their God. This letter to Piscator was much more personal and straightforward concerning what Arndt believed his role and calling to be. Most likely on account of their friendship,

Arndt was able to write more freely. However, if Piscator was a friend with (at least perceived) mutual interests, Arndt's letter to his protégé and confidant would prove to be the most intimate of all.

Letter to Johann Gerhard, August 3, 1607[72]

On August 3, 1607, Arndt wrote to Johann Gerhard, then professor of theology at Jena. It is important to stress that for Arndt, Gerhard was an exemplar of orthodoxy, a defender of confessional fidelity, and a self-styled heir of his brand of spiritual reform. On account of this particular relationship, Arndt's language in this letter was particularly forthcoming. Arndt was not writing an apology or a defense of his work; rather, he was writing to a friend for consolation and affirmation of his calling.

To contextualize this letter, it is important to recall that it was written in 1607 as Arndt was sending copies of *True Christianity* to various theological faculties and being either rejected or told to rewrite or delete major sections.[73] Arndt was also in Braunschweig, where he was under constant threat of military attack and condemnation from his fellow pastors. The letter is uneven in many respects, moving from one thought to the next as he dealt with the depression his station had caused him as well as his own desire to reform the church. Arndt began by writing of the many who had slandered him and not taken his directive to read his works in light of the Lutheran confessions. He wrote, "I have wanted everything that I have written to be understood in light of our symbolic books."[74] At this point, Arndt suggested that he had considered leaving his church, but, as has been established, a standard for the prophet in the church was to be faithful to his calling, and so Arndt stated that he would stay in Braunschweig "if no other calling comes."[75] After explaining more of the difficulties he had endured, he suggested, "Perhaps I could move to Eisleben and take up a private life."[76] While this seems contradictory of his previous affirmation of the importance of the call, it reveals the sorrow out of which Arndt was writing. This sadness becomes most evident as he wrote, "I have not had a single good day in the two years since you were with me."[77] This intensely personal letter gives us a glimpse of Arndt not only as the author who wrote to ingratiate himself and promote a call to spiritual improvement but as one who suffered a crisis of calling. Like most biblical prophets, he was hardly keen to accept his mission. The biblical prophet suffered hardship and disdain. Arndt's understanding of his role as a prophet was not a ploy for fame or to sell books; it came from an existential crisis.

Yet Arndt did remain in his called position and outlined to Gerhard what he intended to do. Arndt wrote that if he was not called elsewhere and had to suffer, then he would become a herald of reform: "And so I will show the way and means, the practice and the process of conversion."[78] Among the confessional Lutherans, it would be suspect to speak of conversion as either a process or a practice. The standard order of salvation placed conversion among the first things to occur, and it was always a passive event. Arndt was writing in a moment of spiritual enthusiasm in which he laid aside his confessional concerns. Arndt was calling for the compounding of practice and conversion, and in this section of fervent prophetic writing, he wrote that he would be the one to testify to the way and that spiritual exercise and justification were to be linked so as to create a spiritual and "true" Christianity.

Arndt continued his shift from depressive crisis to clarion call as he explained to Gerhard that the corrupting agents in the current spiritual predicament were the theologians. He claimed that it was the theologians who were corrupting and evil influences.[79] Arndt was likely upset with many of the theological faculties that had rejected his work or criticized his preaching. This should not be read as if Arndt was contradicting what he expressed to Mentzer—that theological knowledge at the universities and spiritual reform could take place together. Rather, Arndt was writing to one whom he believed to be a kindred spirit to express his alternately dejected and prophetic state of mind. It was not, however, the only time in which Arndt's would come across as seemingly dejected yet invigorated. In a letter to another friend Daniel Dilger fourteen years later, Arndt expressed similar prophetic and personal themes.

Letter to Daniel Dilger, May 4, 1620

On May 4, 1620, Arndt wrote to Daniel Dilger, a member of the company of pastors in Danzig. Dilger, along with Herman Rathmann and Michael Blank, was one the three pastors censured by the synod when one of their followers was found in possession of the writings of Paracelsus, Weigel, and Schwenckfeld. This follower, a certain Gaule, implicated Arndt with the other authors.[80] While the matter was ultimately concluded in favor of Arndt and Dilger by Johann Gerhard and the ministerium at Wittenberg, they had been linked with *schwaermerisch* dissenters and continued to be attacked by certain, more strict Lutherans.[81] Arndt wrote to Dilger to encourage him to fight for their brand of interior spiritual reform. The prophetic voice was more grandiose and had messianic tones; his language was turned internally, and his theology became less dependent on external means. In a pattern seen thus far, Arndt argued that this particular period required a prophet; the wicked age demanded a voice crying out in the wilderness. Arndt wrote of an evil wind that was blowing about but comforted himself that he alone would proclaim "true" Christianity.[82] Furthermore, Arndt claimed that this evil age was not recognized by most, who remain blind.[83] Arndt would thus be the one to preach the word of true repentance and the imitation of Christ, as he had repeatedly claimed this to be the solution for those trapped in blindness. In another of the more remarkable prophetic allusions, Arndt wrote to Dilger, "If my work is the work of man, then it will not last, but if it is from God, then they will not be able to extinguish it."[84] Arndt here was applying the test set by the early Jewish leaders for the early Christian church, thus implying great importance for his prophetic program and suggesting an almost messianic role for himself. In a further qualification of his prophetic status, Arndt stated that his detractors served as a thorn in the flesh to keep him humble, echoing St. Paul. He equates his opponents with Satan's angels.[85] Arndt had thus identified himself with both Christ and St. Paul, an impressive prophetic pedigree.

As Arndt was writing to a friend, and one who had suffered on his account, there are similar enthusiastic moments in which Arndt contradicted what he had written in other letters. For instance, in his letters to Frantzius and Mentzer, Arndt continually specified that his means were external: the Word and Sacraments. However, in this letter, Arndt wrote, "The Kingdom of God is not in words, but in power."[86] This is in direct opposition to his statements to others that he was reliant on the external means of the word. Arndt wrote that this power was "a real, living, and powerful gift and enlightenment."[87]

He continued away from the external means of grace to stress "change of heart" and the "internal testimony of the Holy Spirit."[88] Finally, Arndt placed the fountain of truth not in the confessions but in self-recognition, internal repentance, and moral improvement.[89]

This letter, in which Arndt continued with the familiar themes of his prophetic role for his wicked age, is the most dissonant of his letters. While Arndt has been seen in his letters to Gerhard to be emotive and despondent, this letter shows Arndt's grief over his controversy coupled with conflicting and heterodox statements not found elsewhere in his correspondence. There are a few possible explanations for this. As he was writing to Dilger, who was censured by the church, Arndt did not likely see the need to carefully stay within the confessional standards. Arndt was likely also very upset that the church had attacked his work in a controversy that surrounded authors who were noticeably beyond the pale of the Lutheran confessions. The common themes of internal spirituality, persecution, and the blindness of the current age were all present, but Arndt, writing in his last years, seemed less concerned to present Dilger with a letter of encouragement that was tightly bound to confessional standards. He was writing to a friend who was experiencing the same struggle with which he had been dealing with for at least fourteen years, since *True Christianity* was first published. One can see, without suggesting duplicity on Arndt's part, a certain tone present in his letters to those who knew him and were thus not judging his confessional credibility based on a piece of correspondence.

A collection of letters to various magistrates reveals more of Arndt's prophetic voice. These letters contain themes similar to the previous letters but understandably take on a certain Old Testament model as Arndt saw himself in the mold of those prophets who were called upon to advise the Israelite kings.

Letters to Duke August the Younger, January 28 and 29, 1621[90]

The last surviving letters written by Arndt were sent to Duke August the Younger of Braunschweig-Lüneburg in January 1621. These letters carried with them the language and forcefulness seen in few of his previous letters. Arndt, then superintendent in Celle, wrote to

Duke August with regard to the fallout over the Danzig controversy in 1618. One such fruit of the new controversy, which linked Arndt to Weigel and Schwenckfeld, was a commentary on the apocalypse by Daniel Cramer. Cramer, whose book contained references to Arndt's heterodoxy, wrote to the duke to convince him that Arndt taught another gospel.[91]

It has been suggested that with the encroachment of Calvinism and the Second Reformation in Germany, the Lutheran contingency in Braunschweig was particularly steadfast in its retention of a Lutheran identity.[92] Duke August, who was not known as a strict interpreter of the Lutheran confessions, may well have deferred to the majority to keep peace in his territory. Duke August's close contacts included J. V. Andreae, the sometimes Rosicrucian and mystically inclined Lutheran who wrote a foreword to an edition of Arndt's *True Christianity*, and his court physician Melchior Breller, a major supporter of Arndt after his death and one with connections to Weigelist and Paracelsian groups. While Duke August may certainly have been a sincere Lutheran, and concerned with peace in his territory, he represented an example of a less confessionally inclined Lutheran to whom Arndt could write with an emphasis on the spiritual aspects of his reform.

The letters of Arndt play out his perception of Duke August as a malleable, less rigid supporter of Lutheran reform. Arndt would surely see a supporter such as the duke as the ideal patron for his brand of moral and spiritual reform. Arndt presented himself in these letters not so much as the prophet of Lutheran orthodoxy but more in the mold of an Old Testament prophet. Arndt played the role of the prophet counseling the ruler, claiming authority in religious matters, prophesying, and laying out an ambitious program of reform. Arndt also qualified his voice as authentic by claiming that the Lutheran theologians had fallen away from the true faith into a disputational and bickering scholastic theology.[93] As there were competing voices vying for the duke's attention, Arndt claimed that his opponents were not only incorrect but of a different spirit. Arndt went so far as to claim that many great theologians had less of Christ than they were thought to have.[94] Thus Arndt set up his opponents and the "scholastic" theology as a foil for his true prophetic voice.

In these letters, there is no reference to Luther or the Lutheran confessions. The only citation of an ecclesiastical author comes from St. Bernard. Arndt quoted Bernard, saying that one "sooner embraces Christ when one follows him."[95] Thus Arndt once again stressed the importance of imitation as the solution for a revived Lutheran church.

Gone from Arndt's voice is the carefully confessional language of the previous letters. For the only time in his correspondence, Arndt ventured into the realm, if only briefly and broadly, of predictive prophecy. Arndt had already claimed that a good many theologians do not grasp Christ at all, and he claimed that if they were left unchecked by the authorities, "a time will come when one will weep over the Academies in Germany."[96] While this is perhaps not the boldest of predictions, it represented Arndt playing to the sensibilities of his ruler. It warrants noting that this was also one of the few times that Arndt referenced the German lands. Arndt presented the problem as particularly national and then offered the ruler his prophetic program as a remedy.

Arndt presented his ideal plan in two parts: he claimed that the German church must recover the recognition of true teaching and stress holy living.[97] The central issue for Arndt in this letter to the duke was the teaching of the imitation of Christ. Arndt claimed that this can only be done if one draws back the mind of the student and the pastor from the polemical and disputational theology being taught in the universities.[98] Arndt wrote that what would truly benefit the church were not more universities and confessions but a recognition of the true Christian life and the life of Christ in the soul of the believer.[99] As opposed to what Arndt wrote to his confessional and theologically trained correspondents, he suggested to the duke that this plan of renewal involved a turning from the confessions and the confessional universities. In this letter, we see the eclectic strain of Arndt's thought established in the previous chapter.

Other Magistrates

It has been shown that the previous letters were written with the specific intention of providing a prophetic framework with which the correspondent would understand Arndt in his prophetic role, calling for a renewal of the church. Yet understanding Arndt's prophetic self can also shed light on sections of letters in which Arndt's primary goal was not his particular prophetic representation. There exist in many of Arndt's letters prophetic allusions, as well as seemingly curious inclusions that can best be made sense of in light of this role he had established for himself.

Following his exile from Anhalt, Arndt was employed by the abbess Anna of Stollberg to preach at the St. Nikolaikirche.[100] During the initial phase of his time there, Arndt claimed to have set up a type of refuge for similarly exiled confessional brethren. It was in this period that Arndt's first surviving work, *Ikonographia*, was published. This was Arndt's only published work attacking Calvinism as it documented the theological justification for images and Christian adornments (the controversial issues that led to his exile). During this period, Quedlinburg was struck by plague, an event that Arndt saw in biblical terms, leading him to preach a series of sermons on the ten plagues of Egypt.[101] In comparing his own town to Egypt and preaching against the sins of the people, Arndt would eventually fall into disfavor and subsequently accept a call to Braunschweig. Arndt's unpopularity, coupled with the plague and the claim that he was unfaithful to his calling, would undoubtedly bolster Arndt's own prophetic understanding.

The Quedlinburg Magisterium

One set of letters was to his new church at Quedlinburg. The first and lengthier letter was written to the abbess Anna von Stollberg. Little is known about the abbess, who was Arndt's overseer for nine years in Quedlinburg. The fact that she had accepted Arndt after his exile from Anhalt and promoted him in two years to the position of head pastor suggests that she was concerned with upholding the Lutheran confessions. Arndt had dedicated his *Ikonographia* to the abbess.[102] In writing, Arndt would be certain to affirm his confessional fidelity but also to justify his leaving the church for a new position. Unsurprisingly, Arndt employed his understanding of the persecuted and called prophet to do so. Arndt began the letter by laying the groundwork of his understanding of the call. As has been mentioned, the call was an essential element to the Lutheran understanding of the particular office. Arndt claimed that he had received the call and must be faithful to it.[103] Arndt was also particularly careful to distance himself from the false prophets and claims that he was innocent of the accusations to the contrary.[104] To place himself in the context of the true prophets, Arndt invoked Jeremiah, whom he claimed was also true to the external call, and the Psalmist who testified that God is the guider of paths.[105] Arndt then wrote of the suffering that had befallen him and testified to his authentic experience. Arndt claimed that the office to which men are called is their cross to bear.[106] He claimed that his cross had included the slander of his name that has made him weary of his position.[107] Finally, Arndt echoed the variation of the passage from Ecclesiastes referenced later in his letter to the Braunschweig Council, "*Calumnia enim conturbat sapientem frangitque robur cordis ejus.*"[108] Arndt turned any attention from the content of the complaints against him to the fact that *calumnia* is contrary to Christian practice and weakens the effectiveness of his ministry. Arndt was thus portraying himself in familiar prophetic tones, as called to the office and patiently suffering. While the letter is not as strong in either confessing or dissenting tones and is not primarily a text to establish his prophetic status, the themes align with his prophetic understanding.

The second brief letter was written the following day to the company of pastors in Quedlinburg. Arndt wrote to garner a recommendation from them to help clear his name from a controversy that involved two burgomasters, Paschasi Luderi and Valentine Helmudi. Arndt claimed that he had been slandered, and one record of the controversy claims that the discontent was a result of Arndt's rigorous ethical standards.[109] Arndt did not spend any time in the letter defending himself or proposing his rectitude. Rather, he laid claim to the particular called office and his prophetic status as one called to the office. Arndt attempted to garner a favorable report from the company of pastors by applauding the group's faithfulness to the called office.[110] The letter is brief and hardly a concentrated effort to propose his prophetic status, but by placing himself in the called office, he echoes previous statements that also attempted to exculpate himself from the charges of being a false prophet. This small sample section of letters surrounding Arndt's move from Quedlinburg to Braunschweig shows Arndt using the prophetic language to provide his defense.

The Braunschweig Council

The letter from June 26, 1599, was addressed to the council at Braunschweig to ask release from his position. The first letter began with Arndt's claim that recent controversies have made him weary not only of his position but also of his life and the world.[111] Here, early in his career, we see the sadness and despair that would come out more fully in his letters to his friends. In this context, Arndt referenced a passage from the preacher of Ecclesiastes. While the preacher fits with Arndt's prophetic styling, Arndt altered the passage slightly to reflect his own situation. Arndt claims that *calumnia*, or sophistry, afflicts the wise and saps the strength of the heart. This is a very commonplace claim with Arndt, as there are repeated references to a rejection of what he called "scholastic" and "disputational" theology. The passage Arndt cites from the book of Ecclesiastes is an appropriate prophetic choice, as the preacher in the Old Testament book is also, at times, a beleaguered and despondent voice. Arndt selected a particularly thorny text and presented it in light of his own situation. The passage in Luther's Bible, *"Unrechter Gewinn macht den Weisen zum Toren, und Bestechung verdirbt das Herz,"* follows most translations and suggest that improper gains and bribery corrupt the heart. Yet Arndt quoted, *"Calumnia enim conturbat Sapientem et frangit robur cordis ejus,"* the Latin translation of the verse that supplied the meaning best suited for him.[112] In Arndt's reference, it is not finances or bribery but rather sophistry (*calumnia*) that confuses wisdom and beleaguers the heart. Likewise, Arndt paraphrased the preacher and further added to his status as an oppressed prophet. Arndt further referred to his oppressors and their unfound challenges against his person.[113]

In the second letter, written on the following day, the themes are almost identical. Arndt claims to have been treated unfairly by his parishioners, says he has suffered on account of his poor farming resources and pay, and seeks to be called elsewhere. The one significant addition to this letter is another reference to Arndt's mistreatment on account of his being an exile from Anhalt.[114] This is instantly familiar as Arndt's prophetic trademark and claim to confessional fidelity.

Statius Kahlen

Finally, there are two surviving letters from Arndt to Statius
Kahlen, a burgomaster in Braunschweig, and in both letters, Arndt
was writing to present himself as unfairly persecuted.[115] The prophetic tone in Arndt's letters to Kahlen differs from the previously
examined letters. In these two letters dating from Arndt's time in
Braunschweig, the prophetic voice of Arndt was not overwhelmingly
the central argument of the letter, but it came out in Arndt's presentation of himself as less the prophetic voice of renewal and more the
patient victim.

The first letter dates from 1605, the year *True Christianity* was
first published, and was written on account of Arndt's knowledge
that a colleague, Herman Denecke, had accused him of *schwaermerisch* tendencies.[116] Arndt wrote to Kahlen for support in suppress-
ing the controversy. The familiar prophetic tones appear in Arndt's
claim that he was the target of "*calumniam*," that he has been treated
with ungrounded suspicion and falsely accused of heresy.[117] Arndt
did not offer any theological justification or suggest that the controversy was based on misunderstanding. Rather, in referring to plague,
affliction, and the ploys of the devil, Arndt reprised his representation as the persecuted prophet.

The second letter, from 1608, was written as Arndt received
a call to move to Eisleben.[118] Arndt wrote to the burgomaster to
implore him for a release from his position to take up another. This
situation and the content of the letter parallel those in the letter written to Abbess Anna von Stollberg, when Arndt asked for a release
from his position to move from Quedlinburg to Braunschweig. The
prophetic tone is one of the called servants of God submitting only
to the desires of his master. Arndt qualified his prophetic voice with
familiar references, the first being the divine nature of the call. Arndt
claimed that moving to the new church is not his own wish but the
will of God.[119] This theme of the call, and what Arndt refers to three
times in this letter as his "vocation," was Arndt's manner of establishing his work as set apart, specifically called, and therefore not
open to challenge. The second issue in the letter was his exile from
Anhalt. Arndt listed the ways in which he had been mistreated in
Braunschweig and referenced the similarity to his treatment in his

fatherland.[120] Arndt, in describing his mistreatment and tying it to his prophetic representation, proceeded to bolster the connection in claiming that the only way he had been able to deal with the suffering was his knowledge that his conscience was clear and that he was walking in the footsteps of both Christ and his apostles.[121]

Arndt's letters to Kahlen do not read as primarily prophetic; absent are the confessing or eclectic prophetic voice and details of a program for renewal. Yet when it suited him, Arndt was able to use the prophetic themes to show himself as both a victim and persecuted servant of God.

Conclusion

One of the central realities of Johann Arndt's life was that he believed himself to be a prophet called to his church. Through his life of suffering and exile, as well as his perception of the moral laxity of the church, he was able to forge a distinct understanding of that of which the church needed to be reminded. Theology was not simply right doctrine or an academic exercise, according to Arndt. It included these things, but the word of God, as interpreted through the confessions, needed to be realized in practice; it needed to be manifested in the daily lives of Christians who would devote themselves to renewal and repentance. Ultimately, instruction was not enough; it was the Spirit that was to enlighten and reform the church. This, according to Arndt, was what constituted "true" Christianity.

Thus Arndt's prophetic call embraced the totality of his thought and life. The eclectic and confessional strains, which may seem contradictory, are reconciled with this understanding of Arndt as a prophet in his own context. Arndt imbibed this prophetic call from various sixteenth-century models and adapted what he believed to be his high calling to his various correspondents. Although he was particular, and conscious of what he wrote at times, he was not duplicitous. He believed his calling as a prophet and his summons to the church to repent were what defined him, and he was thus able to employ whatever language or voice he felt necessary to achieve his calling: to proclaim an internal, and spiritually effective, "true" Christianity.

Conclusion

The central question of this book has been, Who did Johann Arndt believe himself to be? The simple yet highly significant answer is that Arndt thought of himself as a confessional Lutheran. The evidence from his correspondence demonstrates that he clearly sought to be read and understood in light of the confessions of the Lutheran church. Recognizing this provides an important corrective to the major interpretative paradigms of Arndt research. The identification of Arndt as a mystic has failed to place him in his historical context and in particular to acknowledge his pastoral duties as an ordained Lutheran minister, a role that was central to Arndt's own understanding of his identity.

While the introduction identified those authors who highlighted mystical elements in Arndt's work, they do not represent the majority of Arndt interpreters. Rather, Arndt has more commonly been referenced in texts pertaining to the Pietist movement. This seems to take Arndt out of his own context. However, in light of the prevalent trend to view Arndt through the lens of the Pietist movement, it seems appropriate to return to the idea of Arndt as a Pietist in light of my work. The issue (as raised in the introduction) lies in the definition of Pietism and the interpretation of a complex figure. As established in the introduction, Pietism has been subject to a varied number of interpretations. In the seventeenth century, Pietism was defined in terms of both theology and personal holiness. In a seventeenth-century poem, Joachim Feller wrote the following:

> Pietist—the name is now well-known throughout the world.
> What is a Pietist? One who studies God's Word
> And also leads a holy life according to it.[1]

If this is the definition of a Pietist, Arndt certainly fits the mold. However, if this rather simplistic definition is accepted, this would fit any pious Christian in any era. A contemporary of Feller, Valentin Löscher, suggested that the essence of Pietism was as follows:

> "The unfounded and general dominion of strange spirits and impulses in 'religious things,' unlimited love for secret, peculiar, and lofty things. This usually disintegrates into mysticism . . ." "[That] there is only one religion, namely piety; the rest are human trifles," "they rail against the names orthodox and orthodoxy . . . they complain that orthodoxy is too highly regarded," "[that] there are really no external means of grace at all," "Pure doctrine . . . works nothing in spiritual men," "they contrast the external things in the worship service with the inner things in such a way that external things are of no value."[2]

As referenced in the introduction, Löscher defended Arndt against these claims. Based on the correspondence of Arndt, it appears that Löscher was correct. One could argue that his definition of Pietism was flawed, but if this rubric is accepted, then Arndt would certainly be beyond the scope of the movement.

Heinrich Schmid differed in his opinion of Pietism as a solely theological movement and suggested the necessity of a particular social outgrowth necessary to the movement: conventicles.[3] These home churches, which suggested an *ecclesiola in ecclesia*, are never mentioned in Arndt's works or correspondence. While Arndt's letters suggest that some (if not many) in the church were not in fact "true" Christians, the social phenomenon of the conventicle blossomed more than half of a century after Arndt's death. If this definition is accepted, Arndt falls beyond the pale of Pietism. Albrecht Ritschl suggested that Pietism was antithetical to Luther's thought.[4] If Pietism was then the rejection of Luther's thought, one cannot come to the conclusion that Arndt was a Pietist. Johannes Wallmann, while preferring the term *Frömmigkeit* to Pietism, nevertheless defined Pietism as both a broad and narrow movement.[5] As a broad movement toward a particularly spiritually affective movement within the Lutheran church, Arndt would certainly fit the definition of a Pietist. Yet as a narrow movement, which required Schmid's social requisite of a conventicle, Arndt cannot be considered a Pietist.

Two historians mentioned earlier, Wilhelm Koepp and Eric Lund, take a different approach to the question by placing Arndt on a continuum between the late medieval mystics and the later Pietist movement.[6] While Arndt's direct connection with the Pietist movement is not made explicit, Lund suggests that Arndt was the developer of a Lutheran spiritual tradition, and Koepp refers to Arndt's mystical *Sonderreligion*. My book owes much to the interpretation of Lund in particular, but through the use of the correspondence it has been possible to extend the argument further. What emerges is a picture of Johann Arndt as a man who cannot be seen simply as a forerunner of pietism, although elements of his thought suggest possible connections. Arndt, as I have attempted to show, believed himself part of the institutional Lutheran church and an adherent to its established theology. What he made of that institution and its theology was distinctively his own.

As this indicates, Arndt's thought—and with it his identity—cannot be divorced from his personal biography and his historical context. Arndt lived in a time of social and theological upheaval within the Lutheran church. The relationship between the Lutheran church and other Protestant bodies was not firmly established. The social and economic upheaval that would contribute to the outbreak of war also provided a devotional author such as Arndt with a context in which he felt comfortable borrowing from a broad spectrum of Christian theology to console his readers. Arndt saw no contradiction here with his own location within the Lutheran church, a view that can only have been reinforced for him by his enormous popularity among the laity.

Many theologians have treated Arndt's work as a type of systematic or dogmatic theology. Two significant modifications of this view have been proposed in this work. Arndt has been viewed here through his correspondence, and with only a few exceptions, these letters were meant for a specific and identified audience. Arndt's self-perception is evident in his crafting of his relationship with the recipient. In the majority of his letters to Gerhard, Arndt was writing to a confirmand and then established theologian within the church. Arndt's perception of Gerhard as a kindred spirit reveals himself as both a confessional and an eclectic pastor dedicated to the renewal of the church. Further investigation of the theological, pastoral, and personal relationship between these two men would likely be highly rewarding.

106

Second, Gerhard's comment to Polycarp Leyser that Arndt "thought better than he wrote" raises the issue of Arndt's education. Although Hans Schneider's recent article has addressed Arndt's *Studienzeit*, we still know little about Arndt's teachers, academic qualifications, or reading. Many sixteenth-century commentators believed that the strength of the *Theologia Deutsch* was that it was written "as out of the mouths of babes," and similarly, it was Arndt's lack of theological sophistication that made him a popular and effective devotional author. This may also, however, account for the theological inconsistencies that have brought criticism from those searching for a systematic theologian.

Arndt may have been the "most read Lutheran author of the seventeenth century," but he has received little attention from historians or editors. There are no critical editions of his work and there is no standard historical biography. As the spotlight is turned increasingly on the Lutheran Reformation after Luther, Arndt's works and context may in turn also receive greater illumination. Viewed through his extant correspondence, it is already apparent that Arndt ultimately believed himself to be a prophet of interior Lutheranism.

Appendix A
List of Correspondence

The following is a list of the letters collected and used for this book. These letters were tracked down using the footnotes and appendices of earlier works on Arndt and with the help of the librarians at the *Forschungsbibliothek* at Gotha. While some letters appear in multiple volumes, I have listed the version I have used (either because it was the entire letter, as opposed to an excerpt or because it was in the original language in which Arndt wrote it). Following the list is a bibliographic key for each of the names in bold on the right. I have also included the libraries where I used each work.

Johann Arndt's Letters

1. September 2, 1579—Theodore Zwinger **Schneider**
2. September 10, 1590—Johann Georg von Anhalt **Rambach**
3. 1591/2—Lyserum Senatorum **Scharff**
4. June 25, 1599—Braunschweig City Council **Rambach**
5. June 26, 1599—Braunschweig City Council **Rambach**
6. July 6, 1599—Abbess Anna II von Stollberg **Rambach**
7. July 7, 1599—Ministerium at Quedlinburg **Rambach**
8. December 25, 1599—Erasmus Wolfhart **Rambach**
9. January 26, 1601—Johann Gerhard **Raidel**
10. March 15, 1603—Johann Gerhard **Rambach**
11. January 27, 1604—Johann Gerhard **Raidel**
12. January 10, 1605—Johann Gerhard **Raidel**
13. June 26, 1605—Johann Gerhard **Raidel**
14. October 17, 1605—Johann Gerhard **Raidel**
15. June 13, 1606—Statius Kahlen **Rambach**

16. June 20, 1606—Johann Gerhard **Rambach**
17. July 5, 1606—Johann Gerhard **Raidel**
18. November 27, 1606—Johann Gerhard **Raidel**
19. January 14, 1607—Petrus Piscator **WC**
20. February 19, 1607—Johann Gerhard **Rambach**
21. March 21, 1607—Petrus Piscator **Rambach**
22. May 4, 1607—Johann Gerhard **Raidel**
23. August 3, 1607—Johann Gerhard **Rambach**
24. August 28, 1607—Johann Gerhard **Raidel**
25. June 29, 1608—Johann Gerhard **MS @ Gotha**
26. March 4, 1608—Johann Gerhard **Raidel**
27. March 8, 1608—Johann Gerhard **Rambach**
28. April 20, 1608—Johann Gerhard **Raidel**
29. April 25, 1608—Johann Gerhard **Raidel**
30. May 13, 1608—Johann Gerhard **Raidel**
31. June 7, 1608—Johann Gerhard **Raidel**
32. June 10, 1608—Johann Gerhard **Rambach**
33. August 28, 1608—Johann Gerhard **Raidel**
34. October 23, 1608—Johann Gerhard **Raidel**
35. November 1, 1608—Statius Kahlen **Rambach**
36. June 6, 1610—Petrus Piscator **Gleich**
37. May 1611—Kanzler Hildebrand **Fr. Arndt**
38. June 3, 1611—Johann Gerhard **Fr. Arndt**
39. July 13, 1612—Johann Gerhard **MS @ Gotha**
40. 1612—Franciscus Herman **Fr. Arndt**
41. November 13, 1614—Johann Gerhard **Ernst Gerhard**
42. June 7, 1615—Christophorus Friccius **Ernst Gerhard**
43. November 28, 1617—Gerhard Colemannus **Fr. Arndt**
44. February 19, 1619—Antonius Buscher **WB**
45. January 18, 1620—Johann Gerhard **Ernst Gerhard**
46. March 29, 1620—Wolfgang Franzius **Fr. Arndt**
47. May 4, 1620—Daniel Dilger **WC**
48. October 23 (9), 1620—Balthasar Mentzer **WC**
49. November 11, 1620—Johann Gerhard **Ernst Gerhard**
50. January 28, 1621—Duke August the Younger **Rambach**
51. January 29, 1621—Duke August the Younger **Rambach**
52. April 20, 1621—Duke August the Younger **Fr. Arndt**

Key

Ernst Gerhard—BSB

Gerhard, Johann Ernst, *Epistola ad amicum de obtrectationibus Arndii* (Giessen, 1705).

Gleich—BSB

Gleich, Johann Andreas, *Trifolium Arndtium: Johannis Arndi tres epistolae* (Wittenberg, 1726).

MS @ Forschungsbibliothek Gotha

Chart. A 121, Bl. 16r-17v-29 January 29, 1608

Chart. A 121, Bl. 18r-19v July 13, 1608

Rambach—BSB

Arndt, Johann, *Johann Arnds Geistreicher Schriften und Werke: Gesammelte Kleine Werke Bd. III*, ed. Johann Jacob Rambach (Leipzig, 1736).

Raidel—GOTHA

Raidelius, Georgius Martinus, *Epistolae Virorum Eruditorum Ad Johannem Gerhardum* (Norimbergae, 1740).

Repitito Apologetica—GOTHA

Arndt, Johann, *Repetitio Apologetica. Das ist: Widerholung und Verantwortung der Lehre vom wahren Christenthumb: zu weiterer Information und Unterweisung derer so Christum oder die Gottseligkeit lieb haben damit sie sich von der Gottlosen Welt nicht lassen abwendig machen* (Magdeburg, 1620).

Scharff—BSB

Scharff, Gottfried Balthasar, *Supplementum historiae litisque Arndianae aliquot inclutorum superioris saeculi theologorum Epistolis constans* (Wittenberg, 1727).

Schneider—UB Basel,   Schneider, Hans, "Johann Arndt als
Frey-Gryn. II 4 Nr. 11   Lutheraner?" in Hans Christoph
                              Rublack, ed., *Die lutherische*
                              Konfessionalisierung in Deutschland:
                              Wissenschaftliches Symposion
                              des Vereins für Reformation Geschichte
                              (Gutersloh, 1992), 274–298.

WB—BSB   Breller, Melchior, *Warhafftiger,*
                              Glaubwurdiger und Gründlicher Bericht
                              von den vier Büchern vom Wahren
                              Christenthumb Herrn Johannis Arndten
                              auss den gefunden brieflichen Urkunden
                              zusammen getragen (Lüneburg, 1625).

WC   Arndt, Johann, *Sechs Bücher vom*
                              wahren Christentum (Bielefeld, 1996).

Appendix B

Important Dates and Printed Works

December 27, 1555—Born in Ballenstedt, Anhalt

November 24, 1565—Johann's father, Jakob, died in Ballenstedt

1576—Arndt studied at the University of Helmstadt

1577-1579—Arndt studied at Strasbourg

September 1579—Arndt at Basel

1582—Arndt married to Anna Wagner

1583—Arndt ordained in Anhalt

1584—Arndt served as pastor at St. Vitus Church in Anhalt

1590—Arndt removed from his pastoral position

Arndt moved to Quedlinburg—took up a position at the St. Nikolai Church

1595 (?)—*De origine sectarum, De magis ex oriente, De antiqua Philosophia*

1596—Arndt preached (and printed?) *De zehn plagis Aegyptorum*

1597—*Ikonographia* printed

Arndt prepared a new edition of the *Theologia Deutsch*

1598—Plague in Quedlinburg

1599—Arndt asked Abbess Anna von Stollberg for a release from St. Nikolai Church

Arndt moved to Braunschweig

1600—Braunschweig under siege by Duke Heinrich Julius

1602-1604—Political turmoil in Braunschweig between burgomasters and patricians

1605—First book of *True Christianity* printed in Frankfurt

Zwei uralte und edle Büchlein (*Theologia Deutsch* and *Imitation of Christ*)

Zwei alte geistreiche Büchlein Doctoris von Staupitz

1606—Revised edition of the first book of *True Christianity* printed in Braunschweig

Second revised edition of the first book of *True Christianity* printed

1607—Second book of *True Christianity* sent to Petrus Piscator

Third revised edition of *True Christianity* printed in Jena

1608—Third and fourth books of *True Christianity* sent to Johann Gerhard

Arndt accepted a call to the Andreas Church in Eisleben

1609—Arndt moved to Eisleben

1610—All four books of *True Christianity* printed together in Magdeburg

1611—Arndt accepted a call to Celle as general superintendent

1612—*Paradiesgartlein* printed in Magdeburg

1613—*Summa und Inhalt ger ganzen heiligen Schrift*

1615—*Postilla*

1616—*Catechismuspredigten*

1617—*Auslegung des gantzen Psalter Davids*

1618—*Huldigungspredigt* and *Landtagspredigt*

Controversy in Danzig concerning *True Christianity*

1620—The Lüneburg Bible appeared with a foreword by Arndt

De Unione Credentium cum Christo Jesu

Lehr- und Trostbüchlein vom wahren Glauben und heiligung Leben

Von der Vereinigung der Gläubigen mit Christo Jesu ihrem Haupt

Von der heiligen Dreifaltigkeit

Repititio Apologetica

May 11, 1621—Arndt died in Celle

Appendix C

September 10 to Duke Johann Georg of Anhalt

Rambach p. 599

Weil mein Gewissen hierinn gefangen, dass die Rechtgläubigen Väter vor dreyzehen hundert Jahren den Exorcissmum zur heil. Tauffe geordnet, und dadurch eine allgemeine Ceremonie der ganzen rechtgläubigen Kirche worden, welche sie auch nach dem Sinn und wahren Verstande der Schrifft genommen; auch mit nichten eine sündliche Ceremonie ist; Auch ich der Kirchen Gottes und hertzlieben Fuerstlichen jungen herrschaft nichts vergeben kan; Auch keine Ursach unter allen mein Gewissen befriediget: So bitte ich unterthänig und demüthiglich, mein gnädiger Fürst und herr wolle mir in Gnaden nicht verdencken, dass ich hierinn nicht kann willigen, und stelle demnach meinen gnädigen Fürsten und herrn unterthänig anheim, nach gnädigen Gefallen mit mir zu handeln.

15 March 1603 to Johann Gerhard

Rambach p. 618

Binas pro accipe, ad tuas geminas, quae ad me advolarunt. Priores meas volante calamo fusas potius, quam scriptas, vereor ut possis legere, nec enim omnem occasionem tabellaririum negligendam ducebam. Ad illa, quae in superioribus non attigi, paucual respondeo. Primum de libris Theologicus comparandis Biblia Vatabli Hebraeo Latina, Lexicon

Hebraeum, vel Pagnini vel Avenarii consilio Professoris Hebraicae Linguae; pro incipientibus sufficit Avenarius: Exstat Biblicum Opus illud Complutense, editions Regiae Antverpianz: in numero illorum Tomorum unus est. qui textum Biblicum continent cum inserta versione Latina interlineari: ad marginem vero omnes radices Hebraeas adnotatas habet. Si hunc tomum seorsim nanciscipotes, quemadmodum puto, sine mora tibi comparator. Interpretes Bibliorum, et Commentatores nescio sane quos tibi commendare debeam quidam sunt adeo populares, ut nihil rerum habeant: quidam tantum in cortice haerent: plurimi, quod pace aliorum dixerim, non ex spiritu, sed ex carne scribunt. Regulum igitur hic hanc habe: In libris seligendis, antequam emas, aliquot pagellas evolvito, et attende, an ex corde et conscientia tua loquator auctor, si precellit animum et penetrate sermo, vivus est, et ex spiritu; sin minus; spiritus Carnis ibi dominator. Bone, quanti hoc mihi constitit? Antequam didici discernere libros illos, qui ex spiritu, et qui ex carne scripti sint. Fastus: avaritia: contentio: origo plurimorum: carnales hi sunt. Bernhardus ex Spiritu scripsit: et Kempisius et Macarius: Spinaeus: et quidam Gratensis: sed Postillam ejus non magni facio: et Augustini quaedam. Inter omnes Philosophos neminem scio, qui ex spiritu scripserit (qui, ubi vult, spirat) praeter unum Senecam: quem si, necdum legisti, per otium quaeso legito: emas autem Godofredi editionem. R. Gwalteri Commentarios, uti et Aretii, nescio sane, an tibi debeam commendare: cogitabo de his altius. Disputationes Theologicas minime disvadeo. Epitomem Historiae Ecclesiasticae, Osiandri usque ad nonum tomum deductam, (nuper etiam 16. Saeculum, prodiit:) ut emas et evolvas, auctor sum. Hebraeae linguae cognitionem tibi commendo et ut et veram pronunciationem assequare, emas Psalterium Hutteri Harmonicum: sed vide, ne nimis scrupulosus sis in illa lingua sufficit fundametum iecisse. Sufficit etiam sic satis familiarem tibi reddidisse textum biblicum. Meditationibus ego sacris plurimum laudis tribuo, praesertimsi ex intimo Dei amore et seria poenitentia proficiscuntur. Hic est meus liber praecipuus: de quoaliquando oretenus: Vale iterum et salve 15. Martii Brunsvigae 1605.

14 January 1607 to Petrus Piscator

In WC pp. 26–29

Heil in unserem einigen Heilende! Ehrwürdiger, Hochachtbarer und Hochgelahrter, Hochzuehrender Herr!

Ich habe vor etlichen Wochen mein Buch vom wahren Christentum Ew. Ehrw. zugesandt, damit ich dero Gutachten und Privantzentur darüber bekäme, aus welchem Unterricht ich mich von mancherlei Argwohn losmachen und in der künftigen Ausgabe dieses und jenes genauer prüfen und examinieren könnte. Da ich aber durch anhaltende Bekümmernisse desgleichen durch den weiten und beschwerlichen Weg verhindert und abgehalten bin, auch seltene Posten und Gelegenheit dorthin habe, so habe ich die Sache nicht nach Wunsch treiben können. Auch habe ich besorget, ich möchte Ew. Ehrw. oder dem ganzen Kollegio der Herren Theologen beschwerlich sein. Indes aber, da ich sehe, es sei mir der gelehrten Theologen Gutachten und Rat nötig, so nehme ich zu Ew. Ehrw. wiederum meine Zuflucht, ob ich gleich, wie Gott weiss, ungerne Mühe und Verdruss mache, und bitte von Herzen, mit guten Rat zu erteilen, wie ich den falschen Argwohn, den man wieder mich gefasset, ablehnen möge. Ich will aber in diesem Briefe mit Ew. Ehrw. erstliche von der Sache selbst, hernach von meinen Umständen handeln, damit man das ganze Werk genauer könne einsehen, und verlasse mich hierin auf Ew. Ehrw. sonderbare Leutseligkeit und Frömmigkeit. Ich führe drei Fundamente an, damit mein Sinn und Reingkeit in dem Artikel vom freien Willen, davon man hier mit mir handelt, wie wider die Synergie kund werde. 1. Habe ich aus dem Texte meine Buchs über zwanzig Örter aufgezeichnet, welche meine Meinung eröffnen und wieder die Synergie Streiten. 2. Die Redensarten meines Buches, die anstössig scheinen möchten, erkläre ich nach meines Herzens aufrichtiger Meinung, und hoffe nicht, dass man aus einer blossen Redensart wider den Sinn den ganzen Buches einen Irrtum erzwingen könne. Ich erbiete mich dasjenige, was nicht bedachtsam genug geredet ist, nach Ew. Ehrw. Gutbefinden in der künftigen Auflage des Buches zu verbessern. 3. In einigen von den ersten Kapiteln des anderen Buches, davon ich den Anfang überschicke, sonderlich im 6. Kapitel vernichte ich gänzlich die menschlichen Kräfte in der Bekehrung, und zwar so deutlich, dass ich den menschlichen Kräften an und für sich selbst weder vor, noch und in nach der Bekehrung das Geringste zuschreibe. Denn ich weiss und lehre, dass die Gnade Gottes alles in uns zur Seligkeit werke und tue, nach dem Zeugnis der apostolischen Worte: Nicht ich, sondern die Gnade Gottes in mir. Hernach beweise ich die Gerechtigkeit des Glaubens aus gnaden mit vielen Gründen in den ersten Kapiteln eben dieses Buches, und zeige deutlich, dass in der Gerechtigkeit des Glaubens aus Gnaden unser höchster und einiger Trost bestehe. Diese drei Gründe, die ich mit meinen Worten aufgezeichnet und meinem Schreiben beigelegt habe, wolle Ew. Ehrw. belieben durchzulesen un mir guten Rat und Instruktion mitzuteilen, und ersuche Sie zugleich, Sie wollten mir nicht übel deuten, dass ich nach meiner vorigen Bitte so lang verzogen, wiederum an Sie zu schreiben, woran sicherlich meine Trübsale schuld sind. Ich rufe den grossen Got, den Herzenskündiger, zum Zeugen an, dass ich nichts geschreiben habe aus einem Gemüt, das von der wahren Religion der Augsburgischen Konfession und der Formula Concordiae abtrete, oder gesinnet sei, falsche Meinungen auszustreuen, viel weniger zu verteidigen, die mit den symbolischen Büchern unsere Kirche stritten. Ich habe ein Mittel erfinden wollen, wider die entsetzliche Bosheit dieser unserer verderbten Zeit, und einen Weg zeigen, wie auch die Wiedergeborenen nach der Bekehrung durch den Geist Gottes die angeborene Verderbnis des Herzens bändigen und zähmen könnten. Und ich schreibe nicht sowohl denen, die noch stehen in dem Stande vor der Bekehrung, als denen, welche Christum schon durch den Glauben erkannt haben und doch hiednisch leben. Diese ermahne ich, dass sie die fleischlichen Lüste durch den Heil. Geist ablegen und töten. Diesen zeige ich die Belohnung der Gottseligkeit und der Furcht des Herrn, nämlich die Erleuchtungdes Geistes und die Vermehrung der geistlichen Gaben Gottes. Diesen erkläre und rekommandiere ich Natur des Glaubens, der die Herzen reiniget und den ganzen Menschen erneuert. Diesen preise ich an die kräftige Wirkung der göttlichen Gnade, dadurch die Wiedergebornen, gestärkt und gefördert werden, dass sie die Werke des Fleisches kreuzigen und töten, Christo im Leben nachfolgen und in Christo immer heiliger leben können. Diesen Zweck habe ich mir vorgenommen, bei dem so grossen Verfall der Gottseligkeit und der Furcht Gottes, und bei der so freien Ausübung der Laster, damit nicht der Herr komme und das Erdreich mit dem Banne schlage, wie der Prophet Malachias weissaget.- Ich komme nun auf den ander punkt meines Briefes. Ich diene der Gemeinde Christi schon 24 Jahre her, bin von Jugend auf in der wahren Religion erzogen, habe viel Elend erfahren, viel betrübte Verfolgung von der Dissentierenden erduldet, bin aus meinem Vaterlande, dem Fürstentum Anhalt, verstossen, als die gegenseitige Partei überhand nahm, da ich sieben Jahre unter mancherlei Nachstellung in meinem Vaterlande gelehret und wider die Bilderstürmerei geschrieben hatte. Als ich von da ausgestossen, bin ich nach Quedlinburg berufen worden, meine Schafe folgeten mir haüfig aus der Nachbarschaft nach und ver langeten von mir mein Amt, und ich habe sowohl denen zu Quedlinburg, als diesen neun Jahre gedienet. Da nun E.E. Rat zu Braunschweig meine Treue erkannte, haben sie mich hierher an die Hauptkirche berufen, daran ich bereits acht Jahre diene. [. . .] Durch diesen Verfall des wahren Christentums bin ich bewogen worden, von der liebe schreiben bei welcher Gelegenheit ich auf solche Gedanken geraten bin, woraus diese meine Bücher erwachsen sind, darübermir, ich weiss nicht, was für Böses beigemessen wird, weil ich aus Unbedacht einige Redensarten und Erinnerungen gebraucht habe. Wenn E.E. dieser meiner Arbeit nicht eine gelindere und billigere Zensur verleihen wird, so scheinet es, dass ich von dem unsinnigen Pöbel der vor aller Gottesfurcht einen Abscheu hat, wenn der Lärmen recht angehet, nichts Gewisseres zu gewarten habe, als ins Elend verstossen zu werden. Ja, der rat selbst, dessen Ansehen ich durch meine Predigten mich eifrigst bemühe zu erhalten, wird zu tun haben, dass er sich halte. Denn die Bürger werden hier ganz entkräftet durch die achtjährigen Pressuren, und sind von neuen ungeduldig wider den unschuldigen Rat. Ich wollte zwar die Verbannung (wenn nicht die Religion selbst darunter litte) mit allen Freuden annehmen, damit ich aus diesen Nöten, die voll Furcht und Neid sind, los käme, aber es kann ein jeder leicht ermessen, was das für ein Elend sei einem Theologen, wegen falschen Verdachts eines Irrtums in der Religion verjagt werden. E.E. weiss Unterschied unter theologischen Disputationen und unter Ermahnungen, welchen zum Volke zur Besserung des Lebens gerichtet werden. In jenen wird das Allergeringste akkurat und genau in den Glaubensartikeln untersuchet, in diesen wird ohne Subilität, wie es am leichtesten zu begreifen, das Hauptsächlichste vor Augen geleget, was die Verbesserung des Lebens betrifft. Ich kann Luther zum Zeugen anführen, der anders redet, wenn er disputiert, anders, wenn er die Laster straft. Es stehen einige Örter in der Kirchenpostille von den guten Werken und von der Gnadenwahl, die er gebraucht, die Busse und Lebensbesserung einzuschärfen, welche ich gewiss mich nicht unterstehen wollte, mit eben den Worten vorzutragen. Aus dieser vielleicht allzu weitläufigen und verdriesslichen Erzählung wird E.E. den Zustand meiner Sachen erkennen, welche zu dem Ende geschieht, damit E.E. von mir gelinder nach dero sonderbaren Leutseligkeit und Gottselgkeit urteile, und mir eine solche Zensur widerfahren lassen, die mein Leiden und verfolgung mässigen und lindern möge. Die Wahrheit der wahren Religion liegt mir so am Herzen, als jemanden auf der ganzen Welt, und ich verteidige keine falsche Meinung; nur dahin bemühe ich mich, dass mit der wahren christlichen Religion auch ein christliches Leben übereinstimme. Werden E.E. sich diesmal gegen mich in meine Elende gütig erzeigen, so werden Sie mich Ihnen zu einer unsterblichen Freundschaft verbindlich machen, die ich bei allen Rechtschaffenen öffentlichwerde zu rühmen haben. Von mir kann ich E.E. nichts anders versichern, als was einem redlichen Diener Jesu Christi in Lehre und Leben gebühret. Unser Syndikus würde in dieser Sache selbst geschrieben haben, wie er mit oft angeboten, er ist aber in wichtigen Angelegenheiten der Republik anjetzo verreiset. Es würde auch zum Behuf meiner Sache dienlich sein, wenn mein anderes Buch auf Ihrer Akademie gedruckt würde, welches ich deswegen gerne E.E. Zensur vor der Auflage übergeben möchte. Denn obgleich hier die ersten Blätter, die ich schicke, gedruckt sind, so wollte ich doch die darauf gewandenten Kosten gerne verschmerzen, und hoffe, das Buch würde abgehen, wenn man den Inhalt der Kapital, den ich schicke, ansehen wird. Er lebe wohl auf späte Jahre. Wenn es also gefällig ist, so will ich ehestens das Buch von neuem rein abschreiben schicken. Gegeben zu Braunschweig den 14. Januar, in dem fatalen 1607ten Jahre, welches ich E.E. glücklich und gesegnet zu sein wünsch.

19 February 1607 to Johann Gerhard

Rambach p. 605

wie gerne wolte ich von der geistlichen Verwandelung schreiben, welche auch in diesem Leben anfängt, wenn wie verwandelt werden, von der Klarheit zur Klarheit, gleich als von dem Geiste des Herrn. Aber sobald ich von vergleichen Dingen in Predigten rede, oder den Saamen dieser lehre in meinem Büchelchen austreue, sobald muss ich die Lästerung hören; Dieser Mann ist ein Enthusiste und Synergiste; da ich doch denen menschlichen Kräften alles benehme, und denenselben nichts, weder vor, noch in und nach der Bekehrung, sondern alles ganz und gar, lediglich der göttlichen Erbarmung und Gnade in Christo Jesu zuschreibe.

21 March 1607 to Petrus Piscator

Rambach p. 605

Ehrwürdiger und Hchberühmter Herr!

Desselben Briefe habe ich mit Freuden empfangen und gelesen, und daraus Ew. Ehrw. Grosse Leutselgkeit und Gottseligkeit ersehen, dafür ich höchlich verbunden bin, werde auch nicht unterlassen, solches bie allen Rechtschaffenen zu rühmen, und mich bemühen, dass es E.E. niemals gereuen mögen solche Liebe und Treue an mir bewiesen zu haben. Uebrigens da ich die Sache tiefer einsehe, missfällt mir nunmehro selbst die Redensart: "Eine evangelische Zerknirschung"; ich meinte zwar, sie könnte entschuldigt werden, soferne durch die inbrünstige Betrachtung des Leidens und Todes unser Heilandes die göttliche Traurigkeit erwecket wird, welche wirket eine Reue, die niemand gereuet. Weil aber der Tod Jesu Christi, soferne er den Zorn Gottes und die Sünden anzeiget, selbst eine Gesetzpredigt ist, welche dergleichen Zerknirschung oder Traurigkeit wirket, so wird vorgedachte Redensart billig verworfen. Doch scheinet Luther einegermassen hiezu sein, Tom. I. Jen. Germ., von der Busse wider die Päpstler. Da aber hiedurch der Unterschied unter Gesetz und Evangelium scheinen verdunkelt zu werden, so mag vielmehr die Reue ganz allein ein Werk des Gesetzes bleiben. Was die Reformierten hievon glauben, ist nicht unbekannt. E.E. tun so wohl und schicken mir ehestens Ihre Disputation. Es stehet allerdings von dieser göttlichen Traurigkeit wohl zu fragen, ob sie einzig und allein aus dem Gesetz entstehe, oder aber aus Betrachtung der Leutseligkeit Gottes und der unermesslichen väterlichen Güte gegen uns, die wir doch beleidiget haben. Braunschweig, den 21. Mart. 1607.

3 August 1607 to Johann Gerhard

Rambach pp. 605–606

Die Ausfertigung meiner übrigen Bücher verhindern meine Colleges, bedienen sich einer gar zu bittern Censur, und verachten meine Schreib-Art nach herausgebung meines ersten Buchs vom W.C. bin ich genug gedrücket, und habe viele Verfolgungen und Verläumdungen erlitten. Unangesehen, das ich es der Einhelligkeit der Lehre wegen, unter der Theologischen Facultät zu Jena Censur und Gutachten daselbst wieder auslegen lassen; alles auch geändert habe, was nur einen Schein wiedriger Meynung, geschweige irriger Lehre haben möchte; und in der Vorrede mich dahin erkläret, das ich alles, was ich geschreiben, nach unsern Symbolischen Glaubens-Büchern wolte verstanden wissen; so konnen dennoch meine Collegen nicht ruhen, sondern wollen mit Gewalt aus einem eintzigen Wort einen Irrthum erzwingen p.334 l.6. Jenischen Drucks, welches also lautet: Wie der Verwundete mit ihm handeln liesse, wie es seinem Arzt dem Samaritter gefällt, das soll Synergia heissen. Weil der natürliche Mensch nicht nur nicht leidet, sondern widerstrebet, welches ich leichtlich zugebe, weil unser natürlicher Wille von Gott abgekehret und feindlich. Allein hiervon handle ich nicht, sondern zeige nur die Art und Weise, die Praxin und den Process oder Lauff der Bekehrung, und schreibe alles der göttlichen Gnade in Christo Jesu zu, gleichwie die folgende Worte und der ganze Context bezeugen. Aber es muss nicht helffen. Ich werde heimlich und öffentlich Ehrenrührig angegriffen, und bey dem rohen Volk verdächtig gemacht, und halte dafür, man wolle mich gern hinaus haben. Wollen aber gerne sie hätten Gelegenheit. Sehet also gehet mirs, und habe seit ihr vor 2. Jahren bey mir gewesen, keinen guten Tag gehabt. Muss mich noch wohl will ich Friede haben, wann ich keinen andern Beruff bekomme, etwa an einem Ort hinbegeben, vielleicht nach Eisleben und ein Privatleben anfangen. Denn die Welt wird gar zu heilloss. Ich hätte es nimmer gemeinet, dass unter den Theologen so gifftige böse Leute wären. Diese nemlich sollen seyn, Wiedergebohrne, Gesalbte und des heil. Geistes Werckzeuge; und muss denn alles um die reine Lehre gethan seyn!

29 January 1608 to Johann Gerhard

Raidel pp. 130–133

Salutem in Christo plurimam, hujusque anni incipientis exitum felicissimum, ex animo precor! Reverende, Clarissime, et in Christo mihi gnesios dilecte! Literas tuas, Calend. Jan. datas, 29. ejusd. Accepi, una cum adjunctis; disputatione nempe tua, de praedestinatione, et concione funebre, disputationeque Libavian, (A) quam postremam illico evolve; et thesi 77. tandem in locum illum incidi, quem verebar. In medio autem, quas ille affert rationes, contra comunem et usitatem Theologorum sententiam, relinquo. Video, illum in tota disputatione singulare quid affectare; quo de, ubi otium, cogitabo altius. Gratias autem ago, pro terno isto munere. Libellos meos ita adornaveram, ut expectarent adventum tui tabellarii. Sed interim, dum hoc negotium maturo, veniunt mihi literae, a Clarissimo viro, Dn. D. Christophoro Schleupnero, Superintendente Islebiense;

quibas mihi offertur vocation nova, et munus pastoratus, in templo Petro-Paulino, eodem in oppido: et quidem ille locus, cui olim M. Conradus Porta, M. Rhote, forte tibi ex scriptis noti, et D. Probus, praefuere. Ego, dum rem in deliberationem voco, et moram necto, astus quidam intercipit successum. Insinuat se enim quidam interim, apud Illustrem Comitem Mansfeldum, Ernestum, qui mittitur illico, cum diplomate, in urbem, ut ex mandato recipiatur: Repugnat Ecclesia; et ita rem urget apud eundem Generosum Comitem, ut ille repulsam passus sit: interim oritur lis de jure vocationis. Ecclesia vero subinde, missis ad me literis, contra morae et turbarum aliquantularum taedim, me animant. Et in hoc statu etiamnum haeret negotium. Quid facium? Liberari quidem ex hoc loco percupio: interim tamen turbas nolo ingredi; sed turbis egredi. Ego de successu ferme despero Differendum igitur parumper negotium libellorum meorum censeo, donec, de successu hujus negotii certior factus fuero. Ut ut autem res cadet, per te edi illos meos libros, vel maxime desidero, quemadmodum ex Epistola ad te, libellis praefigenda, liquido cognosces: cujus descriptionem hodierno vesperi ad lucernam tentabo; si vero absolvere non potere, mittam, una cum libellis, per tabellarium Reipublicae nostrae juratum, qui mittetur a Senatu nostro Ratisbonam ad Comitia, ad nostros legatos ibi jam degentes; hic enim tabellarius per vestros fines, puta Coburgicos, transiturus est. Nobile Medicamentum utrumque, Compositionem nempe extractorum specificorum, contra luem pestiferam, et contra plerasque stomachi affections, quam nostri mixturam vocant stomachalem, et contra pestern, mitto, dono, et peto, ut munusculum animi paterni boni consulas. Item Extractum ligni sancti. Stomachalis, remedium quoque est hypochonriacum. Usus utriusque praeservativus, et curatives: Pro praeservatione mus man eine Nuszschale voll, in ein Löffel giessen, und des Morgens einnehmen, auch wenn man zu Krancken gehen will. Pro curatione: Ein Löffel voll, und darauf ein Schweisz provociren: hac ratione expellit, et non patitur venenum. Stomachalis mane jejuno stomacho parum pro libitu, pota; ventriculum certissime corroborat, et rectificat, adeoque totius corporis systema, et constitutionem emendat. Extractum ligni sancti, in haustulo vini, aut aquae hyperici, si haberi potest, egregie mundificat sanguinem, et praeservat etiam a lue illa, de qua scribes. Optarim haec remedia praesto etiam esse, praestantisimo viro, D.D. Cancell Gerstenbergero; salvum enim tantum virum, et diutissime superstitem unice cupio. D. Schroederum ex scriptis novi: quorum quaedam ad meas venerunt manus; praesertim de negotio sacramentario: illum autem peri

idio koinonias nondum vidi. Dissuaderem et ego aulicam illam voca-
tionem tuam, et mallem, te ad nos retrogradum fore; sed resistere
voluntati Principis difficillimum erit. Epistolam novam dedicatoriam
ad te, libellis meis praefigendam, qua munire me cogor adversus nostros, quod ipsis relunctantibus ediderim, libellos, ad literam celeriter
descripsi: tu, quicquid tibi visum fuerit, dele. Tuum est enim, et in tua
potestate, quemadmodum et libelli, quos propediem accipies. Faxit
D. Jesus, ut finem, quem specto, qui mihi est unicus Jesus noster dil-
lectissimus, te obstetricante, consequantur! Amen. Metus belli nos
urget iterum. Commendo me, tuis precibus. Vale in Christo, et salve.
Eodem quo tuas accepi 29. Jan. 1608. Brunswigae.

10 June 1608 to Johann Gerhard

Rambach pp. 606–608

Eurer E. freundlichen Gesuch zu willfahren, habe ich nicht umhin
gekont, die von mir so offt verlangte drey übrige Büchlein, welche
ich vom den wahren Christenthum geschrieben, als das andere,
dritte und vierdte, endlich überzusenden, das sie wenigstens zu
einem Privat-Gebrauch dienen können. Und weil sie ja E.E. laut
ihres Schreibens, für eine sondere Wohlthat und Geschenk halten
wollen, so sollen sie ihm hiermit verehret seyn, damit ich durch
etwas geringes einen grossen Danck bey ihm verdienen möge. Es
machen es E.E. nach Art der Liebhaber, welche auch das allergeringste Geschenk, wenn es nur von lieber und gewogener hand
kommt, hoch zu schätzen pflegen. Es soll aber dieses ein Privat-und
Haus-Geschenk seyn, das sie nicht durch öffentlichen Druck heraus kommen. Denn ich sehe, dass die Ausfertigung des ersten Buchs
einigen misshage, derer Urtheilte und Gedancken ich gerneich gern
höher achte, als meine eigene, auch nicht übel nehme, dass man mir
desswegen einen Missfallen bezeigen oder gar hassig werden will,
weil ich ja mir selber, mit aller meine Arbeit nicht gefallen kan. Man
siehet zu Basel eine Grabschrifft über den weyland sehr berühm-
ten Mann, Adam von Bodentstein, welche vortreffliche Theodorus
Zwingerus, desgleichen ich, da ich den freyen künsten noch oblag,
an Gelahrtheit nicht gesehen, verfertiget, davon ich etliche Zeilen im
Gedächtnis behalten habe, die also lauten:

Non omnibus nec omni mihi
Placuere: quinam ego omnibus?
Non omnibus
Non Eremita Spagirus
Num tu viator omnibus?
Deo placere cura. Abi.

Das ist: Wie nicht allen, also auch mir gefällt nicht alles. Wie solte
ich den allen gefallen können? Nicht allen gefällt der Einsiedlerische
Alchymist. Und du Wandersmann, woltest allen gefallen? Sorge nur,
wie du Gott gefallen mögest. Gehe fort. Und also bin ich auch gesinnet: Gnug, dass ich Gott durch Christum gefalle.

In dessen haben einige Leute in ihren an mich gegebenen sonderbah-
ren Schreiben bekannt, dass, nach dem sie mein schlechtes Büchlein
gelesen, sie nicht wenig in der Gottseligkeit zugenommen haben. So
nun hierdurch ein desto grösserer Eyffer zur Gottseligkeit in ihnen
erwecket, auch einige Fussstapfen zur Nachfolge des Lebens Christi
ihnen gezeiget, und ihr lebennach dem Exempel Christi eingerichtet
worden, so habe ich Gott, der solches gethan, dafür zu dancken.
Denn ja diss der Christen hauptzweck seyn soll, also zu leben, wie der
gelebet hat, an welchen sie glauben. Dannenhero ich nicht etwa
geschreiben habe den noch unbekehrten heyden, die die Salbung
des Geistes nicht empfangenhaben, und daher auch keine besondere
Regung des Heil. Geistes empfinden: sondern den Schriften, bey
welchen die Bekehrung ihren täglichenWachsthum und Stuffen
machen und haben muss, als womit das Braut-Bette und der Busen
des Herzens dem Seelen-Bräutigam Christo, durch den Heil. Geist
und die tägliche Ubungen der Gottseligkeit und Busse je mehr und
mehr eröffnet, und der innere Mensch zu Erlangung desto grössern
Lichtes und der Geistes Gaben von Tage zu Tage erneuert wird.
Welches so man vom dem Stande vor der Bekehrung, oder dem
Werck der Bekehrung selbst, oder dero ersten Grade, verstehen wolte,
man sehr ihren und die Klippen der Synergisten anstossen würde.
Von welchen Graden oder Stuffen der Bekehrung und Erneuerung die
liebens-würdige Disputation E.E. de Praedestinatione, das ist von der
Gnaden-Wahl, aus unserm Chemnitio sehr nett und mitt allem Fleiss
handelt; Wie viele Beweissthümer solcher Stuffen der Bekehrung und
des geistlichen Wachsthums findet man sowohl beym Augustino, als

Bernhardo, sonderlich in Libro amorum oder in der Eklärung des hohen Lieds-Salomonis von dem Russ des Bräutigams? Also bezeuget auch der Tuicensis im Buch de Providentia ausdrücklich, und spricht: Ich empfinde in mir selbst etwas Göttliches, ein Licht und Flämmlein, so mich bewegt. Diese Dinge, welche mit der bösen Gewohnheit der Schreib-Begier nichts gemein haben, könten mich zur Ausfertigung meiner übrigen Büchlein gar wohl aufmuntern; allein, wie gesagt, ich mag anderer Urtheilen, (dass ichs aufs glimpflichste gebe) gern weichen. Wobey man aber die Schrifften so vieler Scribenten recht könne erkennen, davon habe ich an E.E. allbereit geschrieben, und werden sie wohl und weis thun, wenn sie dabey betrachten, wie der innerliche Mensch werde aufgerichtet, hingegen der äusserliche vernichtet, ingleichen die Salbung und Gabe des Geistes erwecket. Derowegen setze ich anitzo diejenige hinzu, welches das fürnehmste und innerste Stück der Theologie ist: Nemlich, das man alle art zu lehren und zu schreiben dahin anwenden müsse, dass man den Manschen in sich kehre, den Abgrund seines Elendes zu erkennen, darnach ihn zu Jesu Christo, dem Gnaden-Schatze hin weise, wie nemlich derselbe inwendig ins hertz mit Glauben müsse gefasset und verwahret werden. Denn inwendig ist das Rein Gottes mit allen seinen Gütern: Inwendig ist der Tempel Gottes: Inwendig ist der wahre Gottesdienst: Inwendig ist das rechte Bethauss, im Geist in der Wahrheit: Da ist die Schule des heil. Geistes; da ist die Werckstatt der heil. Dreyeinigkeit, daraus Aechzen und Seuffzen, Lehren, Tröstungen, Rath, Verstand, das gesamte Tugend Thor und die ganze Gesellschaft guter Wercke hervor gehet, nemlich aus der Gnaden-Quelle, die sich in einer gläubigen Seele hervor thut und daraus entspringet. Von welchen herrlichen Stück und kern der zur Ubung gebrauchten Theologie ich in meinem gantzen dritten Büchlein deutlicher und weitläufftiger gehandelt habe. Alldieweil ich nun diese meine Büchlein E.E. als ein Geschenk zu eigen gebe, so muss ich wenigen erinnern, wohin bey deren Ausfertigung mein Absehen gerichtet sey. Ich hoffe aber, er werde mir diese Freyheit micht übel nehmen, weil ich, ausser E.E. sonst niemanden habe, der hierinnen mit mir gleich gesinnet sey, und sich um die Erneurung des neuen Menschen rechtschaffen bekümmere. Das erste Büchlein bahnet und öffnet den Weg zum inner Menschen: Das andere führet etwas näher zu demselben, nemlich zum Geschmack der geistlichen Dinge, durch die Gedult des Creutzes: Das dritte lehret den Menschen in sich und in sein Innerstes einkehren, und zeiget, dass dass Reich Gottes inwendig in unssey: Das vierdte aber leitet, durch die grosse

Welt und das Buch der Natur, Gott, als den Urheber und Schöpfer der Natur, in das innerste der menslichen hertzen. Denn der Mensch, als kurtzer Begriff des ganzen Welt-kreises, die kleine Welt, ist der Haupt-zweck und Mittel-Punct der grossen welt, darin Gott und die Natur alles zusammen trägt, wie solches des Menschen selbst eigenes Gewissen bezeuget. Siehe da drey grosse Zeugen, die inwendig reden, und den Menschen inwendig überzeugen! Es benimmet aber diese Lehre gar nichts der Reinigkeit des Glaubens, so in den Symbolischen Büchern der Augspurgischen Confession enthalten ist, dazu ich mich mit E.E. beständigbekenne, so ich auch, wenn es nöthig, wider alle Irrthümer, sie mögen Namen haben, wie sie wollen, zu verthätigen bereit bin. Vielmehr zeiget sie die Ubung und den Gebrauch unsers Bekäntnisses sie machet den rechten Safft und Krafft des innern Lebens daraus, sie führet uns auf den inwendigen Menschen und machet ihn Christo gleichförmig, das Christus eine Gestalt in uns gewinne, das ist, dass wir innerlich in Christo werden wiedergebohren, und er in uns lebe, uns inwendig, als unser Leben, lebendig mach, als das Wort des lebens inwendig, in uns rede, als das Seelen-Licht inwendig Leuchte, als unser geistlichen König und Ertz Bischof der Seelen, sein Reich und Priesterthum inwendig verwalte, weil ja das Reich Gottes nicht stehet in Worten, sondern in Krafft: Welche geistliche Frucht, wenn sie von dem äusserlichen Bekäntniss nicht in meine Seele dringet, so ist zu besorgen, dass sie nicht recht könne gefättiget werden. Von andern will ich nicht urtheilen. Indem ich aber hieran gedencke, ängste ich mich im herzen und gehe in mich, bedenckend, wie weit ich noch von dem hafen entfernet sey. Denn andere richte ich nicht, Strafft sie auch nicht, und lehre sie nicht, sondern ich habe dieses mit ängsten Sorgen und Meditiren, bloss zu meiner eigenen Wohlfahrt, untersuchen wollen. Nachdem mir aber Gott ein solches Pfündlein verliehen, müste ich befürchten, dass, wenn ich die von mir verlangte Büchlein E.E. versagen wolte, Gott mich wegen des vergrabenen Pfündleins straffen würde. Wenn nun der Herr unser Gott dermaleinst von mir, seinem geringsten Knecht, sein mir anvertrautes Pfündlein mit Wucher wieder fordern wird, so wilt ich vor dessen Angesichte nur E.E. als einen grossen und reichen Wucher (weil ich nicht anders kan) darstellen. Denn ich zweiffete nicht, E.E. werden, ihme von Gott geschenckten Lehr-reichen Gemüths- und Verstandes. Gaben des heil. Geistes, diesen handel besser ausführen, ob schon viele Lästerungen denselben zu begleiten pflegen. Glaubet mir, der ichs selbst erfahren habe. Indessen hofe ich, es werden die schweren Anfechtungen, die E.E. (wie aus dero Schreiben

erheilet) so viel Schlaff-lose Nächte verursachen, durch diese meine
Gedancken etwas gemildert werden. Denn die, auf welche E.E. in
ihrem Schreiben zielen, handeln die Sache nicht recht ab, und treiben
dabey nicht die reine Lehre, sondern verwandeln mehren theils die
Wercke des innern Menschen, welche aus enime freywilligen Geist
und innerlichen Sabbath herrühren, in lauterGesetz-Wercke und
Knechtische Gebote, und machen verdienstlich, indem sie des Geistes,
der Liebe und der Kindschaffe vergessen haben. Kinder verrichten
ihre Geschäffte aus Trieb innerliche Liebe. Die Knechte aber aus
Trieb und hoffnung einer Belohnung. Kinder lieben den Vater frey-
willig und um seinet willen, weil er der Vater ist. Die Knecte aber um
des Lohns willen. Welche damnach auf die Belohnung sehen, die lieben nicht Gott, als einer Vater, sondern sich selbst, und sind von der
Natur der Kinder weit entfernet, daher machen sie sich auch verlustig
der ihnen aus Ganden zugedachten Erbschaft: Davon ich in meinem
andern Buch mit Fleiss gehandelt habe in der Capitel von der edlen
Tugend der Liebe, als dero Adel bestehet, dass sie nicht verdienstlich
ist. Endlich mag vielleicht wohl etwas seyn, daran E.E. noch kein völ-
liges Vergnügen haben, sonderlich in dem dritten Buche, als welches
durchgehends von dem inner Menschen handelt. So gestehe ich gern,
dass ich noch nicht alle die verborgenen Dinge oder tieffen Geheimnis
begreiffen könne, welche einige Theosophi und Gotts-Gelehrte der
Seelen undihrem innersten Grunde zuschreiben. Man weiss ja, dass
etliche Blumen im Frühlinge, andere mitten im Sommer, noch andere
im Herbst, ja einige auch gar im Winter beym Schnee hervor blühen:
Also bin ichauch noch nicht so weit kommen, dass ich die Tiefe der
Seelen, wie sie Taulerus heisset, solte begriffen haben: Andere nen-
nen es das göttlich Dunckel, so durch jenes Dunckel, in welches sich
Moses (2. B Mos. 20,21) hinzu gemacht hat, Sey voergebildet worden.
Denn weil Gott ein Licht ist, welches keine Creatur begreiffen kan, so
muss auch unser Sinn und Verstand bey diesen aufgeheden unaus-
sprechlichen Lichte nur verdunckelt stehen, gleichwie das helle
Mittags-Licht den Nacht Eulen eine Dunckelheit ist. So ist demnach
dieses Dunckel das unaussprechliche Licht. Denn gleichwie bey
Aufgang der Sonnen die Sterne verdunckelt werden; also wenn das
göttliche Lichtin der Seelen leuchtet, so gehen all Kräffte der Seelen
unter, auf dass Gott allein in dem Gemüthe leuchte, wie die Sonne
allein mitten am himmel leuchtet. Aber diese hohe Sachen überlasse
ich andern, und bin mit dem Mittelmässigen zufrieden. Mich ver-
gnüget wenn ich nur meinem Jesum rechtschaffen liebe, welches
alle Wissenschaft übertrifft. Aus diesem Brief werden E.E. meine

Meynung verhoffentlich vollkommen verstanden haben. Ich wün-
sche, nebst hertzlichem Grusse in Christo, dass E.E. alle traurigkeit
des Gemüths möge fahren lassen, sich in dem Herrn freuen, die Welt
und den Teuffel verachten, die Anfechtungen mit gedult und Glauben
überwinden, in der alleinigen Liebe Christi stille und ruhig leben.
Denn dieses ist unser Reichthum, unsere Freude und Lust, unser
Paradiess, der Himmel, und alles. Gegeben zu Braunschweig den
10ten Jun 1608.

29 March 1620 to Wolfgang Franzius

Fr. Arndt pp. 34–37

"Ehwürdiger, hochachtbarerund hochgelahrter Herr Doktor, günstiger
vielgeliebter Herr und werther Freund, dass E.E. mir diese Freundschaft
bezeiget, und die Calumnien, so zu Danzig wider mein Büchlein vom
wahren Christehthum ganz böslich ausgesprengt, mir wohlmeinend
wissen gemacht, auch dawider ein wahrhaftiges und gründliches
Schreiben abgehenlassen, thue gegen dieselben ich mich herzlich bedan-
cken, mit freundlichem Erbieten, solche brüderliche Treuherzigkeit bes-
ten Vermögen nach hinwieder zu beschulden. Und weil ich vermerkt
dass vielen Leuten solche schädliche Nachreden allbereit eingebildet sein
sollen, habe ich in deutscher Sprache auf E.E. brüderliches Schreiben
antworten wollen, damit jedermann diese meine Entschuldigung lesen
könne, ob E.E. belieben möchte, dieselbe als eine apologiam und
Errettung meiner Unschuld zu publicieren. Und ist zwar nicht ohne,
dass ich vorlängst vermerket, dass sich die Welt wider solche eifrige
Schriften heftig gesperret und aufgelehnt, sonderliche solche junge
Leute, die nicht durch Gewohnheit haben geübte Sinnen zum
Unterschiede des Guten und des Bösen, Erb. 5, 14. Weil ich aber ein freu-
diges Gewissen habe vor dem Herrn, Aller herzenkündiger, auch eine
treu eifrige Absicht, nämlich der grossen beharrlichen Unbussfertigkeit
und Gottlosigkeit der Welt durch solche meine Büchlein zu widersprechen, (ob Gott etlichen wo nicht Vielen, Gnade zur Busse hierdurch
geben wolle) so habe ich viel solcher Ungewitter darüber ausgestanden
und in grosser Geduld vorüber gehen lassen. Denn ich habe wohl vermerket, dass etwas hierüber müste gelittensein, sonderlich giftige
Fersenstiche, weil der alten Schlange dadurch auf den Kopf getreten ist.
Unterdessen habe ich erfahren, dass diese meine geringen Schriftlein bei

hohen und niedrigen Standes-Personen durch Gottes Gnade vielen
Nutzen geschafft haben, derowegen auch Etliche bei mir um
Schutzschriften wider die Calumnianten angehalten; habe mich aber
bisher durch nichts bewegen lassen, weil ich gewiss bin, dass wer in
Christo leben will, und dem heiligen Geist die herrschaft in seinem herzen gönnet, und nicht dem Fleisch oder dem Satan, denselben würde
sein eigen Gewissen überzeugen, dass es also ist und sein muss, und
nicht anders, als die Büchlein melden; will er anders nicht mit einem
Schein- und heuchel- oder gefärbten Glauben ine Verderben fahren.
Ach, mein lieber Herr Doktor, sollte man nicht eifern wider die Bosheit,
die nun so gross ist, dass sie in den Himmel steiget und schreiet, darauf
entwedereine blutige und giftige Sündfluth, oder das Feuer zu Sodom,
oder der Hunger zu Samaria und Jerusalem gehöret? Niemand will den
Abgrund aller Bosheit, die Erbsünde recht erkennen lernen; Niemand
will erkenne, das die Bosheit, so im Herzen ist und heraus gehet in die
That, ein Werk ist des Satansund dass der böse Geist selbst da ist, wo
seine Werke sein. Niemand will ablassen von seinen bösen Gedanken,
wie der Prophet Jesauas 55,6 erfordert. Jedermann zärtelt und spielet mit
seiner Sünden, da sie dochh ein so heftiges, grosses, eingewurzeltes Gift
ist, dass sie mit eifernen Griffeln und spitzigen Diamanten in die Tafeln
des Herzens geschrieben ist. Jer. 17, 1. Wahrlich, der Zorn Gottes wird
sich mit schlechter Heuchelbusse nicht lassen abwenden. Wo ist das zerbrochene herz? Wo sind die heissen Thränen? Wo ist das einsame
Vögelein auf dem Dache, das da wachet und seufzet? Wo ist jemand, der
wider den Riss stände, und sich zur Mauer machte wider den Zorn
Gottes? Das wäre besser, als dass man unschuldige Leute und Buss-
Prediger mit secterischen, ketzerischen Namen Befleckte, und um sich
wirft mit Enthusiasten, Weigelianern, Osiandristen, Schwenkfeldisten,
Papisten. Mit solchen Teufelslarven wird man bei weitem nicht das Reich
Gottes frommen Leuten aus dem Herzen reissen. Oder meinen sie, dass
Christus zur rechten hand Gottes sein Reich nicht mehr auf Erden habe
in den Herzen der Gläubigen? Meine geringen Büchlein, als äusserliche
Zeugnisse des inwendigen Reichs Gotte, könnten leicht aus den
Händen der Menschen gerissen werden; aber das inwendigen Zeugniss
des Geistes lässt sich so leicht nicht heraus reissen, es wäre denn, dass
der Geist Christi, der von ihm zeuget, in dem Gläubigen kraftlos oder
ohnmächtig geworden wäre. Und was plagt man sich doch mit
des Enthusiasterei? Kann man auch derselben beschuldigt werden, wenn
man mit der Schrift sagt: Werdet voll Geistes, erfüllet mit aller Gottes
Fülle? Sind den die Propheten und Apostel Enthusiasten gewesn, da sie
voll Gottes und voll Geistes worden sind, da sie mit Kräften aus der Höhe

angethan, und mit dem heiliger Geist getauft worden sind? War S. Stephanus auch ein Enthusiast, als er Enthusiast, als er vor dem Rath zu Jerusalem voll heiligen Geistes war, und sahe den Himmel offen, und die Herrlichkeit Gottes? Haben nicht alle Christen solche Verheissungen, da der Herr spricht: Wir werden zu ihm kommen, und Wohnung bei ihm machen? Item: Vielmehr wird mein himmlischer Vater den heiligen Geist geben allen, die ihn darum bitten? Haben wir nicht die Herrlichen Mittel dazu, das Wort Gottes, das Gebet, das herzliche Verlangen nach Gott, davon in meinem Lehr- und Trostbüchlein das vierte Kapitel, vom Worte Gottes, zu lesen ist? Ist das Enthusiasterei, wenn gelehrt wird, man soll täglich in sich selbst gehen, sein Elend bedenken, die zukünstige Herrlichkeit betrachten, sich in Gott erfreuen? Sagt nicht der Prophet: Ihr Übelthäter, gehet in euer Herz, Jesaia 46, 8? Der heilige David wird ein Enthusiast sein, da er Psalm 5, 4 spricht: Frühe will ich mich zu dir schicken und darauf merken. Was sind alle Meditationes und Soliloquia Augustini und anderer heiligen Gottes auch zu dieser Zeit? Aber weil solche heilige Übungen der Andacht vergessen und verloschen sind, muss es bei den ungelehrten Sophisten Enthusiasterei heissen. Was sagt aber der Herr: Gehe in dein Kämmerlein, schleuss die Thur nach dir zu, und bete im Verbrogenen. Was ist die Zukunft des Reichs Gottes, darum wir täglich bitten? Was hat man denn an dieser Lehre zu lästern? Was plagt man sich denn auch mit den Wiegelianern? Sollden die apostolische Regel nicht mehr gelten: Prüfet alles, das Gut behaltet. Was gehen mich des Weigels Irrthümer an, darüber ich gegen vornehme Leute oft geklagt, dass er wider die Schrift die zuzurechnende Gerechtigkeit (Justitiam imputativam) spöttlich ausmachet, dadurch Abraham vor Gott ist gerecht erkännt. Und S. Paulus will von keiner andern Gerechtigkeit wissen, als von der, die dem Glauben wird zugerechnet. Von der Person und menschlichen Natur Christi hat Weigel einen gefährlichen Irrthum. Item von der Auferstehung unsers Fleisches wider das 15. Kapitel der ersten Epistel an die Corinther, und was der unschrift-mässigen Händel mehr sein mögen, denn ich seiner Schriften wenig gelesen habe. Mit Osianders Irrthum habe ich weniger als nichts zu thun, wie mein Lehr-und Trostbüchlein vom Glauben, von Vergebung der Sünden, von der Gerechtigkeit des Glaubens, neben andern meinen Schriften überflüssig bezeugen. Wider den Schwenkfeld habe ich die Kraft des göttlichen Worts im ermeldeten Büchlein deutlich genug behauptet, und die Lehre vom inwendigen neuen Menschen aus der Schrift ausgeführt. Man wolle doch um Gottes willen die Prinzipien und Grundlehren meiner Büchlein vom wahren Christenthum, nämlich, den unergründlichen Sündenfall, das verlorne Bild Gottes, Busse und

Glauben, die neue Creatur, das Leben Christi in den Gläubigen, den Streit des Fleisches und des Geistes, das zerbrochene Herz, die Nachfolge des Exempels Christi; und mögen sich meine Lästerer wohl bedenken, was und wie lästern, oder mögen die Gegenlehre beweisen, dass die Christo angehören, ihr Fleisch nicht kreuzigen sollen, sammt den Lüsten und Begierden (Gal. 5, 24): und dass der nicht eine neue Creatur sein muss, der in Christo Jesu sein will; und dass die so zu Christo kommen solle, sich nicht selbst verläugnen, und ihr eigen Leben hassen dürfen; (Luc. 9, 24 Matth. 20, 39.) item, dass diejenigen auch den Namen Gottes wohl anrufen könne, die nicht abtreten von der Ungerechtigkeit; item, dass ohne göttliche Traurigkeit eine Reue zur Selgkeit könne gewirkt werden (2. Cor. 7, 10), und dass die Liebe der Welt bei Gottes Liebe stehen könne (1. Joh. 2, 15), und das derjenige ein wahrer Christ sein könne, der die Früchte des Geistes nicht habe. Dieweil sie meine Büchlein verwerfen, so mussen sie auch meine Prinzipien verwerfen, und weil dieselben bei ihnen flasch sein müssen, so muss ja die Antithesis (Gegenlehre) bei ihnen wahr sein. Mein Postille, Psalter, Catechismus und Auslegung der Passion sind öffentlich Zeugnisse und Verantwortungen meiner Unschuld wider meine Lästerer, welche ich dem gerechten Gerichte Gottes befehle, und mit ihnen nicht weiter zu zanken gendenke. E. Ehrw. wolle keinen Verdruss haben über mein langes Schreiben, unterwerfe solches Deroselben hochverständigen Censur, und bitte auf meine Unkosten die Publikation zu befördern. Erbiete mich zu allen möglichen brüderlichen Diensten, und befehle E.E. dem gnadigen Schuss des Allerhöchsten! Datum Zelle, den 29. Martii Anno 1620. E.E. freundwilliger Johann Arndt, Superintendens des Fürstenthums Lüneberg man. pr.

23(9) October 1620 to Balthasar Mentzer

In WC pp. 40–42

Meinen herzlichen Gruss in Christo Jesu!

Wohlehrwürd, Hoсachtbarer und Hochgelahrter etc . . .

Euer E. sage ich unsterblichen Dank für das neulichan mich abgelassene sehr freundliche Schreiben, in welchem der Schwenkdeldischen

Irrtümmer halber einige Meldung geschehen. Gewisslich sind dergleichen Irrtümmer nicht geringt, nämlich von der Heiligen Schrift
von der Person Christi, von den beiden Sakramenten und von dem
evangelischen Predigtamt, welche ingesamt teils in der augsburgischen Konfession, teils in der Konkordienformel, nachdem die reine
Lehre auf festen Fuss gesetzet, öffentlich verdammet und verworfen
worden. Ich meines Orts habe, nach dem von Gott mir verliehenen
Pfündlein, in meinen evangelischen Predigten, welche im öffentlich
Drucke sind, von der Frucht und Kraft der heiligen Schrift, als welche
das lebendige Wort Gottes ist, an unterschiedlichen Stellen gehandelt, und mit vielen Gründen aus dem Munde Christi gelehret, dass
dieser unvergängliche Same, wenn er nur einen guten Acker findet,
nicht fruchtlos sei. So habe ich auch wider den volkommenen
Gehorsam des Gesetzes, davon auch heutzutage einige Schwärmer
träumen, hin und wieder, in Ansehung des verlorenen Ebenbildes
Gottes, und der aufs äusserste verderbten menschlichen Natur, deutlich und mit allen Fleiss geredet. Die reine Lehre von der Person
Christi habe ich nach der Richtschnur der Konkordienformel gar
nicht schläfrig verteidigt. Von den beiden Sakramenten habe ich
mein Bekenntnis nach unser symbolischen Büchern, sowohl in meiner Postille, als in der Katechismuserklärung, nicht ohne Eifer abge-
stattet. Was aber das evangelische Predigtamt betrifft, so habe ich
auch an unterschiedlichen Orten die Christengläubigen beständig
davon unterrichtet, dass es der Heilige Geist durch seine schwachen
Werkzeuge kräftig verrichte, und dass solche Kraft nicht an den
Personen liege. Ja, ich habe gar, um einiger Lassdünkel böse Nachrede
zu vermeiden, ein Büchlein herausgegeben, darin ich die meisten
Stücke kürzlich wiederhole und ein rechtgläubiges Bekenntnis anfüge
von der hochheiligen Dreieinigkei, von der Person Christi, von der
geistigen Vereinung Christi, des Hauptes der Kirchen, mit seinen
gläubigen Gliedmassen, dass ich das gänzliche Vertrauen habe, ich
werde allenreinen, der augsburgischen Konfession zugetanen Lehren,
Genüge getan haben. Denn ich bin ja durch Gottes Gnade so unbe-
dachtsam und unvorsichtig nicht, dass ich in so vielen Jahren nicht
sollte gelernet haben das Gold von dem Kote zu unterscheiden: da, so
niemand, insonderheit ich, doe Wohlfahrt der Seelen mir höchsten
Fleisses angelegen sein lasse. Dass aber einige mich gar in bösen
Verdacht ziehen wollen, dessen Ursach ist, dass sie meine Büchlein
von dem wahren Christentum nur obenhin gelesen und daher in die
Gedanken geraten, als wenn ich die Übung des christlichen Lebens,
auf welches ich so sehr dringe, ohne Absicht auf die hiezu benötigten

Mittel, als da sind das Wort Gottes und die heiligen Sakramente, triebe; in welchem Stücke sie sich sehr betrogen finden. Denn weil man nicht eher von einem Baum kann Früchte haben, er sei denn vorher gepflanzet, daher fordere ich auch alsdann mit allem Ernst die Früchte der Gerechtigkeit, des Glaubens und der wahren Bekehrung oder Busse, nachdem man die Wahrheit aus dem Worte Gottes erkannt hat. Das wahre Christentum bestehet nicht nur in der Lehre und in Untersuchung und Widerlegung der Streitigkeiten und Irrtümer, wiewohl ihrer viele sich einbilden, sondern auch in der Gottseligkeit, in der Besserung des Lebens, in wharhafter und ernster Busse und deren Früchten, in Erkenntnis der Sünde, sonderlich der Erbsünde, als einer abscheulichen, sehr tiefen und gänzlichen Verderbung der menschlichen Natur, und aller deren Kräfte, ohne welcher genaue Erkenntnis keine wahre Busse oder Bekehrung, auch keine Besserung der so gar sehr verderbten Begierden des Herzens entspringen, noch des Bild Gottes jemalen neu aufgerichtet werden kann. Nachdem nun diese verborgene und innerliche Bosheit erkannt, welche unter Tausenden kaum einer recht erkennet, so muss alsdann gezeiget werden, die Schwach- und Unvermögenheit der menschlichen Kräfte, welche aus der angeborenen Verderbnis, aus dieser aber die Eitelkeit des ganzen fleischlichen Lebens der Menschen herfliesset. Darnach muss man den Glauben an Christum weisen und die Eigenschaften des Glaubens erklären, deren vornehmste ist, dass, er mit Ausschliessung aller Kreaturen und menschlichen Verdienste, allein hange an der Gnade Gottes un dem Verdienste Christi; die andere aber, dass er den Menschen nach dem Ebenbilde Gottes erneure. Hierauf nun muss die Nachfolge des Lebens Christi vorgestellt werden, welche durch Wirkung des Heiligen Geistes allein genug ist, die Gottseligkeit auszuüben und zu lieben. Endlich muss man auch dringen auf die ernstliche Betrachtung des göttlichen Wortes und dessen fleissiges Nachdenken, ingleichen, wie unser Heiland befiehlet Luk. 8.15 die Bewahrung des göttlichen Samens in einem reinen Herzen. Daher entspriessen letzlich die guten Werke und Früchte der Rechtfertigung, nämlich von den Bäumen, die recht gepflanzet und neu zugerichtet worden. Ist demnach der Gärtner Auslachens wert, wie heutigen Tages meisten sind, welche wollen Früchte haben und doch keine Bäume haben, und wollen durch das Gesetz erzwingen, was doch ein Werk göttlicher Gnaden und des Heiligen Geistes ist. Indem ich nun dieses treibe und das andere Stück des wahren Christentums abhandele, bloss zu dem Ende, dass der gemeine Mann zum wenigsten im christlichen Leben recht unterricht und von den sehr verderbten Sitten abgebracht werde: so muss ich von den unverständigen Leuten, wieder mein Verschulden, ein Enthusiast und Schwenkfelder heissen. Denn wenn ich lehrete, dass die Bekehrung des Menschen ohne Mittel nämlich ohne das Wort Gottes, geschähe, so hätten diese Unverständige zu schmähen und zu lästern Ursache; nun ich aber gottselig lehre, dass Gott sei in dem Worte und durch das Wort wirke, auch durchs Wort in uns wohne, durchs Wort mit uns vereiniget werde, durchs Wort die Herzen erleuchte, tröste, Seufzer erwercke, das Feuer der Andacht hege, Seelengespräche eingebe, Herzensfreude und einen süssen Vorschmack des ewigen Lebens empfinden lasse; so fahen die solcher Sachen unerfahrenen Leute, aus blosser Unwissenheitdie geistlichen Lebens, an, mich zu lästern und der Enthusiasterei zu beschuldigen, damit sie sich aber selbst verraten, dass sie den Nutzen und die Kraft des Wortes nicht verstehen, noch einige Gemeinschaft mit Gott haben. Sie bedenken nicht, dass das rechte Christenlebensie geistlich, welches nicht könne gelehret, gefördert und getrieben werden, es sei dann, dass der Grund vorher dazu gelegt worden, und zwar durch das geoffenbarte Wort Gottes, durch Christi Verdienst und Exempel, durch die Wirkung des Heiligen Geistes, durch den vorleuchtenden Glauben und die Rechtfertigung. Denn was hat man nicht für Sprüche heiliger Schrift, welche die Lehre des Glaubens und der Gottseligkeit mit einander verknüpfen? (1 Tim. 6, 3) Gewisslich, sobald die Apostel den Grund der Lehren geleget, kommen sie alsofort auf das christliche Leben und die Gottseligkeit, als Früchte des Heiligen Geistes, welche, so sie versäumet werden, ist alle diejenige Mühe und Arbeit verloren, die, obgleich noch so eifrig zur Erhaltung reiner Lehre angewandt wird. Es muss traun! bei der Reinigkeit der Lehre zugleich die Wiedergeburt getrieben werden, ohne welche alles theologische Wissen unfruchtbar ist, daraus keine Frucht der wahren Busse hervorkommen kann. Der Bau der Seelen und die Verbesserung der alten, eingewurzelten Bosheit erfordert eine grosse Übung der Gottseligkeit, ein Exempel und geistliche Klugheit. Daher setzet der Apostel 2. Tim. 3, 16 Lehre und Besserung zusammen ohne welche beide Stücke die wahre Kirche keineswegs kann erbauet werden. Ich Schreibe darum hievon so weitläuftig, damit E.E. mich desto eigentlicher verstehen, und ich desto deutlicher möge dartun, dass ich gegen die Kirche nichts gesündiget habe, sondern dass meine harten Zensoren und Richter vielmehr anzuklagen sind, weil sie meinen, man habe in der Kirchesonst mit nichts, als nur mit Diputieren zu tun. Es seien demnach E.E. gänzlich versichert, dass ich von meiner

Jugend an bis in das graue Alter (denn ich bin durch Gotttes Gnade
nunmehr fast aus meinem fünfundsechzigsten Jahre ausgetreten),
keinem einzigen Irrtum, der wider die augsburgische Konfession und
die Konkordienformel laufen, oder dem Wort Gottes zugegen sein
sollte, zugetan gewesen, und dass ich deswegen aus meinem
Vaterlande, dem Fürstentum Anhalt, vertrieben worden, weil ich
denen, so in Glaubenslehren mit uns streitig sind, nicht beipflichten
konnte. Gleichwie ich nun vorhin in meinen Büchern vom wahren
Christentum öffentlich bezeuget habe, also bezeuge ich auch noch
jetzo, dass ich solche meine Büchlein und die alten deutschen
Redensarten, daran ich mich ergötze, nicht anders wolle verstanden
haben, als nach dem Worte Gottes, dem Glauben an Christum und
ohne Verletzung des Grundes der Rechtfertigung, so aus Gnaden
geschieht. Meine Zensoren (Richter) und Beurteiler aber ermahne
ich, dass sie auch zugleich mit mir in diese Fechtschule treten, und
den Atheismus (Gottlosigkeit) zu vertreiben mit mir sich bemühen;
dabei sie doch nichts destoweniger ihre Kontroversen treiben können, ob sie schon das zerfallene Christentum wieder aufzurichten
sich zugleich werden angelegen sein lassen. Beides erfordert die
Heilige Schrift; beides hat Christus gelehret; beides haben die Apostel
fortgesetzet. Was ist aber für Aufrichtigkeit und theologische Klugheit
bei denen zu finden, die, aus einer Begierde zu widersprechen und
was recht geredetist, zu verkehren, ihrem Glaubensgenossen und
Bruder eines anmachen wollen? Ich weiss, dass alles, was ich geschrieben, mit dem Grunde des Glaubens übereinstimme, wenn nur die
Lästerung davon bleibet. Was noch übrig, kann E.E. aus meiner
Repitione Apologetica, das ist Wiederholung und Veranrwortung der
Lehre vom wahren Christentum, ersehen. Ergebe E.E. dem allwalten-
den Gott, nächst herzlichem Wunsche, das E.E. bis ins späte Alter
vergnüglich leben mögen. Zelle, den 29. Oktober Anno 1620.

29 January 1621 to Duke August

Rambach pp. 617–618

Euer Fürstl. Gnaden habe ich zwar am gestringen Sonntage mit dem
eilenden Boten geantwortet, damit er nicht ganz ledig zurückkäme.
Nachdem der aber wegen der allzustrengen Kälte noch übernacht all-
hie verbleiben müssen, habe ich dieses meinem vorigen hinzuthun

und auf das von mir gefasste Bedencken D. Crameri völliger antworten
wollen. Es irret sich der gute Mann, dass er meynet, als habe ich in
meinem Büchlein Christum unsern Heyland nur als Exempel, nicht
aber als eine Gabe und Geschenck, vorgetragen. Denn das Gegentheil
kan man lesen im 5. Cap. des 1. Buchs, vom Glauben; imgleichen
Cap. 19 und 21. von dem wahren Gottesdienste, wie auch Cap. 34.
Hauptsächlich aber im 2. Buch. Cap. 1.2.3.6.8.9.10. In diesen Capiteln
habe ich Christum, als das höchste, beste und gröste Geschenck Gottes
des Vaters, also beschrieben, erläutert und gepriesen, dass ich mich
von Herzen erfreuen würde, wenn ich solte sehen, dass diss beste
Geschenck von jemanden also, oder auch noch mehr solte gepriesen und erläutert seyn. Denn dieses meine einzige Lust, Freude und
Wonne ist. Hiezu kommt auch das 3. Cap. des. 3 Buchs, von dem selig-
machenden Glauben, und dessen Eigenschafften. Wenn nun hievon
die fürnemsten Capitel besonders solten gedrucket werden, solte das
allertröstlichste Büchlein daraus erwachsen, welches mit allen andern,
sie mögen aus neuen (unter welche er auch mich verächtlich zählet)
oder alten Scribenten zusammen getragen seyn, einen Wett-Kampff
anstellen möchte. Welches ich doch ohn eiteln Ruhm will gesagt haben,
weil ich eine gerechte Sache habe. Dannenhero Herr D. Cramer meines
Namen wohl hätte schonen mögen. Allein ich muss es geschehen lassen;
die Wahrheit redet das Wort für mich. Es hat aber dieser sonst hochgelahrter Mann die Absicht und den Zweck meiner Bücher nicht begriffen, welcher dieser ist: Erstlich habe ich die Gemüther der Studenten
und Prediger wollen zurück ziehen von der gar zu disputir- und streitsüchtigen Theologie, daraus fast wieder eine Theologia Scholastica
ist. Zum andern habe ich mir vorgenommen die Christgläubgen
von dem todten Glauben ab-und zu dem Fruchtbringenden anzu-
führen. Drittens, sie von der blossen Wissenschafft und Theorie zur
würcklichen Ubung des Glaubens und der Gottseligkeit zu bringen:
Und viertens zu zeigen, was das rechte Christl. Leben sey, welches
mit dem wahren Glauben übereinstimmet, und was da bedeute, wenn
der Apostel saget: Ich lebe, aber doch nun nicht ich, sondern Christus
lebet in mir, Gal. 2, 20. Welches alles zu erklären mehr erfordert, als
das blosse Exempel Christi. Derowegen dieses nicht die Absicht meiner Bücher ist, wie sich der Herr Doctor träumen lässet, dass ich,
nach Art der Münche, Christum nur als ein Exempel wolte vorgestellet haben; sondern dass der Glaube an Christum müsse aufwachsen
und seine Früchte bringen, damit wir nicht in dem Gerichte Gottes als
unfruchtbare Bäume erfunden werden. Darnach hat der sonst gelehrte
Mann nicht begriffen, was der heil. Bernhardus mit diesem schönen

Spruche andeuten wollen: Christum sequendo citius apprehendes, quam legendo. Das ist: man wird Christum eh ergreifen, wenn man ihm nachfolget, als wenn man von ihm lieset. Denn er meynet, Christo nachfolgen, sey nur so viel, als seinem Exempel folgen. Es begreiffet aber die Nachfolge Christi in sich den Glauben an Christum und alles, was zum Glauben gehöret, nemlich all sein Vertrauen Trost Hoffnung und Heyl auf Christum setzen, ihn aufrichtig lieben, sein Creuz ihm gedultig nachtragen. Wie es also der Heyland selber erkläret, Matth. 16, 24 Wer mir will nachfolge, der nehme sein, das ist, mein Creuz auf sich. Nun bedencke ein jeder redlicher Biedermann, ob Christus allein durch lesen könne ergriffen werden. Denn so wir wissen, dass Christus sey unsere Gerechtigkeit, Weissheit, und Erlösung 1. Cor. 1, 30 so müssen ja die Ubungen des wahren Glaubens nothwendig bewerckstelliget werden. Und so wir erkennen, dass Christus nichts sey, als lauter Liebe, Demuth, Sanfftmuth, Gedult so wird gewiss niemand der solchesnur lieset, Christum ergreiffen; sondern er muss auch ihme Christi Exempel lassen belieben, seine süsseste Liebe schmecken, seine Gerechtigkeit umfassen, und ihme im Glauben zueignen, und ausüben was Christus befohlen und verheissen hat. Ach! Ich besorge, gnädiger Fürst und Herr, ich sorge, sage ich, dass viele grosse Theologi weniger von Christo haben, als man vermeynet, dass sie haben. Aber gnug hievon.

20 April 1621 to Duke August

Fr. Arndt pp. 180–183

Durchlautiger, Hochgeborner, gnädiger Fürst und Herr, das von Ew. Fürstl. Gn. Überstandte Convolut, habe ich nebst Derselben gnädigen Schreiben versiegelt, mit gebürlicher Reverenz wohl empfangen, und sage unterthänigst Dank für alles, will die Exemplare der Reformation unter unsere evangelischen Confession confirmiren. Nächst diesem habe ich herzlich gern mit grossen unterthänigem Dank empfangen und gelesen Herrn Matthias Lauterwaldts Censur über den Taulerus; denn im folgenden Tractat wider Osiander, habe ich aus dem Stil gesehen, dass es ein Autor ist, Ich lobe ihn wegen seiner Sorgfältigkeit, denn er sich besorget, es möchten die Leute oder die Leser dadurch von unserer wahren Gerechtgkeit des Glaubens und vom Worte Gottes abgeführt werden auf sonderliche ungewisse Offenbarungen, unterscheidet auch gar artig am Ende die Gerechtigkeit von den Werken, welches alles an seinem Ort recht und christlich ist.

Dass aber Taulerus darum so sehr verdächtig zu halten, als ob er Fundament unserer Seligkeit gar zuwider sei, wie dieser vornehme fromme Mann meint, ist gar zu ein zu mildes Urtheil, und dem zuwider, was vornehme Theologen aus Taulers Schriften, von der Rechtfertigung, dem Verdienste Christi und seiner Genugthuung für unsere Sünden geschlossen haben, unter denen Herr Michael Neander und D. Glaserus die vornehmsten sind. Erstlich belangend die Geschichte von der Bekehrung des Tauler durch einen Laien, halte ich für meine Einfalt eines grosses Theil für Fabeln, von Mönchen hinzu gesetz, wie solcher Sachen im Papstthum viel geschehen sind Was aber anreichet den Zweck des Tauler, so kann derselbe an seinem Orte wohl mit und bei den Fundamenten des frommen Lauterwalds bestehen. Dies ist aber des Taulers Zweck, durch Selbstverläugnung und Selbstentsagung näher und so Gott in sich selbst zu empfinden. Dass kann gar wohl mit dem vorigen Fundament bestehen. Dies Fundament bleibet in Ewigkeit: Niemand kommt zum Vater, denn durch mich. Wenn demnach Tauler nicht Christo, als Weg, Wahrheit und Leben, gefolgt ware, hätte er nicht zu solchen geistlichen Reichthümern sich erheben können. Gott also in sich fühlen und seine überreiche Gnade, ist keine Entzückung; ist auch nicht vonnöthen, wie der fromme Herr Lauterwaldt meint, und hat mit S. Pauli Entzückungen nichts zu thun, sondern es ist ein schönes Theil oder Erstling des Reiches Gottes, das in uns ist, ist eine kräftige Wirkung und lebendiges Zeugniss Gottes in uns; und ist nicht unsere Gerechtigkeit, wie Lauterwaldt dem armen Tauler zumisset, sondern es ist eine hohe Gabe Gottes, und eine Frucht und Zeugnis der Gerechtigkeit und Gnade Gottes; welche ob sie der fromme Lauterwaldt und seines Gleichen nicht gehabt hat, oder verstanden, sollte sie deswegen verwerflich sein?

Zum andern, so viel mir bewusst, hat Taulerus mit der wesentlichen Gerechtigkeit nichts zu thun, sonder das leibliche Wesen Gottes empfinden, (Ps. 16) ist viel ein anderes; es ist eine hohe, edle, geistliche Gabe, und Vorschmack der himmlischen Wonne, davon viel in den Psalmen zu finden, worauf dieser andächtigen Leute Abziehung oder Entziehung von der Welt gerichtet ist. Es ist keine Entzückung, sondern eine geistliche Empfindung der wahren wesentlichen Liebe und Freude Gottes, und ist das Wort Wesentlich im Taulero entgegen gesetz der falschen und eingebildeten Überzeugung und Voraussetzung, wie auch die Psalmen redden: Herr, meine Freude, mein Licht, meine Stärke, meine Kraft.

Wundert mich demnach nicht wenig, dass neben diesem andere Theologen solches dem Teufel zuschreiben, da es doch nichts anders ist als eine Offenbarung des Reich Gottes in uns, und ein Zerstörung des Reichs des Teufels. Es ist auch keine eigene gesuchte Plage, wie der fromme sorgfältige Lauterwaldt schreibt, sondern es ist die angenehmste Erhebung des Gemüths zu Gott, Ps. 25 Zu dir, o Herr, habe ich meine Seele erhoben, und Ps. 43 die Gerechten werden es hören und sich freuen. Das ist die höchste Freude und Lust der gläubigen Seelen, und keine Plage. Es ist auch viel zu schwach geurtheilt, dass solche geistliche Übungen sollten von Gottes Wort abführen; denn ohne Betrachtung des göttlichen Worts könnte nie eine solche Andacht und Erhebung des Gemüths zu Gott Statt finden; der ganze Psalter ist wahrlich eine Anleitung zu dieser geistlichen Übung.

Ich vermerke auch, dass des herrn Lauterwaldts Urtheil von den hohen geistlichen Anfechtungen, wie sie Taulerus empfindet, viel zu geringe sei, dadurch Gott in die Hölle führt und wieder heraus. Der heilige David hat's nicht ohne Ursach im Psalter so treulich beschrieben.

Zum Beschluss muss ich auch dieses gedencken, dass der fromme Herr Lauterwaldt allein dringt auf das Gehör göttlichen Wortes: Sie haben Mosen und die Propheten; lass sie dieselbigen hören. Wie auch Viele der Unsern das ganze Werk der Religion in das Gehör des Wortes setzen. Aber wo bleibt die Frucht des Gehörs? Unser Heiland verbindet das Gehör des Worts mit der Bewahrung des Worts, und zwar in einem guten und feinen Herzen; fügt auch das Fruchtbringen in Geduld hinzu. Sollten das die Laien practiciren, es thun's die Gelehrten nicht.

Ich Schliesse endlich und wiederhole den Inhalt meiner Vorrede, welche ich neulich bei der herausgabe des Tauler auf Verlangen voraufgeschickt habe, und die so lautet: Ein Herz so Christum zum Grunde gelegt hat, wird im Taulero ein solches Licht der Besserung, der Andacht, der Heiligkeit, der Frömmigkeit, der Gottseligkeit, der Furcht Gottes, der geistlichen Weisheit finden, dass er's fruchtbarlich zur köstlichen Seelenarznei wird zu geniessen haben.

Bibliography

Manuscripts

Forschungsbiblothek Gotha   A 121, 16r-17v
Johann Arndt to Johann Gerhard, January 29, 1608

Forschungsbiblothek Gotha   A 121, 18r-19v
Johann Arndt to Johann Gerhard, July 13, 1608

Primary Sources

Andreae, Johann Valentin, *Christianopolis*, trans. Emil Held (New York, 1916).

Andreae, Johann Valentin, *Selbstbiographie Joh. Valentin Andreä's* (Winterthur, 1799).

Arndt, Johann, *Ikonographia; Gruendlicher und Christlicher Bericht von Bildern* (Halberstadt, 1596).

Arndt, Johann, *Johann Arnds Geistreicher Schriften und Werke I, II, III*, ed. Johann Jacob Rambach (Leipzig, 1736).

Arndt, Johann, *Repetitio Apologetica. Das ist: Widerholung und Verantwortung der Lehre vom wahren Christenthumb: zu weiterer Information und Unterweisung derer so Christum oder die Gottseligkeit lieb haben damit sie sich von der Gottlosen Welt nicht lassen abwendig machen* (Magdeburg, 1620).

Arndt, Johann, *Sechs Bücher vom wahren Christentum* (Bielefeld, 1996).

Arndt, Johann, *True Christianity*, trans. Peter Erb (New York, 1979).

Arndt, Johann, *Vier Alte und Geistreiche Büchlein: Das Erste: Die Deutsche Theologia. Ein edles Büchlein Vom rechten Verstande,*

Das Ander: Die Nachfolgung Christi. Wie man alle Eytelkeit dieser Welt verschmehen soll. Durch D. Thomam a Kempis beschrieben. Das Dritte: Von Trost und Hülff in Trübsalen, Das Vierdte: Von Zuberaitung deß Todts (Linz, 1621).

Arndt, Johann, *Zehen Lehr- und Geistreiche Predigten: von den Zehen grausamen und schröcklichen Egyptischen Plagen* (Frankfurt am Main, 1657).

Breller, Melchior, *Mysterium Iniquitatis Pseudoevangelicae: Hoc est: Dissertatio Apologetica Pro Doctrina Beati Joannis Arnd, Ducatus Lunaeburgensis Superintendentis generalis. Adversus Centauros Quosdam Pseudoevangelicos et sophisticam illorum Theologiam, Ad Nobilissimum Virum Oligerum a Rosencrantz* (Lüneburg, 1621).

Breller, Melchior, *Vindiciae Pro Mysterio Iniquitatis Pseudoevangelicae: Adversus Pseudoevangelicum Declamatorem, et Postillatorem Hamburgensem* (Goslar, 1623).

Breller, Melchior, *Warhafftiger, Glaubwurdiger und Gründlicher Bericht von den vier Büchern vom Wahren Christenthumb Herrn Johannis Arndten / auss den gefunden brieflichen Urkunden zusammen getragen* (Lüneburg, 1625).

Buscher, Anton, *Geistlich Hertz- und Hauszkirch: Wie das Reich Gottes in uns nach Anlaß der Zeit / Orts / und Geschäffte alle Stunde des Tages / und alle Tage der Wochen durch Andacht und Gebet zu bawen . . . Sampt einer Vorrede Von Ursachen deß jetzt falschen Christenthumbs . . . Herrn Johann Arndes* (Lüneburg, 1624).

Castellio, Sebastian, *Theologia Germanica: Ex Germanico Translatus Joanne Theophilo Vero Nomine Sebastiano Castellione Interprete* (Leipzig, 1630).

Cramer, Daniel, *Apocalypsis, oder Offenbarung S. Johannis* (Stettin, 1619).

Dame, Friedrich, *Vom Alten und Newen Menschen: Woher dieser Unterscheid entstanden / und das alleine newe Menschen die wahre Kirche Christi* (Lübeck, 1632).

Denck, Hans, *Die teutsche Theologia. Das ist Ein edles buechlein vom rechten verstande was Adam vnd Christus sey und wie Adam in uns sterben und Christus in uns leb* (Halberstadt, 1597).

Dilger, Daniel, *Des Ehrwürdigen / Achtbaren und Hochgelarten Herrn Johannis Arndes, im Löblichen Fürstenthumb Lüneburg General Superintendenten, Richtige / und in Gottes Wort wolgegründete*

Lehre / in den vier Büchern vom wahren Christenthumb: In etlichen Puncten auß dringenden / Nothwendigen ursachen/ die in der Vorrede angezogen repetiret und wiederholet (Stettin, 1620).

Egardus, Paulus, *Ehrenrettung Johannis Arndten / Das ist / Christliche und in Gottes Wort wolgegründete Erinnerung/ was von D. Lucae Osiandri, Theologiae Professoris zu Tübingen Urtheil und Censur, uber Johan Arndten wahres Christenthumb / sey zu halten / Allen Frommen und Gottfürchtigen* (Lüneburg, 1624).

Franck, Sebastian, *Paradoxa CCLXXX. Das ist: Zwey hundert und achtzig Wunder-Reden Aus der Heiligen Schrifft: So vor allem Fleisch unglaublich und unwahr seynd doch wider der gantzen Welt Wahn . . . wahr: Jtem Aller . . . Christen recht Göttliche Philosophia, und Teutsche Theologia . . . ausgeführt und an Tag gegeben Durch Sebastian Francken von Wörd* (s.l., 1690).

Gerhard, Johann, *Loci Theologici* 6, ed. Eduard Preuss (Berlin, 1869).

Gerhard, Johann, *Meditationes Sacrae* (Oxford, 1633).

Gleich, Johann Andreas, *Trifolium Arndtium: Johannis Arndi tres epistolae* (Wittenberg, 1726).

Löscher, Valentin Ernst, *The Complete Timotheus Verinus*, trans. James L. Langebartels (Milwaukee, 1998).

Meldenius, Rupertus, *Paraenesis votiva pro pace ecclesiae ad theologos Augustanae confessionis* (S.I., 1625).

Müntzer, Thomas, *The Collected Works of Thomas Müntzer*, ed. and trans. Peter Matheson (Edinburgh, 1988).

Osiander d.J., Lucas, *Theologisches Bedencken / Und Christliche Trewhertzige Erinnerung / welcher gestalt Johann Arndten genandtes Wahres Christenthum / nach anleitung des H. Wortes Gottes / . . . anzusehen und zuachten sey. / Allen Gottseligen Christen . . . zu nothwendiger Nachrichtung / gestellet und Publiciert / Durch Lucam Osiandern / . . .* (Stettin, 1624).

Rachelius, Mauritius, *Schola Arndiana Das ist: Arndtische Schule: Darinnen vier unterschiedliche Classes oder Hauffen gefunden werden / derjenigen/ welche des . . . Herrn Johannis Arndten / gewesenen General-Superintendenten des löblichen Fürstenthumbs Lünenburg . . . Bücher un[d] Schrifften . . . gebrauchen/ Allen . . . Schülern wolmeindlich eröffnet und auffgerichtet Durch M. Mauritium Rachelium, Pastorn zu Lunden in Dithmarschen* (Rostock, 1627).

Raidelius, Georgius Martinus, *Epistolae Virorum Eruditorum Ad Johannem Gerhardum* (Norimbergae, 1740).

Rostius, Georg, *Amica ac fraterna Admonitio Super Controversiis De Vero Dn. Joannis Arndten, generalis in Ducatu Luneburgico Superintendentis, p.m. Christianismo, inter D.D. Lucam Osiandrum et M. Henricum Varenium, Dn. Paulum Eggardum, aliosq[ue] Theologos et politicos ortis: In qua non tantu[m] pax et concordia fatiscentis Ecclesiae summopere commendatur, sed dissentientes quoq[ue] ad eamdem fraterne revocantur* (Rostock, 1626).

Rostius, Georg, *Examen Brevis Considerationis Varenianae Apopologeticum, Seu Iusta ac modesta defensio amicae ac fraternae Admonitionis supercontroversiis de vero Arndi p.m. Christianismo ortis: In Qua Arndiani Christianismi orthodoxia approbatur, heterodoxia fraterne emendatur, et . . . corruptelis M. Henrici Varenii vindicantur . . . / Adornata ac remissa a Georgio Rostio Concionatore Aulico Meg.* (Rostock, 1628).

Spener, Philipp Jacob, *Postilla, Das ist: Geistreiche Erklärung Der Evangelischen Texte / durchs gantze Jahr/ auff alle Sonn- Hohe- und andere Fest- und Apostel-Tage: Sampt einer dreyfach- durchgehenden Betrachtung über die gantze Passions-Historia; Alles also eingerichtet / Daß durchgehends auff jeden Text zwo / drey / vier / auch zuweilen fünff unterschiedliche Predigten zu finden / Mit höchstem Fleiß Zur Ehre Gottes und Erbauung deß wahren Christenthumbs / Gestellet durch Herrn Johann Arndten / weiland General-Superintendenten deß Fürstenthumbs Lüneburg / und Pfarrherrn zu Zella. Jetzo mit dem vom Authore selbst zuletzt revidirt- und augirten Exemplar abermahl auffs fleissigste conferiret . . . auch mit viel schönen Kupfferstücken und noth- wendigen Registern auffs neue außgezieret. Nebens einer neuen Vorrede an den Leser von gegenwertiger Edition, Hn. Philipp Jacob Speners / der H. Schrifft Doct. et Ministerii Francofurt. Senioris* (Frankfurt, 1675).

Varenius, Heinrich, *Brevis Consideratio Admonitionis Georgii Rostii Super Controversiis De Vero B. Arndi Christianismo Ortis In qua B. Arndi innocentia eiusdemq[ue] Christianismi orthodoxa ver- itas asseritur, et a Phlyariais et corruptelis G. Rostii vindicatur, quaestionesq[ue] motae dextre et solide explicantur/ Adornata et remissa A M. Henrico Varenio, Ecclesiaste Hitzackerano* (Lüneburg, 1626).

Werenberg, Jacob, *Vindiciae Ecclesiae Lutheranae Dei Gratia A Mysterio Superstitionis Pontificiae Superiore Seculo liberatae: A Mysterio Apostasiae Haereticae ab eo tempore conservatae Contra Mysterium Iniquitatis Pseudoevangelicae . . . / susceptae a M. Jacobo Werenbergio, ad D. Mar. Magdal. Pastore, et Professore in inclyto Gymnasio Hamburgi* (Lüneburg, 1622).

Secondary Sources

Abray, Lorna Jane, *The People's Reformation; Magistrates, Clergy, and Commons in Strasbourg, 1500–1598* (Ithaca, 1985).

Allbeck, Willard Dow, *Studies in the Lutheran Confessions* (Philadelphia, 1952).

Altman, Janet, *Epistolarity: Approaches to a Form* (Columbus, 1982).

Anetsberger, Werner, *Troestende Lehre: die Theologie Johann Arndts in seinem Predigtwerken* (Munich, 2001).

Appelby, Andrew B., "Epidemics and Famine in the Little Ice Age," *Journal of Interdisciplinary History* 10 (1980), 643–663.

Arndt, Friedrich, *Johann Arndt—ein biographischer Versuch* (Berlin, 1838).

Arndt, G., "Die Berufung Johann Arndts nach Halberstadt," *Zeitschrift des Vereins für Kirchengeschichte in der Provinz Sachsen* 2 (1905), 23–34, 228–236.

Arndt, Joachim, *Das Leben und Wirken von Johann Arndt: Der Reformator der Reformation* (Bielefeld, 1998).

Atkinson, James, *Martin Luther: Prophet to the Church Catholic* (Exeter, 1983).

Axmacher, Elke, *Johann Arndt und Paul Gerhardt: Studien zur Theologie, Froemmigkeit und geistlichen Dichtung des 17. Jahrhunderts* (Tübingen, 2001).

Baring, Georg, *Bibliographie der Ausgaben der Theologia Deutsch* (Baden, 1963).

Baring, Georg, "Valentin Weigel und die Deutsche Theologie," *Archiv für Reformationsgeschichte* 55 (1964), 5–17.

Barnes, Robin Bruce, *Prophecy and Gnosis: Apocalypticism in the Wake of the Lutheran Reformation* (Stanford, 1988).

Batten, J. Minton, "Political Factors in Movements towards Christian Unity in Seventeenth Century Europe," *Church History* 12 (1943), 163–176.

Beck, Hermann, *Die religiöse Volksliteratur der ev. Lutherische Kirche Deutschlands* (Gotha, 1891).

Bente, Friedrich, *Historical Introductions to the Book of Concord* (St. Louis, 1965).

Bepler, Jill, "Vicissitudo Temporum: Some Sidelights on Book Collecting in the Thirty Years' War," *Sixteenth Century Journal* 32 (2001), 953–968.

Beyer, Jürgen, "A Lübeck Prophet in Local and Lutheran Context," in Bob Scribner and Trevor Johnson, eds., *Popular Religion in Germany and Central Europe* (London, 1996), 166–182.

Blaschke, Karl Heinz, "Religion und Politik in Kursachsen 1591–1686," in Heinz Schilling, *Die Reformierte Konfessionalisierung in Deutschland—Das Problem der "Zweiten Reformation"* Wissenschaftliches Symposium des Vereins für Reformationsgeschichte 1985 (Gütersloh, 1986), 79–97.

Bodemann, Friedrich Wilhelm, *Leben Johann Arndts weil General-Superintendenten des Furstenthums Lüneberg* (Bielefeld, 1871).

Bornkamm, Heinrich, *Mystik, Spiritualismus und die Anfange des Pietismus im Luthertum* (Giessen, 1926).

Brady, Thomas A., "Confessional Europe," in Thomas A. Brady, Heiko A. Oberman, and James D. Tracy, eds., *Handbook of European History* 2 (Brill, 1995), 641–681.

Braw, Christian, *Buecher im Staube: die Theologie Johann Arndt in ihrem Verhaeltnis zur Mystik* (Leiden, 1986).

Braw, Christian, "Das Gebet bei Johann Arndt," *Pietismus und Neuzeit* 13 (1988), 25–46.

Brecht, Martin, "Das Aufkommen der neuen Frömmigkeitsbewegung in Deutschland," in Martin Brecht, ed., *Der Pietismus vom siebzehnten bis zum frühen achtzehnten Jahrhundert* 1 (Göttingen, 1993).

Brecht, Martin, ed., *Der Pietismus vom siebzehnten bis zum fruehen achtzehnten Jahrhundert* (Göttingen, 1993).

Brcucr, Dicter, *Froemmigkeit in der fruehen Neuzeit* (Amsterdam, 1984).

Cizevskij, Dimitri, "Das Wahre Christentum in Russland," *Evangelium und Osten* 8 (1935), 41–47.

Cohn, Norman, *The Pursuit of the Millennium* (Oxford, 1970).

Cotton, Hannah M. "Greek and Latin Epistolary Formulae: Some Light on Cicero's Letter Writing," *American Journal of Philology* 105 (Winter 1984), 409–425.

Derrida, Jacques, *The Postcard: From Socrates to Freud and Beyond*, trans. Arthur Bass (Chicago, 1987).

Dickson, Donald, "Johann Valentin Andreae's Utopian Brotherhoods," *Renaissance Quarterly* 49 (1996), 760–802.

Dixon, C. Scott, "Narratives of German History after the Reformation," *Historical Journal* 41 (1998), 875–883.

Drickamer, John, "Johann Arndt and True Christianity," *Concordia Journal* 8 (1982), 98–104.

Drummond, Andrew, *German Protestantism since Luther* (London, 1951).

Duncker, Heinrich, *Anhalts Bekenntnisstand 1570–1606* (Dessau, 1892).

Eskhult, Josef, "Latin Bible Versions in the Age of Reformation and Post Reformation: On the Development of New Latin Versions of the Old Testament in Hebrew and on the Vulgate as Revised and Evaluated among the Protestants," in Anders Jarlert, ed., *Kyrkohistorick Aarsskrift 2006* (Lund, 2006), 31–66.

Fantazzi, Charles, "Vives versus Erasmus on the Art of Letter Writing," in Toon Van Houdt et al., eds., *Self-Presentation and Social Identification. The Rhetoric and Pragmatics of Letter Writing in Early Modern Times* (Leuven, 2002), 39–56.

Fischer, E. R., *The Life of Johann Gerhard*, trans. Richard J. Dinda and Elmer Hohle (Malone, 2000).

Fitzmaurice, Susan M., *The Familiar Letter in Early Modern English* (Philadelphia, 2002).

Forster, Marc, "With and Without Confessionalization," *Journal of Early Modern History* 1 (1997), 315–343.

Geyer, Hermann, *Verborgene Weisheit: Johann Arndts "Vier Bucher vom Wahren Christentum" als Programm einer spiritualistisch-hermetischen Theologie* (Berlin, 2001).

Gilroy, Amanda, and W. M. Verhoeven, eds., *Epistolary Histories* (Charlottesville, 2000).

Gordon, Bruce, *The Swiss Reformation* (Manchester, 2002).

Gruebner, Birgit, *Gott und die Lebendigkeit in der Natur: eine Interpretation des dritten und vierten Buches von Wahres Christentum* (Rheinbach, 1998).

Guggisberg, Hans R., *Sebastian Castellio, 1515-1563: Humanist Defender of Religious Toleration in a Confessional Age*, trans. Bruce Gordon (Aldershot, 2002).

Gutman, Myron P., "The Origins of the Thirty Years War," *Journal of Interdisciplinary History* 18 (1988), 749-770.

Haaglund, Bengt, ed., *The Theologia Germanica of Martin Luther* (New York, 1980).

Hamm, Berndt, "Johann Arndts Wortverstaendnis. Ein Beitrag zu den Anfängen des Pietismus," *Pietismus und Neuzeit* 8 (1983), 43-73.

Holborn, Hajo, *A History of Modern Germany* 2 (New York, 1959).

Hsia, R. Po-Chia, *Social Discipline in the Reformation Central Europe 1550-1750* (London, 1989).

Hubbard, Alice Philena, "The Bible of Vatable," *Journal of Biblical Literature* 66 (1947), 197-209.

Hughes, Michael, *Early Modern Germany 1477-1806* (London, 1992).

Koch, Ernst, "Striving for the Union of Lutheran Churches: The Church-Historical Background of the Work Done on the Formula of Concord at Magdeburg," *Sixteenth Century Journal* 8 (1977), 105-122.

Koepp, Wilhelm, *Johann Arndt, eine Untersuchung ueber die Mystik im Luthertum* (Berlin, 1912).

Koepp, Wilhelm, *Johann Arndt und sein "Wahres Christentum": Lutherisches Bekenntnis und Oekumene* (Berlin, 1959).

Kolb, Robert, *Luther's Heirs Define His Legacy: Studies on Lutheran Confessionalization* (Aldershot, 1996).

Kolb, Robert, *Martin Luther as Prophet, Teacher, and Hero* (Grand Rapids, 1999).

Kolb, Robert Timothy J. and Wengert, eds., "Editors' Introduction to the Formula of Concord," in *The Book of Concord* (Minneapolis, 2000).

Langebartels, James L., "Historical Introduction," in Valentin Ernst Löscher, *The Complete Timothy Verinus*, trans. James L. Langebartels and Robert J. Koester (Milwaukee, 1998).

Leinhard, Marc, "Luther and Beginnings of the Reformation," in Jill Raitt, ed., *Christian Spirituality: High Ages and Reformation* (New York, 1988), 268-299.

Lindberg, Carter, ed., *The Pietist Theologians* (Oxford, 2005).

Löscher, Valentin Ernst, *The Complete Timotheus Verinus*, trans. James L. Langebartels (Milwaukee, 1998).

Lund, Eric, "The Problem of Religious Complacency in Seventeenth Century Lutheran Spirituality," in Bernard McGinn, ed., *Modern Christian Spirituality* (Atlanta, 1990), 139–159.

Lund, Eric, "Second Age of the Reformation: Lutheran and Reformed Spirituality, 1550–1700," in Louis Dupre and Don E. Saliers, eds., *Christian Spirituality: Post Reformation and Modern* (New York, 1989), 213–239.

Maag, Karin, *Seminary or University? Genevan Academy and Reformed Higher Education, 1560–1620* (Aldershot, 1995).

Mager, Inge, "Gottes Wort schmecken und ins Leben verwandeln: Johann Arndts Schriftverstaendnis," *Finnische Literaturbeziehungen* 24 (1992), 149–158.

Mager, Inge, "Johann Arndts Bildfroemmigkeit," in Udo Straeter, *Pietas in der Lutheran Orthodoxie* (Wiesbaden, 1997).

Marius, Richard, *Martin Luther: Man between God and Death* (London, 1999).

Montgomery, John Warwick, *Cross and Crucible: Johann Valentin Andreae Phoenix of the Theologians* (The Hague, 1973).

Morris, John G., *The Life of Johann Arndt* (Baltimore, 1853).

Mueller, David L., *An Introduction to the Theology of Albrecht Ritschl* (Philadelphia, 1969).

Murray, Scott, "What Did It Mean to Be Lutheran among the Orthodox Lutheran Fathers?," in John A. Maxfield, ed., *The Pieper Lectures Volume 4: What Does It Mean to Be Lutheran?* (St. Louis, 2000).

Nicolson, John, "Cicero's Correspondence: A Literary Study," *American Journal of Philology* 121 (Spring 2000), 159–162.

Nischan, Bodo, "The Exorcism and Baptism Controversies in the Late Reformation," *Sixteenth Century Journal* 18 (1987), 31–52.

Nischan, Bodo, "The 'Fractio Panis': A Reformed Communion Practice in Late Reformation Germany," *Church History* 53 (1984), 17–29.

Nischan, Bodo, "Germany after 1550," in Andrew Pettegree, ed., *The Reformation World* (London, 2000).

Nischan, Bodo, *Prince, People, and Confession: The Second Reformation in Brandenburg* (Philadelphia, 1994).

Oberman, Heiko, *Martin Luther: Man between God and the Devil* (New Haven, 1989).

Oberman, Heiko, "Preface," in Johann Arndt, *True Christianity*, trans. Peter Erb (New York, 1979).

Ozment, Steven, *Mysticism and Dissent: Religious Ideology and Social Protest in the Sixteenth Century* (New Haven, 1973).

Pfefferkorn, Oliver, "Predigt, Andachtsbuch und Gebetbuch bei Johann Arndt," *Zeitschrift für Mittelalterliche Deutsche Literatur* 28 (1999), 347–385.

Pfitzer, Christian, "The Little Ice Age: Thermal and Wetness Indices for Central Europe," *Journal of Interdisciplinary History* 10 (1980), 665–696.

Pleijel, Hilding, "Die Bedeutung Johann Arndts für das schwedische Frömmigkeitsleben," in Heinrich Bornkamm, Fredrich Heyer, and Alfred Schindler, eds., *Der Pietismus in Gestalten und Wirkungen, Martin Schmidt zum 65. Geburtstag* (Bielefeld, 1975), 388–399.

Pleijel, Hilding, *The Devotional Literature of the Swedish People* (Lund, 1955).

Preus, Robert, *The Theology of Post-Reformation Lutheranism* (St. Louis, 1972).

Rabe, Horst, *Reich und Glaubensspaltung, Deutschland 1500–1600* (Munich, 1989).

Ramsey, P., "The European Economy in the Sixteenth Century," *Economic History Review* 12 (1960), 458–459.

Rice-Henderson, Judith, "Erasmus on the Art of Letter Writing," in James J. Murphy, ed., *Renaissance Eloquence* (Berkeley, 1983), 331–355.

Rice-Henderson, Judith, "Humanist Letter Writing: Private Conversation or Public Forum?," in Toon Van Houdt et al., eds., *Self-Presentation and Social Identification* (Leuven, 2002), 17–38.

Ritschl, Albrecht, *Geschichte des Pietismus* (Bonn, 1880).

Röbbelen, Ingeborg, *Theologie und Frömmigkeit im deutschen evangelischen-lutherischen Gesangbuch des 17. und frühen 18. Jahrhunderts* (Göttingen, 1957).

Rublack, Hans-Christoph, "Der wohlgeplagte Priester: Vom Selbstverständnis Lutherischer Geistlichkeit im Zeitalter der Orthodoxie," *Zeitschrift für Historische Forschung* 16 (1989), 1–30.

Rublack, Hans-Christoph, *Die lutherische Konfessionalisierung in Deutschland: Wissenschaftliches Symposion des Vereins für Reformationsgeschichte* (Gütersloh, 1992).

Rummel, Erika, "Erasmus' Manual of Letter-Writing: Tradition and Innovation," *Renaissance and Reformation* 25:3 (1989), 299–312.

Schaff, Phillip, *History of the Christian Church VIII: Modern Christianity. The Swiss Reformation* (Grand Rapids, 1988).

Scharff, Gottfried Balthazar, *Supplementum historiae litisque Arndianae aliquot inclutorum superioris saeculi theologorum Epistolis constans* (Wittenberg, 1727).

Schmauk, Theodore E. and C. Theodore Benze, *The Confessional Principle and the Confessions of the Lutheran Church* (St. Louis, 2005).

Schmid, Heinrich, *Die Geschichte des Pietismus* (Nördlingen, 1863).

Schmidt, Martin, *Der Pietismus als theologische Erscheinung* 2 (Göttingen, 1984).

Schneider, Hans, "Johann Arndt als Lutheraner?," in Hans Christoph Rublack, ed., *Die lutherische Konfessionalisierung in Deutschland: Wissenschaftliches Symposion des Vereins für Reformationsgeschichte* (Gütersloh, 1992), 274–298.

Schneider, Hans, "Johann Arndts Studienzeit," *Jahrbuch der Gesellschaft für niedersächsische Kirchengeschichte* 89 (1991), 133–175.

Schneider, Hans, *Der fremde Arndt: Studien zu Leben, Werk und Wirkung Johann Arndts (1555–1621)* (Göttingen, 2006).

Schubart, U. N., "Johann Arndt: Ergaenzungen und Berichtigungen zu der Geschichte seines Lebens und Wirkens in Anhalt," *Neue kirchliche Zeitschrift* 9 (1898), 456–472.

Schwager, Hans Joachim, *Johann Arndts Bemuehen um die rechte Gestaltung des neuen Lebens der Glaeubigen* (unpublished PhD dissertation, Münster, 1961).

Scribner, R. W., "Incombustible Luther: The Image of the Reformer in Early Modern Germany," *Past and Present* 110 (1986), 38–68.

Seebass, Friedrich, *Johan Arndt: Ein Kaempfer fuer das wahre Christentum* (Giessen, 1955).

Sheele, C., *Plato und Johann Arndt. Ein Vortrag* (Berlin, 1857).

Sommer, Wolfgang, *Gottesfurcht und Fürstenherrschaft—Studien zum Obrigkeitsverständnis Johann Arndts und lutherischer Hofprediger zur Zeit der altprotestantischen Orthodoxie* (Göttingen, 1988).

Sommer, Wolfgang, "Johann Arndt im Amt des Generalsuperintendenten in Braunschweig-Lüneberg," in Hans Christoph Rublack, ed., *Die lutherische Konfessionalisierung in Deutschland: Wissenschaftliches Symposion des Vereins für Reformationsgeschichte* (Gütersloh, 1992).

Sommer, Wolfgang, *Politik, Theologie und Froemmigkeit im Luthertum der frühen Neuzeit* (Gottingen, 1999).

Stoeffler, F. Ernest, "Johann Arndt," in Martin Greschat, *Orthodoxie und Pietismus* (Stuttgart, 1982), 37–49.

Stoeffler, F. Ernst, *The Rise of Evangelical Pietism* (Leiden, 1965).

Stupperich, Robert, *Melanchthon*, trans. Robert H. Fischer (Philadelphia, 1960).

Taithe, Bertrand and Tim Thornton, "The Language of History: Past and Future in Prophecy," in Bertrand Taithe and Tim Thornton, eds., *Prophecy: The Power of Inspired Language in History: 1300–2000* (Gloucestershire, 1997).

Vogler, Bernard, "Die Gebetbücher in der lutherischen Orthodoxie 1550–1700," in Hans-Christoph Rublack, ed., *Die lutherische Konfessionalisierung in Deutschland* (Gütersloh, 1988).

Wallmann, Johannes, "Johann Arndt," in Carter Lindberg, ed., *The Pietist Theologians* (Oxford, 2005), 21–37.

Wallmann, Johannes, "Johann Arndt und die protestantische Frömmigkeit," in *Jahrbuch der hessischen kirchengeschichtlichen Vereinigung* 35 (1984), 371–379.

Weber, Edmund, *Johann Arndts Vier Bücher vom wahren Christentum als Beitrag zur protestantischen Irenik des 17. Jahrhunderts* (Marburg, 1969).

Weeks, Andrew, *Valentin Weigel (1533–1588): German Religious Dissenter, Speculative Theorist, and Advocate of Tolerance* (Albany, 2000).

Weigelt, Horst, "Interpretations of Pietism in the Research of Contemporary German Historians," *Church History* 39 (1970), 236–241.

Wildenhahn, Carl August, *Johann Arndt; ein Zeitbild aus Braunschweigs Kirchen- und Stadtgeschichte in den ersten Jahren des Siebenzehnten Jahrhunderts* (Leipzig, 1858).

Winter, Friedrich Julius, *Johann Arndt, der Verfasser des "Wahren Christentums," ein christliche Lebensbild* (Leipzig, 1911).

Witt, Ronald, "Medieval 'Ars Dictaminis' and the Beginnings of Humanism: A New Construction of the Problem," *Renaissance Quarterly* 35:1 (Spring 1982).

Yates, Frances A., *The Rosicrucian Enlightenment* (London, 1972).

Zeller, Winfried, "Lutherische Lebenszeugen," in Winfried Zeller, ed., *Evangelisches und orthodoxes Christentum in Begegnung und Auseinandersetzung* (Hamburg, 1952).

Unpublished Theses

Holt, Bradley Paul, *Perspectives on the Self in Devotional Writing: Augustine, Rudbeckius and Arndt* (unpublished PhD dissertation, Yale University, 1973).

Kohl, Manfred Waldemar, *Studies in Pietism. A Biographical Study of Research since 1958* (unpublished PhD dissertation, Harvard University, 1969).

Lund, Eric, *Johann Arndt and the Development of a Lutheran Spiritual Tradition* (unpublished PhD dissertation, Yale University, 1979).

Spink, George Samuel, *John Arndt's Religious Thought: A Study in German Proto-Pietism* (unpublished PhD dissertation, Temple University, 1970).

Wiebe, Orlando, *Johann Arndt: Precursor of Pietism* (unpublished PhD dissertation, University of Iowa, 1965).

Endnotes

Introduction

1 Thomas Sprat, *An Account of Life and Writings of Mr. Abraham Cowley. Written to Mr. M. Clifford in the Works of Abraham Cowley. Consisting of those which were formerly printed: and those which he designed for the Press* (London, 1968), quoted in Susan M. Fitzmaurice, *The Familiar Letter in Early Modern English* (Philadelphia, 2002), 16.

2 Amanda Gilroy and W. M. Verhoeven, "Introduction," in Amanda Gilroy and W. M. Verhoeven, eds., *Epistolary Histories* (Charlottesville, 2000), 1.

3 Fitzmaurice, *The Familiar Letter*, 18–19.

4 Ronald Witt, "Medieval 'Ars Dictaminis' and the Beginnings of Humanism: a New Construction of the Problem," *Renaissance Quarterly* 35, 1 (Spring 1982): 5.

5 Ibid., 7. See also Hannah M. Cotton, "Greek and Latin Epistolary Formulae: Some Light on Cicero's Letter Writing," *American Journal of Philology* 105 (Winter 1984): 409–425; John Nicolson, "Cicero's Correspondence: A Literary Study," *American Journal of Philology* 121 (Spring 2000): 159–162.

6 Les Perelman, "The Medieval Art of Letter Writing: Rhetoric as Institutional Expression," in Charles Bazerman and James Paradis, eds., *Textual Dynamics of the Professions: Historical and Contemporary Studies of Writing in Professional Communities* (Wisconsin, 1991), 106.

7 Witt, "Medieval 'Ars Dictaminis,'" 30.

8 George Hinge, "Linguistic Consciousness in Erasmus Desiderius' *De conscribendis epistolis* and *De recta Latini Graecique sermonis pronuntione*" (paper presented at the conference *Texts and Contexts IV: The Role of Latin in Early Modern Europe*, Aarhus, Denmark, May 17–20, 2007). The full text of this paper is available at Dr. Hinge's personal webpage, http://www.georgehinge.com/erasm.html. See also Erika Rummel, "Erasmus' Manual of Letter-Writing: Tradition and Innovation," *Renaissance and Reformation* 25:3 (1989): 299–312; Charles Fantazzi, "Vives versus Erasmus on the Art of Letter Writing," in Toon Van Houdt et al., eds.,

Self-Presentation and Social Identification. The Rhetoric and Pragmatics of Letter Writing in Early Modern Times, Supplementa Humanistica Lovaniensia xviii (Leuven, 2002), 39–56; Judith Rice-Henderson, "Erasmus on the Art of Letter Writing," in James J. Murphy, ed., *Renaissance Eloquence* (Berkeley, 1983), 331–355; Judith Rice-Henderson, "Humanist Letter Writing: Private Conversation or Public Forum?," in Toon Van Houdt et al., eds., *Self-Presentation and Social Identification*, 17–38.

9 *CWE* 25, 14.

10 Ibid., 20.

11 Modern epistolary criticism seems predominantly housed in the schools of literary criticism and philosophy. Some of the more widely cited texts include Janet Altman, *Epistolarity: Approaches to a Form* (Columbus, 1982); David Barton and Nigel Hall, *Letter Writing as a Social Form* (Philadelphia, 2000); and Jacques Derrida, *The Postcard: From Socrates to Freud and Beyond*, trans. Arthur Bass (Chicago, 1987).

12 Using the VD17; the bibliographies in Wilhelm Koepp, *Johann Arndt ein Untersuchung über die Mystik im Lutherthum* (Berlin, 1912), 306–310; and the bibliography in Hans Schneider, *Der Fremde Arndt: Studien zu Leben, Werke und Wirkung Johann Arndts (1555–1621)* (Göttingen, 2006), 265–278, I was able to count the number of books written about Arndt in every decade since his death. After the 1620s (16), the decade with the second most printed books on Arndt was the 1710s (9) and the 1850s (9), third was the 1700s (8), fourth was the 1970s (7), and fifth was the 1980s and the 1730s (6). When journal articles are added to the list, the runaway decade is the 1990s (55) followed by the 1980s (23) and the first half of this decade (19).

13 Lucas Osiander d.J., *Theologisches Bedencken Und Christliche Trewhertzige Erinnerung welcher gestalt Johann Arndten genandtes Wahres Christenthum nach anleitung des H. Wortes Gottes anzusehen und zuachten sey Allen Gottseligen Christen . . . zu nothwendiger Nachrichtung* (Stettin, 1623).

14 ADB 24, 45.

15 Osiander, *Theologisches Bedencken*, 49, 184, 194.

16 A list of these works is found in Koepp, *Johann Arndt*, 306–307.

17 Heinrich Varenius, *Christliche Schrifftmässige wolgegründete Rettung der Vier Bücher vom wahren Christenthumb des seligen umb die Kirche Christi wolverdienten recht Lutherischen Evangelischen Theologi H. Johannis Arndten / weiland general Superintendenten der Kirchen im löblichen Fürstenthumb Lüneburg und Pfarrherrn in Zell Verfertiget und D. Lucae Osiandri Theologischem Bedencken entgegen gesetzt* (Lüneburg, 1624).

18 Paulus Egardus, *Ehrenrettung Johannis Arndten, Das ist Christliche und in Gottes Wort wolgegründete Erinnerung was von D. Lucae Osiandri,*

Theologiae Professoris zu Tübingen Urtheil und Censur, uber Johan Arnd-ten wahres Christenthumb sey zu halten (Lüneburg, 1624).

19 "Darauff greiffet er den todten Löwen an mit macht, den Sieg über ihm zu erhalten." "dass ist ein Gut zeichen und eine Anzeigung dass dieselbige vom heiligen Geist sey." Ibid., 22.

20 ADB 5, 656.

21 Melchior Breller, *Warhafftiger Glaubwirdiger und gründlicher Bericht von den vier Büchern vom Wahren Christenthumb Herrn Johannis Arndten auß den gefundenen brieflichen Urkunden zusammen getragen. Darauß Sonnen-klar zu beweisen ist daß gedachte Bücher vom Wahren Christenthumb . . . zur ungebür bezüchtiget und außgeruffen werden. Nebenst Herrn Johann Arndten kurtzen Bedencken uber V. Weigelii Dialogum de Christianismo. Entgegen gesatzt. Den . . . unwarhafften Beschuldigungen . . . Insonderheit aber dem untheologischen Bedencken D. Lucae Osiandri . . . an den tag gegeben* (Lüneburg, 1625).

22 Georg Rostius, *Examin brevis considerationis Varenii* (Rostock, 1628).

23 Koepp, *Mystik im Lutherthum*, 125.

24 Johannes Wallmann, *Philipp Jakob Spener und die Anfänge des Pietismus* (Tübingen, 1986), 247.

25 Quoted by Hans-Joachim Schwager, *Johann Arndts Bemühen um die rechte Gestaltung des neuen Lebens der Gläubigen* (unpublished PhD dissertation, Münster, 1961), 95.

26 Ibid.

27 Koepp, *Mystik im Lutertum*, 19.

28 James L. Langebartels, "Historical Introduction," in Valentin Ernst Loscher, *The Complete Timothy Verinus*, trans. James L. Langebartels and Robert J. Koester (Milwaukee, 1998), viii.

29 Valentin Ernst Löscher, *The Complete Timotheus Verinus*, trans. James L Langebartels (Milwaukee, 1998), 11, 12, 51, 52, 64.

30 Ibid., 15.

31 One of the few works was the book by Johann Friedrich Gauhe, *Gesprä-che im Reich Todten Zwischen Zweyen Hochberühmten Gottesgelehrten der Evangelischen Kirche, Johann Arndten und D. Philipp Spenern . . . Darinnen die Lebens-Geschichte des Weltbekandten Johann Arndts, ingleichen ver-schiedenes von denen Streitigkeiten wegen seines wahren Christenthums angeführet, auch von andern seinen Büchern gehandelt wird* (unknown, 1732). This work has not survived, but it followed a literary tradition of imagining a conversation between two great men in the afterlife.

32 Johann Andreas Gleich, *Trifolium Arndtianum; seu, L. Ioannis. Arndti, tres epistolae hactenus ineditae de libris verum Christianismum concernen-tibus ad D. Petrum piscatorem . . . quibus annexa est peculiaris epistola D. Ioannis Gerhardi* (Wittenberg, 1726).

33 Gottfried Balthasar Scharff, *Supplementum historiae litisque Arndianae aliquot inclutorum superioris saeculi theologorum Epistolis constans* (Wittenberg, 1727).

34 Johann Arndt, *Johann Arnds Geistreicher Schriften und Werke I, II, III,* ed. Johann Jacob Rambach (Leipzig, 1736).

35 Johannes Wallmann, "Johann Arndt," in Carter Lindberg, ed., *The Pietist Theologians* (Oxford, 2005), 22.

36 Ibid.

37 Robert Preus, *The Theology of Post-Reformation Lutheranism* 1 (St. Louis, 1970), 16; ADB 84, 54.

38 Heinrich Schmid, *Die Geschichte des Pietismus* (Nördlingen, 1863), 3.

39 "Der evangelische-reformierte, dem evangelisch-lutherischen Charakter entgegengesetzte und ihn an der Wurzel bedrohende Ausgangspunkt und die entsprechende Grundeinstellung wurden hervorgehoben." Ibid.

40 Ibid.

41 "Zum ersten Male wurde Valentin Ernst Löschers theologische Ablehnung des (hallischen) Pietismus in der modern Forschung ernstgenommen, wenngleich sich Heinrich Schmid vorschnell mit ihr identifizierte." Martin Schmidt, *Der Pietismus als theologische Erscheinung* 2 (Göttingen, 1984), 46–47.

42 "Das Wesen des Pietismus wurde weitgehend auf die 'Konventikel' festgelegt." Schmid, *Geschichte*, 3.

43 David L. Mueller, *An Introduction to the Theology of Albrecht Ritschl* (Philadelphia, 1969), 109.

44 Ibid., 19–20.

45 Eric Lund, *Johann Arndt and the Development of a Lutheran Spiritual Tradition* (unpublished PhD dissertation, Yale University, 1979), 2.

46 Albrecht Ritschl, *Geschichte des Pietismus* 2 (Bonn, 1880), 52.

47 "Die Unvollstaendigkeit seiner ethischen Orientirung, die Zersplitterung seiner Gesammtanschauung in die Reihe der einzeln Dogmen, die vorwiegende Auspraegung seines Besitzes in sproeder Verstandigkeit sind Maengel, welche den Protestantismus bald im Nachteil gegen die Fuelle der mittelaeltrigen Theologie und Asketik erscheinen liessen." Ibid.

48 John G. Morris, *The Life of John Arndt; author of the work on True Christianity* (Baltimore, 1853).

49 Karl August Wildenhahn, *John Arndt: A Historical Life Picture* (Easton, 1882).

50 Koepp, *Mystik im Luthertum*.

51 "Das Lutherthum gibt den Grund, aber die Höhe der Frömmigkeit und ihr eigentliches Ziel und das eigentlich Wertgebende ist erst die Mystik." Ibid., 257.

52 "eine energische Verbindung von ausgeprägter Orthodoxie der Lehre und ethischem ... Rigorismus der Praxis." Ibid., 21.

53 "In seiner Grundintention kann sich Arndt zu recht auf Luther berufen." Hans Joachim Schwager, *Johann Arndts Bemuehen* (unpublished PhD thesis, Münster, 1961), 71.

54 F. Ernst Stoeffler, *The Rise of Evangelical Pietism* (Leiden, 1971), 202. Stoeffler's view reflected a number of dissertations written in the period that made Arndt the forefather of Pietism. Orlando Wiebe, in his *Johann Arndt: Precursor of Pietism* (unpublished PhD dissertation, University of Iowa, 1965), suggested that Arndt was a necessary link between the theology of Luther and Spener while not quite labeling Arndt a Pietist (but certainly not a Lutheran). George Samuel Spink, in his dissertation *John Arndt's Religious Thought: A Study in Proto-Pietism* (unpublished PhD dissertation, Temple University, 1970), suggested a new term, *Proto-Pietist*, and while this may have been seen as a concession to the slightly different positions of Stoeffler and Wiebe, it was merely a suggestion that Arndt was a "Pietist without conventicles."

55 Lund, *Johann Arndt*, 299.

56 Johannes Wallmann, "Johann Arndt und die protestantische Frömmigkeit," in *Jahrbuch der Hessischen Kirchengeschichtlichen Vereinigung* 35 (1984): 371–379.

57 Johannes Wallmann, "Die Anfange des Pietismus," in *Pietismus und Neuzeit* 4 (1977): 11–53.

58 Hans Schneider, "Johann Arndt als Lutheraner?" in Hans Christoph Rublack, ed., *Die lutherische Konfessionalisierung in Deutschland*, Wissenschaftliches Symposion des Vereins für Reformation Geschichte (Gütersloh, 1992), 298.

59 Wolfgang Sommer, "Johann Arndt im Amt des Generalsuperintendenten in Braunschweig-Lüneburg," in Rublack, *Die lutherische Konfessionalisierung*, 300.

60 "Neben den grossen Predigtwerken kommt ihr eine wichtige, in der Arndt Forschung viel zu wenig beachtete Bedeutung zu, wenn Arndts Stellung in seiner Zeit und seine Wirkung als Prediger und Organisator des Kirchenwesens, nicht nur als Erbauungsschriftsteller ..." Ibid., 307.

61 "Die Arndtsche Frömmigkeit ist in ihrem Ansatz kirchliche Frömmigkeit!" Ibid.

62 "Den Höhepunkt der Konfessionalisierung ... Johann Arndt war [ein] orthodoxer, bekenntnisbewusster Lutheraner." Ibid., 310.

63 Quoted in Joachim Arndt, *Das Leben und Wirken von Johann Arndt: Der Reformator der Reformation* (Bielefeld, 1998), 6.

64 Christian Braw, "Das Gebet bei Johann Arndt," in *Pietismus und Neuzeit* 13 (1998): 9–24. Braw also wrote a monograph on Arndt in which he

examined Arndt's writings in relation to medieval mysticism: Christian Braw, *Bücher im Staube* (Leiden, 1997). It is my contention that for the overall shift in emphases in Arndt research, his article examining only Arndt's prayers is more significant.

65 Braw, "Das Gebet," 9.

66 Werner Anetsberger, *Troestende Lehre: die Theologie Johann Arndts in seinen Predigtwerken* (Munich, 2001).

67 Ibid., 61.

68 Ibid., 374–375.

Chapter 1: Johann Arndt: Hero or Heretic?

1 Joachim Arndt, *Das Leben und Wirken von Johann Arndt. Der Reformator der Reformation* (Bielefeld, 1998). Arndt claims in the forward to be a direct descendant of Johann Arndt and recounts various *Wundergeschichten*. The biographical information is almost identical to Friedrich Arndt, *Johann Arndt, weiland General-Superintendent des Fürstentums Lüneberg. Ein biographischer Versuch* (Berlin, 1838). While this Arndt does not claim to be a direct descendent, his work, which attempted to recount Arndt's life through his correspondence only included nine letters and presented a picture of Arndt as a mystic.

2 See Hans Schneider, "Johann Arndt's Studienzeit," *Jahrbuch der Gesellschaft für niedersächsische Kirchengeschichte* 89 (1991): 133–175. Schneider is an active Arndt scholar, and this article clears up a few of the conflicting reports as to where and when Arndt matriculated at various universities.

3 Arndt, *Das Leben und Wirken*, 23.

4 Schneider, "Studienzeit," 133.

5 Eric Lund, *Johann Arndt and the Development of a Lutheran Spiritual Tradition* (unpublished PhD dissertation, Yale University, 1979), 89.

6 Arndt, *Das Leben und Wirken*, 24.

7 Schneider, "Studienzeit," 130. The Pappus-Sturm debates are detailed in Lorna Jane Abray, *The People's Reformation. Magistrates, Clergy, and Commons in Strasbourg, 1500–1598* (Ithaca, 1985).

8 Schneider, "Studienzeit," 114.

9 Ibid., 131–132.

10 ADB, 155.

11 The letter has been reproduced in Schneider, "Studienzeit," 126.

12 Ibid., 127.

13 Arndt, *Das Leben und Wirken*, 25.

14 Johann Arndt, *Ikonographia; Gruendlicher und Christlicher Bericht von Bildern* (Halberstadt, 1596).

15 Hans-Joachim Schwager, *Johann Arndts Bemuehen um die rechte Gestaltung des Neuen Lebens der Glaeubigen* (unpublished PhD dissertation, Münster, 1961).

16 This crucial early confessional moment for Arndt has been written off by a few historians with a theological bias against what they would consider uncharacteristic of Arndt. Stoeffler only makes a passing reference to the events and leaves out the issue of exorcism, simply stating that there were "certain difficulties." Ernst F. Stoeffler, *The Rise of Evangelical Pietism* (Leiden, 1965), 203. Koepp suggested that this was an example of Arndt temporarily caught up in the disputational fervor of his day. Wilhelm Koepp, *Johann Arndt eine Untersuchung ueber die Mystik im Luthertum* (Berlin, 1912), 19.

17 Friedrich Wilhelm Bodemann, *Leben Johan Arndts, weiland General Superintendenten des Fürstentums Lüneberg* (Bielefeld, 1847), 444.

18 Lund, *Johann Arndt*, 102.

19 Bodo Nischan, "The Exorcism and Baptism Controversies in the Late Reformation," *Sixteenth Century Journal* 18 (1987): 44.

20 Martin Brecht, "Das Aufkommen der neuen Frömmigkeitsbewegung in Deutschland," in Martin Brecht, ed., *Der Pietismus vom siebzehnten bis zum frühen achtzehnten Jahrhundert* 1 (Göttingen, 1993), 132.

21 See Robin Bruce Barnes, *Prophecy and Gnosis: Apocalypticism in the Wake of the Lutheran Reformation* (Stanford, 1988). In contrast to his orthodox contemporaries, Arndt seems to have devoted little attention to questions of the second coming and apocalypse.

22 Ibid., 228–260. Barnes includes a lengthy discussion of Lutheran orthodoxy and the reading of celestial events as foretelling the end of the world. He discusses Arndt and places his work in opposition to this kind of prophecy.

23 See chapter 3 for an analysis of Arndt's edition of the *Theologia Deutsch*.

24 *WC*, 830.

25 F. J. Winter, "Johann Arndt; der Verfasser des Wahren Christenthums, ein christliches Lebensbild," *Schriften des Vereins für Reformationsgeschichte* 101 (1911): 19.

26 See chapter 3 and the explication of this letter to Gerhard.

27 Erdmann Rudolph Fischer, *The Life of Johann Gerhard*, trans. Richard J. Dinda and Elmer Hohle (Texas, 2000), 426.

28 Brecht, "Das Aufkommen," 133.

29 Letter to Abbess Anna von Stollberg, July 6, 1599, in *Rambach*, 600–602.

30 Eric Lund, "Second Age of the Reformation: Lutheran and Reformed Spirituality, 1550–1700," in Louis Dupre and Don E. Saliers, eds., *Christian Spirituality: Post Reformation and Modern* (New York, 1989), 223.

31 Lund, *Johann Arndt*, 112.

32 Bodemann, *Leben Johann Arndts*, 465.

33 See the letter to Gerhard from July 5, 1606, in *Raidel*. This letter is referenced and examined in chapter 4.

34 "Muss mich noch wohl will ich Friede haben, wann ich keinen andern
Beruff bekomme, etwa an einem Ort hinbegeben, vielleicht nach Eisleben
und ein Privatleben anfangen. Denn die Welt wird gar zu heilloss. Ich
hätte es nimmer gemeinet, dass unter den Theologen so gifftige böse Leute
wären." Letter to Johann Gerhard, August 3, 1607, *Rambach*, 605–606.

35 "Erat homo ingenio vafro, callido et vulpino, pluris favorem et gratium
senatus quam ministrii autoritatem et salutem faciens quo abuente
ministerium magno onere levatum est." Quoted from the *Catalogous
Ministrorum Brunsvicensium* in Koepp, *Mystik im Luthertum*, 68.

36 Schneider, "Studienzeit," 95.

37 Lund, *Johann Arndt*, 123.

38 Winter, "Johann Arndt, der Verfasser," 46–48.

39 Ibid., 124.

40 Arndt, *Das Leben und Wirken*, 48–49.

41 Brecht, "Das Aufkommen," 143.

42 Ibid., 143.

43 Winter, "Johann Arndt, der Verfasser," 76.

44 Ibid., 77.

45 Lucas Osiander d.J., *Theologisches Bedencken Und Christliche Trewhertzige
Erinnerung welcher gestalt Johann Arndten genandtes Wahres Christenthum
nach anleitung des H. Wortes Gottes . . . anzusehen und zuachten sey. Allen
Gottseligen Christen . . . zu nothwendiger Nachrichtung* (Stettin, 1623).

46 Brecht, "Das Aufkommen," 146.

47 Ibid., 142–151.

48 Paulus Egardus, *Ehrenrettung Johannis Arndten Das ist Christliche und in
Gottes Wort wolgegründete Erinnerung was von D. Lucae Osiandri, Theologiae Professoris zu Tübingen Urtheil und Censur, uber Johan Arndten wahres
Christenthumb sey zu halten* (Lüneburg, 1624); Friedrich Dame, *Vom Alten
und Newen Menschen: Woher dieser Unterscheid entstanden/ und das alleine
newe Menschen die wahre Kirche Christi* (Lübeck, 1632); Melchior Breller,
*Warhafftiger, Glaubwurdiger und Gründlicher Bericht von den vier Büchern
vom Wahren Christenthumb Herrn Johannis Arndten / auss den gefunden
brieflichen Urkunden zusammen getragen* (Lüneburg, 1625).

49 Robert Preus, *The Theology of Post-Reformation Lutheranism* (St. Louis,
1972).

50 This most recent English translation is Johann Arndt, *True Christianity*,
trans. Peter C. Erb (New York, 1979).

51 Johannes Wallmann, "Johann Arndt," in Carter Lindberg, ed., *The Pietist
Theologians* (Oxford, 2005), 21.

52 Lund, *Johann Arndt*, 115.

53 Ibid., 118.

54 Ibid.

55 Ibid.

56 Printing records for the sixteenth century editions from Koepp, *Johann Arndt*, 302–303.

57 Brecht, "Das Aufkommen," 150.

58 Koepp, *Johann Arndt*, 306–309.

59 Brecht, "Das Aufkommen," 150.

60 Ibid.

61 See Orlando Wiebe, *Johann Arndt: Precursor of Pietism* (unpublished PhD dissertation, University of Iowa, 1965).

62 Heiko Oberman, "Preface," in Johann Arndt, *True Christianity*, trans. Peter Erb (New York, 1979), xi.

63 *WC*, 64.

64 Currently, no critical edition of this work exists. In the course of my research, I used a variety of editions, depending on the availability of the text in the area. I have revised this text and standardized all references to the most recent edition printed in Bielefeld in 1996. The modest proposals and interpretation of the text do not suggest any critical rereadings of the text that a critical or first edition might require.

65 *WC*, 64.

66 Ibid. 65.

67 Ibid. 67.

68 Ibid.

69 Ibid.

70 Ibid.

71 Friedrich Bente, *Historical Introductions to the Book of Concord* (St. Louis, 1965), 115.

72 Preus, *Post-Reformation Lutheranism*, 41.

73 *WC*, 67.

74 Ibid.

75 Peter Erb, "Introduction," in Johann Arndt, *True Christianity*, trans. Peter Erb (New York, 1979), 3–4.

76 *WC*, 72.

77 Ibid.

78 *FC*, 511.

79 *WC*, 72.

80 Ibid., 74.

81 FC, 527.

82 *WC*, 118.

83 *WC*, 243–244.

84 Johann Gerhard, *Sacred Meditations*, trans. C. W. Heisler (Philadelphia, 1896). See Meditation XII.

85 Lund, *Johann Arndt*, 181.

86 Erb, "Introduction," 10–12.

87 Fischer, *The Life of Johann Gerhard*, 427.

88 *FC*, 495.

89 *WC*, 505.

90 Albrecht Ritschl, *Geschichte des Pietismus* (Bonn, 1880).

91 *WC*, 536.

92 Ibid.

93 *FC*, 504.

94 *WC*, 537.

95 Steven Ozment, *Homo Spiritualis* (Leiden, 1969), 13–46; and Lund, *Johann Arndt*, 204.

96 Lund, *Johann Arndt*, 208.

97 *WC*, 573.

98 Ibid.

99 Ibid., 572.

100 Fischer, *The Life of Johann Gerhard*, 426.

101 *WC*, 584–642.

102 Ibid., 643.

103 See the introductory chapter in John Warwick Montgomery, *Cross and Crucible: Johann Valentin Andreae (1586–1654), Phoenix of the Theologians* (The Hague, 1973), 1–22.

104 *WC*, 690.

105 Ibid., 690–694.

106 Ibid., 698.

107 Ibid., 714–719.

108 Ibid., 759.

109 Ibid., 762.

110 Ibid., 776–777.

111 All of these letters have been most recently published in *WC*, 25–48.

112 Ibid., 818–830.

113 An analysis of the foreword can be found in chapter 3.

Chapter 2: Johann Arndt as a Confessional Lutheran

1 The clearest representatives of these positions are Wilhelm Koepp, *Johann Arndt und sein "Wahres Christentum" Lutherisches Bekenntnis und Oekumene* (Berlin, 1959), and Ernst F. Stoeffler, *The Rise of Evangelical Pietism* (Leiden, 1965).

2 R. Po-Chia Hsia has referred to this era as the "orphaned years" of the Lutheran church, lacking the bloodshed of France and the Netherlands in R. Po-Chia Hsia, *Social Discipline in the Reformation Central Europe 1550–1750* (London, 1989), 1.

3 Robert Preus, *The Theology of Post-Reformation Lutheranism* (St. Louis, 1972), 42.

4 Ibid., 29.

5 Robert Kolb, "Dynamics of Party Conflict in the Saxon Late Reformation, Gnesio-Lutherans vs. Philippists," *Journal of Modern History* 49 (1977): 1290.

6 Thomas A. Brady, "Confessional Europe," in Thomas A. Brady, Heiko A. Oberman, and James D. Tracy, eds., *Handbook of European History* 2 (Brill, 1995), 643.

7 C. Scott Dixon, "Narratives of German History after the Reformation," *Historical Journal* 41 (1998): 878.

8 Marc Forster, "With and Without Confessionalization," *Journal of Early Modern History* 1 (1997): 316.

9 Horst Rabe, *Reich und Glaubensspaltung, Deutschland 1500–1600* (Munich, 1989), 258; Hajo Holborn, *A History of Modern Germany* 2 (New York, 1959), 228.

10 Willard Dow Allbeck, *Studies in the Lutheran Confessions* (Philadelphia, 1952), 242. Holborn, *Modern Germany*, 238, 242.

11 Rabe, *Reich*, 295, 300ff., 342; J. Minton Batten, "Political Factors in Movements towards Christian Unity in Seventeenth Century Europe," *Church History* 12 (1943): 164; Michael Hughes, *Early Modern Germany 1477–1806* (London, 1992), 61.

12 On Ferdinand I see Rabe, *Reich*, 304. On Maximilian II see Rabe, *Reich*, 306; Holborn, *Modern Germany*, 249.

13 Maximilian presided over an attempt to build a pan-confessional German nationalism with the backing of Lutherans Duke John V of Jülich-Cleves, Elector August I of Saxony, and Elector Joachim II. Hughes, *Early Modern Germany*, 63; Holborn, *Modern Germany*, 250.

14 Bodo Nischan, "Germany after 1550," in Andrew Pettegree, ed., *The Reformation World* (London, 2000), 392.

15 Ibid., 396–400.

16 Ernst Koch, "Striving for the Union of Lutheran Churches: The Church-Historical Background of the Work Done on the Formula of Concord at Magdeburg," *Sixteenth Century Journal* 8 (1977): 106; Allbeck, *Lutheran Confessions*, 245; Holborn, *Modern Germany*, 262.

17 Bodo Nischan, "The Exorcism and Baptism Controversies in the Late Reformation," *Sixteenth Century Journal* 18 (1987): 31–52. Nischan compiled a number of these stories throughout his work on post-1555 Germany.

This article explores the depths to which the theological controversies affected the lay population.

18 Bodo Nischan, *Prince, People, and Confession: The Second Reformation in Brandenburg* (Philadelphia, 1994), 179.

19 Rabe, *Reich*, 334–335; Holborn, *Modern Germany*, 274.

20 Holborn, *Modern Germany*, 260.

21 Karin Maag, *Seminary or University? Genevan Academy and Reformed Higher Education, 1560–1620* (Aldershot, 1995), 193.

22 Preus, *Post Reformation Lutheranism*, 65. Preus mentions that Leipzig and Jena had a slightly milder tone than the other three. Also see Rabe, *Reich*, 331; Holborn, *Modern Germany*, 255; Allbeck, *Lutheran Confessions*, 243.

23 Myron P. Gutman, "The Origins of the Thirty Years War," *Journal of Interdisciplinary History* 18 (1988): 762; Hughes, *Early Modern Germany*, 78.

24 Rabe, *Reich*, 345; Hughes, *Early Modern Germany*, 78.

25 P. Ramsey, "The European Economy in the Sixteenth Century," *Economic History Review* 12 (1960): 458–459; Christian Pfitzer, "The Little Ice Age: Thermal and Wetness Indices for Central Europe," *Journal of Interdisciplinary History* 10 (1980): 685; Hughes, *Early Modern Germany*, 75.

26 Andrew B. Appelby, "Epidemics and Famine in the Little Ice Age," *Journal of Interdisciplinary History* 10 (1980): 645; Hughes, *Early Modern Germany*, 76.

27 C. Scott Dixon, *The Reformation in Germany* (Oxford, 2002), 93–95.

28 Bernard Vogler, "Die Gebetbücher in der lutherischen Orthodoxie 1550–1700," in Hans-Christoph Rublack, ed., *Die lutherische Konfessionalisierung in Deutschland* (Gütersloh, 1988), 424. Vogler traces the development of personal piety through the use of private devotional material.

29 Robert Stupperich, *Melanchthon*, trans. Robert H. Fischer (Philadelphia, 1960), 134.

30 Ibid., 135.

31 Robert Kolb, *Luther's Heirs Define His Legacy: Studies on Lutheran Confessionalization* (Aldershot, 1996). This collection of Kolb's works deals heavily with the gulf (real and imagined) between the so-called Philippists and Gnesio-Lutherans.

32 Friedrich Bente, *Historical Introductions to the Book of Concord* (St. Louis, 1965), 104.

33 Allbeck, *Lutheran Confessions*, 243.

34 Bente, *Historical Introductions*, 115.

35 Ibid., 134.

36 Allbeck, *Lutheran Confessions*, 243.

37 Bente, *Historical Introductions*, 144.

38 Theodore E. Schmauk and C. Theodore Benze, *The Confessional Principle and the Confessions of the Lutheran Church* (St. Louis: 2005), 551.

39 Schmauk and Benze, *Confessional Principle*, 653; Robert Kolb and Timothy J. Wengert, eds., "Editors' Introduction to the Formula of Concord," in *The Book of Concord* (Minneapolis, 2000), 484.

40 Schmauk and Benze, *The Confessional Principle*, 653; Kolb and Wengert, eds., "Editors' Introduction," 484.

41 Schmauk and Benze, *Confessional Principle*, 654; Kolb and Wengert, eds., "Editors' Introduction," 484.

42 As Luther himself noted, "The proper subject of theology is man guilty of sin and condemned, and God the Justifier and Savior of man the sinner. Whatever is asked or discussed in theology outside this subject is error and poison." *LW* 12, 311.

43 *FC*, 467.

44 Ibid., 470.

45 Ibid., 471.

46 Ibid., 473.

47 Ibid., 474.

48 Ibid., 477–478.

49 Ibid., 478.

50 Ibid., 479.

51 Ibid., 479–480.

52 Ibid.

53 Ibid.

54 Ibid., 482.

55 Ibid.

56 Bodo Nischan displayed the manner in which this understanding permeated even the lower social classes as the disputes over the "Fractio Panis" split Lutheran and Calvinist Germans. The Calvinistic practice of breaking the bread before the celebration of the Eucharist was seen as an offense to the Lutheran Christians who believed it to be an affront to the understanding of the real presence. Bodo Nischan, "The 'Fractio Panis': A Reformed Communion Practice in Late Reformation Germany," *Church History* 53 (1984): 17–29.

57 *FC*, 487.

58 Ibid., 492.

59 Bente, *Historical Introductions*, 110.

60 *FC*, 494.

61 Ibid.

62 Ibid., 498.

63 Ibid., 499.

64 Ibid., 500.

65 "Sollte man nicht eifern wider die Bosheit, die nun so gross ist, dass sie in den Himmel steiget und schreiet, . . . Niemand will den Abgrund aller

Bosheit, die Erbsünde recht erkennen lernen." Letter to Wolfgang Frantzius, March 29, 1620, *Fr. Arndt*, 159. The full text of this letter can be
found in appendix C.

66 Ibid.

67 Ibid.

68 Ibid.

69 *FC*, 533.

70 "So habe ich auch wider den volkommenen Gehorsam des Gesetzes,
davon auch heutzutage einige Schwärmer träumen, hin und wieder,
in Ansehung des verlorenen Ebenbildes Gottes, und der aufs äusserste
verderbten menschlichen Natur, deutlich und mit allen Fleiss geredet."
Letter to Balthasar Mentzer, October 23, 1620, *WC*, 27. The full text of
this letter can be found in appendix C.

71 "In Erkenntnis der Sünde, sonderlich der Erbsünde, als einer abscheulichen, sehr tiefen und gänzlichen Verderbung der menschlichen Natur,
und aller deren Kräfte, ohne welcher genaue Erkenntnis keine wahre
Busse oder Bekehrung, auch keine Besserung der so gar sehr verderbten
Begierden des Herzens entspringen, noch des Bild Gottes jemalen neu
aufgerichtet werden kann." Ibid.

72 "Die entsetzliche Bosheit dieser unserer verderbten Zeit . . . die angeborene Verderbnis des Herzens." Letter to Petrus Piscator, January 14,
1607, *WC*, 27. The full text of this letter can be found in appendix C.

73 "Dass man den Manschen in sich kehre, den Abgrund seines Elendes zu
erkennen, darnach ihn zu Jesu Christo, dem Gnaden-Schatze hin weise."
Letter to Johann Gerhard, June 10, 1608, *Rambach*, 608. The full text of
this letter can be found in appendix C.

74 Letter to Johann Gerhard, February 19, 1607, *Rambach*, 605. The full text
of this letter can be found in appendix C.

75 "Da ich doch denen menschlichen Kräften alles benehme, und denenselben nichts, weder vor, noch in und nach der Bekehrung, sondern alles
ganz und gar, lediglich der göttlichen Erbarmung und Gnade in Christo
Jesu zuschreibe." Ibid.

76 Letter to Johann Gerhard, August 3, 1607, *Rambach*, 605–606. The full
text of this letter can be found in appendix C.

77 "So konnen dennoch meine Collegen nicht ruhen, sondern wollen
mit Gewalt aus einem eintzigen Wort einen Irrthum erzwingen . . .
welches also lautet: Wie der Verwundete mit ihm handeln liesse, wie
es seinem Arzt dem Samaritter gefällt, das soll Synergia heissen." Ibid.,
606.

78 "Weil der natürliche Mensch nicht nur nicht leidet, sondern widerstrebet,
welches ich leichtlich zugebe, weil unser natürlicher Wille von Gott abgekehret und feindlich." Ibid.

79 "Und schreibe alles der göttlichen Gnade in Christo Jesu zu, gleichwie die folgende Worte und der ganze Context bezeugen." Ibid.

80 Letter to Johann Gerhard, June 10, 1608, *Rambach*, 608.

81 "Dannenhero ich nicht etwa geschreiben habe den noch unbekehrten heyden, die die Salbung des Geistes nicht empfangenhaben, und daher auch keine besondere Regung des Heil. Geistes empfinden: sondern den Schriften, bey welchen die Bekehrung ihren täglichenWachsthum und Stuffen machen und haben muss, als womit das Braut-Bette und der Busen des Herzens dem Seelen-Bräutigam Christo, durch den Heil. Geist und die tägliche Ubungen der Gottseligkeit und Busse je mehr und mehr eröffnet, und der innere Mensch zu Erlangung desto grössern Lichtes und der Geistes Gaben von Tage zu Tage erneuert wird." Ibid., 606.

82 "Habe ich aus dem Texte meine Buchs über zwanzig Örter aufgezeichnet, welche meine Meinung eröffnen und wieder die Synergie Streiten." Letter to Petrus Piscator, January 14, 1607, *WC*, 27.

83 "Die Redensarten meines Buches, die anstössig scheinen möchten, erkläre ich nach meines Herzens aufrichtiger Meinung, und hoffe nicht, dass man aus einer blossen Redensart wider den Sinn den ganzen Buches einen Irrtum erzwingen könne. Ich erbiete mich dasjenige, was nicht bedachtsam genug geredet ist, nach Ew. Ehrw. Gutbefinden in der künftigen Auflage des Buches zu verbessern." Ibid.

84 "In einigen von den ersten Kapiteln des anderen Buches, davon ich den Anfang überschicke, sonderlich im 6. Kapitel vernichte ich gänzlich die menschlichen Kräfte in der Bekehrung, und zwar so deutlich, dass ich den menschlichen Kräften an und für sich selbst weder vor, noch und in nach der Bekehrung das Geringste zuschreibe." Ibid.

85 "Denn ich weiss und lehre, dass die Gnade Gottes alles in uns zur Seligkeit werke und tue, nach dem Zeugnis der apostolischen Worte: Nicht ich, sondern die Gnade Gottes in mir." Ibid.

86 Letter to Duke August, April 20, 1621, *Fr. Arndt*, 180–183. The full text of this letter can be found in appendix C.

87 "Ich lobe ihn wegen seiner Sorgfältigkeit, denn er sich besorget, es möchten die Leute oder die Leser dadurch von unserer wahren Gerechtgkeit des Glaubens und vom Worte Gottes abgeführt werden auf sonderliche ungewisse Offenbarungen, unterscheidet auch gar artig am Ende die Gerechtigkeit von den Werken, welches alles an seinem Ort recht und christlich ist." Ibid., 180.

88 Ibid.

89 "Hoc totius fidei systema . . . qui hos fidei effectus, imo vim fidei ac rem fidei, nempe applicationem, imputationem, apprehesionem, remissionem peccatorum etc. neglexut, et in inhabitatione essentialis justitiae Christi justitiam nostram collocavit, non in applicatione meriti Christi, quod est

proprium fidei et summa nostra consolatio." Letter to Gerhard Colemannus, 1612, *Fr. Arndt*, 74.

90 "Nonne Christus fit totus noster per fidem?" Ibid.

91 "Fidei igitur substantium, qua de imprimis quaeris, sic intellige; arbitror
a theologis plerisque (excepto unico Luthero) frigidiuscule de fide justifi-
cante disputatum." Ibid.

92 "Scriptura enim loquitur de spiritu fidei . . . additque multos praeclaros
fidei effectus. Considera: an haec fides nuda sit qualitas?" Ibid.

93 "Ponendam igitur arborem bonam, expectandos postea fructus." Ibid.

94 Letter to Peter Piscator, March 21, 1607, *Rambach*, 605. The full text of
this letter can be found in appendix C.

95 "Weil aber der Tod Jesu Christi, soferne er den Zorn Gottes und die Sünden anzeiget, selbst eine Gesetzpredigt ist, welche dergleichen Zerknirschung oder Traurigkeit wirket, so wird vorgedachte Redensart billig
verworfen." Ibid.

96 "Da aber hiedurch der Unterschied unter Gesetz und Evangelium
scheinen verdunkelt zu werden, so mag vielmehr die Reue ganz allein ein
Werk des Gesetzes bleiben." Ibid.

97 *FC*, 480.

98 *FC*, 474.

99 "Denn so wir wissen, dass Christus sey unsere Gerechtigkeit, Weissheit, und Erlösung 1. Cor. 1, 30 so müssen ja die Ubungen des wahren
Glaubens nothwendig bewerckstelliget werden." Letter to Duke August,
January 29, 1621, *Rambach*, 616. The full text of this letter can be found in
appendix C.

100 "Derowegen dieses nicht die Absicht meiner Bücher ist . . . dass ich, nach
Art der Münche, Christum nur als ein Exempel wolte vorgestellet haben."
Ibid.

101 "Einen Weg zeigen, wie auch die Wiedergeborenen nach der Bekehrung
durch den Geist Gottes die angeborene Verderbnis des Herzens bändigen
und zähmen könnten." Letter to Petrus Piscator, January 14, 1607, *Rambach*, 605.

102 "Nicht ich, sondern die Gnade Gottes in mir." Ibid.

103 "Oder meinen sie, dass Christus zur rechten hand Gottes sein Reich nicht
mehr auf Erden habe in den Herzen der Gläubigen?" Letter to Wolfgang
Frantzius, March 29, 1620, *Fr. Arndt*, 159.

104 "Gewisslich sind dergleichen Irrtümmer nicht geringt, nämlich von der
Heiligen Schrift von der Person Christi, von den beiden Sakramenten
und von dem evangelischen Predigtamt, welche ingesamt teils in der
augsburgischen Konfession, teils in der Konkordienformel, nachdem die
reine Lehre auf festen Fuss gesetzt, öffentlich verdammet und verworfen
worden." Letter to Balthasar Mentzer, October 23, 1620, *WC*, 40.

105 "Die reine Lehre von der Person Christi habe ich nach der Richtschnur der Konkordienformel gar nicht schläfrig verteidigt." Ibid.

106 "Dass die Rechtgläubigen Väter vor dreyzehen hundert Jahren den Exorcissmum zur heil. Tauffe geordnet, und dadurch eine allgemeine Ceremonie der ganzen rechtgläubigen Kirche worden, welche sie auch nach dem Sinn und wahren Verstande der Schrifft genommen; auch mit nichten eine sündliche Ceremonie ist." Letter to Duke Georg, September 10, 1590, *Rambach*, 599. The full text of this letter can be found in appendix C.

107 "Von welchen Graden oder Stuffen der Bekehrung und Erneurung die liebens-würdige Disputation E. E. de Praedestinatione, das ist von der Gnaden-Wahl, aus unserm Chemnitio sehr nett und mitt allem Fleiss handelt." Letter to Gerhard, June 10, 1608, *Rambach*, 607.

108 "Besser, als dass man unschuldige Leute und Buss-Prediger mit secterischen, ketzerischen Namen Befleckte, und um sich wirft mit Enthusiasten, Weigelianern, Osiandristen, Schwenkfeldisten, Papisten." Letter to Wolfgang Frantzius, October 29, 1620, *Fr. Arndt*, 159.

Chapter 3: The Eclectic Arndt

1 E. R. Fischer, *The Life of Johann Gerhard*, trans. Richard J. Dinda and Elmer Hohle (Malone, 2000), 426.

2 This idea of Arndt as uneducated was also suggested by Lucas Osiander and Georg Rostius (see chapter 1) and in the twentieth century by Wilhelm Koepp, *Johann Arndt eine Untersuchung ueber die Mystik im Luthertum* (Berlin, 1912), and John Drickamer, "Johann Arndt and True Christianity," *Concordia Journal* 8 (1982): 98–104.

3 The best study on Arndt's student years is Hans Schneider, "Johann Arndt's Studienzeit," in Hans Schneider, *Der Fremde Arndt: Studien zu Leben, Werk und Wirkung Johann Arndts (1555–1621)* (Göttingen, 2006), 83–129.

4 Letter to Johann Gerhard, March 15, 1603, *Rambach*, 618. The full text of this letter can be found in appendix C.

5 Letter to Gerhard, March 15, 1603, *Rambach*, 618. Some collections have dated this letter from 1605. The 1603 dating seems more likely due to the fact that by 1605, Gerhard would have been nearing the end of his studies. Arndt wrote this letter to advise Gerhard on the books he would need to begin his study of theology.

6 Gerhard had recently switched from the study of medicine to theology.

7 Habermann was a Lutheran and taught at Wittenberg, while Pagninus was a Catholic and editor of the Vulgate. Arndt does not show a preference for either one; he simply recommends that Gerhard select one of them.

8 Alice Philena Hubbard, "The Bible of Vatable," *Journal of Biblical Literature* 66 (1947): 197.

9 Ibid., 198.

10 Ibid., 200.

11 ADB 1, 699.

12 Phillip Schaff, *History of the Christian Church VIII: Modern Christianity. The Swiss Reformation* (Grand Rapids, 1988), 144.

13 Josef Eskhult, "Latin Bible Versions in the Age of Reformation and Post Reformation: On the Development of New Latin Versions of the Old Testament in Hebrew and on the Vulgate as Revised and Evaluated among the Protestants," in Anders Jarlert, ed., *Kyrkohistorick Aarsskrift 2006* (Lund, 2006), 44.

14 Letter to Johann Gerhard, March 15, 1603, *Rambach*, 618.

15 "Disputationes Theologicus minime disvadeo." Ibid.

16 Letter to Johann Gerhard, January 10, 1605, *Raidel*, 39.

17 Ibid., 39.

18 Ibid.

19 Ibid., n. (b).

20 Steven Ozment, *Mysticism and Dissent: Religious Ideology and Social Protest in the Sixteenth Century* (New Haven, 1973), 14–60.

21 Johann Arndt, *Vier Alte und Geistreiche Büchlein: Das Erste: Die Deutsche Theologia. Ein edles Büchlein Vom rechten Verstande, Das Ander: Die Nachfolgung Christi. Wie man alle Eytelkeit dieser Welt verschmehen soll. Durch D. Thomam a Kempis beschrieben. Das Dritte: Von Trost und Hülff in Trübsalen, Das Vierdte: Von Zuberaitung deß Todts* (Linz, 1621).

22 Bengt Haaglund, ed., *The Theologia Germanica of Martin Luther* (New York, 1980), 43. The full title was *Die Deutsche Theologia, Das ist Wie Adam in uns sterben und Christus in uns leben sol.*

23 Ozment, *Mysticism*, 25.

24 Ibid.

25 Ibid., 28.

26 Ibid., 32.

27 Sebastian Franck, *Paradoxa CCLXXX. Das ist: Zwey hundert und achtzig Wunder-Reden Aus der Heiligen Schrifft: So vor allem Fleisch unglaublich und unwahr seynd doch wider der gantzen Welt Wahn . . . wahr: Jtem Aller . . . Christen recht Göttliche Philosophia, und Teutsche Theologia . . . ausgeführt und an Tag gegeben Durch Sebastian Francken von Wörd* (S. I., 1690).

28 Sebastian Castellio, *Theologia Germanica: Ex Germanico Translatus Joanne Theophilo Vero Nomine Sebastiano Castellione Interprete* (Leipzig, 1630).

29 On Castellio's thought and a brief context to Castellio's translation of the *Theologica*, see Hans R. Guggisberg, *Sebastian Castellio, 1515–1563:*

Humanist Defender of Religious Toleration in a Confessional Age, trans. Bruce Gordon (Aldershot, 2002).

30 Haaglund, *Theologia Germanica*, 25.

31 Georg Baring, "Valentin Weigel und die Deutsche Theologie," *Archiv für Reformationsgeschichte* 55 (1964): 5.

32 Ibid., 10.

33 Ozment, *Mysticism*, 48.

34 Hans Denck, *Die teutsche Theologia. Das ist Ein edles buechlein vom rechten verstande was Adam vnd Christus sey und wie Adam in uns sterben und Christus in uns leb* (Halberstadt, 1597).

35 "Liegen viel im Staube verborgen, wie Joseph im Kerker." *WC*, 824.

36 "Ob dir nun das Buechlein dunkel und unverstaendlich wird vorkommen, wird dir's doch das andere erklaeren. Wirst auch in meinem Buechlein vom wahren Christentum und Paradeisgaertlein hierueber gute und nuetzliche Auslegung finden." *WC*, 830.

37 "Der turm zu Babel ist eine gewaltige Vorbildung ins Neue Testament und bedeutet den geistlichen Stand . . . also will ein jeder Geistloser mit seinen Buechern jetzo einen Turm in den Himmel Bauen . . . von Buechern und vielen Disputationen erbauet." Ibid., 824.

38 Ibid., 820.

39 "Dass wir auserserhalb der heiligen Bibel wenig Buecher beduerften." Ibid., 820–821.

40 "Die einige Wahrheit ist Christus selbst, und Er selbst ist auch der einige Weg dazu . . . wir beduerften nicht viel Buecher und Wegweiser." Ibid., 821.

41 "Derowegen ein grosser Fehler ist, dass man sich bemuehet, die reine Lehre allein mit Schreiben und Disputieren in den Schulen und Kirchen zu erhalten und des christliche Lebens vergisset." Ibid., 818.

42 "Was ist es nun, dass man so heftig streitet fuer Christi Lehre und vergisset seines Lebens . . . Aber man muss es gleichwohl nicht allein auf Buecherschreiben setzen, sonder es muss auch das Volk zu wahrer Busse getrieben werden [und] Leben Christi an sich nehmen." Ibid., 819–820.

43 "Du wirst in diesem Buechlein nicht viel Gezank, unnuetzes Geschrei, unartige Begierden oder stachlichte Reden finden, sondern lauter reine Liebe, Verlangen nach dem hoechsten ewigen Gut, Absagen und Verschmaehung der eiteln Welt . . . die Kreuzigung [deines] Fleisches, die Gleichformigkeit mit Christo." Ibid., 826–827.

44 "Sehet das Exempel der Korninther an: da sie nicht mehr folgten dem demuetigen Leben Christi und seinen Fusstapfen . . . wenn ich mit Engel- und Menschenzungen redete, und haette . . . alle Erkenntnis . . . und hatte der Liebe nicht, so waere ich nichts, und waere mir alles nichts nuetze." Ibid., 822.

45 "Dies Bleiben in der Rede Christi ist nicht allein von der Lehre zu verstehen, sondern vornehmlich vom Leben." Ibid., 823.

46 "Mit denselben decken sich viel falsche Christen, die viel Worte und Sakramenten gebraucht haben, aber nicht um ein Haerlein besser worden sind. Darum muss man notwendig auch das dritte Kennzeichen hinzu tun, naemlich die Liebe." Ibid., 819.

47 Eric Lund, *Johann Arndt and the Development of a Lutheran Spiritual Tradition* (unpublished PhD dissertation, Yale University, 1979), 9.

48 Commenting on the age of Lutheran orthodoxy, Robert Preus wrote, "There is nothing in evangelical orthodoxy that is withdrawn from practical church life or inimical to piety, nothing in the theology of the day that ignores the importance of the Christian life and piety . . . Christian piety was to be formed and incited by theology." Robert Preus, *The Theology of the Post-Reformation Lutheranism* 1 (St. Louis, 1970), 29.

49 Albrecht Ritschl, *Geschichte des Pietismus* (Bonn, 1880), and F. Ernst Stoeffler, *The Rise of Evangelical Pietism* (Leiden, 1965) are two examples of works that see the period between Luther's death and Spener's *Pia Desideria* as a time of inflexible, dry orthodoxy, with Arndt among the very few spiritually sensitive authors. Andrew Drummond's survey of German history sums up a general consensus: "The reader who explores for the first time the terra incognita of German Protestantism since Luther must be prepared for initial disappointment. He starts with a vision of the world regenerated by the glorious Gospel. Presently, however, he finds himself wandering in an arid theological wilderness, his nostrils assailed by the acrid smoke of harsh polemics; no unifying pillar of fire directs his steps with radiant glow; discordant guides speaking unintelligible jargon compete in offering their services." Andrew Drummond, *German Protestantism since Luther* (London, 1951), 1.

50 "Orthodoxy is difficult to define. To its enemies, such as Arndt, it was seen as dry, polemical, intolerant defence of a single denomination's positions, lacking any concern with issues relevant to religious life or the practice of Christian virtue or devotion." Peter Erb "Introduction," in Johann Arndt, *True Christianity*, trans. Peter Erb (New York, 1979), 3–4.

51 "Arndt's critique is . . . not against Lutheran Orthodoxy as such which proves to be much more alert to affective theology than the usual designation tends to suggest." Heiko Oberman, "Preface," in Johann Arndt, *True Christianity*, trans. Peter Erb (New York, 1979), xi.

52 "Non ex spiritu, sed ex carne scribunt." Letter to Gerhard, March 15, 1603, *Rambach*, 618.

53 "Discrimen esse inter ornamenta et corpus ipsum." Letter to Johann Gerhard, January 10, 1605, *Raidel*, 63.

54 "Optarium etiam, te studiam Theologicum." Ibid., 40.

55 "Quae circa interioris hominis culturam, et *paliggenesian* versetur." Ibid., 39.

56 Ibid.

57 Letters to Johann Gerhard, June 20, 1606, *Rambach*, and to Petrus Piscator, January 14, 1607, *WC*, 26–29.

58 Letter to Johann Gerhard, November 27, 1606, *Raidel*, 61–65.

59 "In futura enim iterata editione, per Dei gratiam, quid vel limitius, vel emandatius, aut rectius sit exprimendum videboe." Ibid., 63.

60 Ibid.

61 "Non enim in verbis, sed in operibus." Ibid., 63–64.

62 Ibid., 64.

63 "Weil der natürliche Mensch nicht nur nicht leidet, sondern widerstrebet." Letter to Johann Gerhard, August 3, 1607, *Rambach*, 606. This claim, that Arndt believed his writings only useful to the converted, is echoed in the preface to the first book of *True Christianity*. As a side note, this is one additional point of divergence from the Pietist movement and Arndt. The Pietist's missionary zeal is absent in all of Arndt's work.

64 "Allein hiervon handle ich nicht, sondern zeige nur die Art und Weise, die Praxin und den Process oder Lauff der Bekehrung, und schreibe alles der göttlichen Gnade in Christo Jesu zu." Ibid.

65 Letter to Duke August, April 20, 1621, *Fr. Arndt*, 180–183. The full text of this letter can be found in appendix C.

66 "Leben und Wirken Johann Arnds." *WC*, 42.

67 "Eine Offenbarung des Reich Gottes in uns, und ein Zerstörung des Reichs des Teufels." Letter to Duke August, April 20, 1621, *Fr. Arndt*, 182.

68 "Will die Exemplare der Reformation unter unsere evangelischen Confession confirmiren." Ibid., 180.

69 "Es ist eine hohe Gabe Gottes, und eine Frucht und Zeugnis der Gerechtigkeit und Gnade Gottes" and "ein Herz so Christum zum Grunde gelegt hat, wird im Taulero ein solches Licht der Besserung, der Andacht, der Heiligkeit, der Frömmigkeit, der Gottseligkeit, der Furcht Gottes, der geistlichen Weisheit finden, dass er's fruchtbarlich zur köstlichen Seelenarznei wird zu geniessen haben." Ibid., 182–183.

70 "Durch Selbstverläugnung und Selbstentsagung näher und so Gott in sich selbst zu empfinden." Letter to Duke August, January 29, 1621, *Rambach*, 617. The full text of this letter can be found in appendix C.

71 Ibid., 617.

72 Ibid.

73 Letter to Duke August, January 28, 1621, *Fr. Arndt*, 177.

74 "Das wahre erkenntnis Christ schaffe auch sofort eine Nachfolgi Christi." Ibid.

75 Jill Bepler, "Vicissitudo Temporum: Some Sidelights on Book Collecting in the Thirty Years' War," *Sixteenth Century Journal* 32 (2001): 953. Other variations are included in *Rambach*.

76 R. W. Scribner, "Incombustible Luther: the Image of the Reformer in Early Modern Germany," *Past and Present* 110 (1986): 38–68.

77 Lund, *Johann Arndt*, 243.

78 Johannes Wallmann, "Johann Arndt," in Carter Lindberg, ed., *The Pietist Theologians* (Oxford, 2005), 21.

79 Ibid., 22.

80 Hilding Pleijel, "Die Bedeutung Johann Arndts fuer das schwedische Froemmigkeitsleben," in Heinrich Bornkamm, Fredrich Heyer, and Alfred Schindler, eds., *Der Pietismus in Gestalten und Wirkungen, Martin Schmidt zum 65. Geburtstag* (Bielefeld, 1975), 388–399.

81 Beginning with Ritschl and his *Geschichte des Pietismus*, with virtually every work on Arndt in the twentieth century citing Arndt in relationship to Pietism.

82 Richard van Dülmen, *Die Utopie einer christlichen Gesellschaft: Johann Valentin Andreae* (Stuttgart, 1978), 118.

83 John Warwick Montgomery, *Cross and Crucible: Johann Valentin Andreae* (1586–1654), *Phoenix of the Theologians* (The Hague, 1973), 29.

84 Ibid., 53.

85 Johann Valentin Andreae, *Christianopolis*, trans. Emil Held (New York, 1916) 131.

86 Van Dülmen, *Die Utopie*, 119.

87 Ibid.

88 Ibid., 120.

89 Letter to Herzog August d. J, November 6, 1650, quoted in Montgomery, *Cross and Crucible*, 130.

90 Johann Valentin Andreae, *Selbstbiographie Joh. Valentin Andreä's* (Winterthur, 1799), 277.

91 Van Dülmen, *Die Utopie*, 118.

92 A full list of authors is provided in Montgomery, *Cross and Crucible*, 92–96.

93 Representing the polar opposite opinions of Andreae are Frances A. Yates, *The Rosicrucian Enlightenment* (London, 1972), and Montgomery, *Cross and Crucible*.

94 See Donald Dickson, "Johann Valentin Andreae's Utopian Brotherhoods," *Renaissance Quarterly* 49 (1996): 760–802.

Chapter 4: Johann Arndt and the Prophetic Voice

1 Two of the more recent monographs dealing with Luther's self-estimation are Heiko Oberman, *Martin Luther: Man between God and the Devil* (New Haven, 1989), esp. chapter 6, and Richard Marius, *Martin Luther: Man between God and Death* (London, 1999). A cursory look at the books

and articles reveals a strong tendency to refer to Luther as a prophet. Yet in none of these works is there any explanation or attempted designations of what the prophetic office entailed in the sixteenth century. A prime example of this is James Atkinson, *Martin Luther: Prophet to the Church Catholic* (Exeter, 1983), in which no reference to what constitutes the office of the prophet is made.

2 Robert Kolb, *Martin Luther as Prophet, Teacher, and Hero* (Grand Rapids, 1999). Kolb's work references Luther's prophetic persona in reference to his nationalistic themes and the weight of his voice, yet no specific criterion is established. The value of the book lies in its documenting the transition in the late Reformation period from Luther's particular thought to that of the accepted confessions.

3 Norman Cohn, *The Pursuit of the Millennium* (London, 1970). This work laid the groundwork for the spate of works documenting the radical and revolutionary tendencies in prophetic eschatology. Robin Bruce Barnes, *Prophecy and Gnosis: Apocalypticism in the Wake of the Lutheran Reformation* (Stanford, 1988), represents the most modern and most convincing (if sometimes narrow) approach to the dominant prophetic and eschatological schemas of the sixteenth century.

4 Franz Lau, "Die prophetische Apokalyptik Thomas Müntzers und Luthers Absage an die Bauernrevolution," in Abraham Friesen and Hans-Jürgen Goertz, eds., *Thomas Müntzer* (Darmstadt, 1978), 3–15.

5 Bertrand Taithe and Tim Thornton, "Bibliographical Essay," in Bertrand Taithe and Tim Thornton, eds., *Prophecy: the Power of Inspired Language in History: 1300–2000* (Gloucestershire, 1997), 202–206.

6 Hans-Christoph Rublack, "Der wohlgeplagte Priester: Vom Selbstverständnis lutherischer Geistlichkeit im Zeitalter der Orthodoxie," *Zeitschrift für Historische Forschung* 16 (1989): 1–30. This work, and a number of others like it, deal with Gerald Strauss's "failed Reformation" thesis. The theme of the beleaguered pastor is established to present evidence that the pastoral and visitation records are flawed historical documents insofar as they represent the pessimistic opinions of a position that necessarily sees itself in a prophetic position. Unfortunately, the scope and definition of the prophetic position is not examined.

7 Luther, and more clearly the Lutheran confessions, refer to the prophet and prophesy as teaching and preaching. There is a similar example in Switzerland, where prophecy was established and linked to the established preaching hours. See Bruce Gordon, *The Swiss Reformation* (Manchester, 2002), 232–239.

8 "First of all, since they bear witness of themselves, one need not immediately accept them; according to John's counsel, the spirits are to be tested." *LW* 2, 366.

9 Ibid.

10 Ibid.

11 Ibid.

12 *LW* 26, 17.

13 Ibid.

14 As could be expected with Luther, there are seemingly dissonant passages regarding his own sense of his prophetic role. Perhaps most famous was his writing on the Monchkalb at Freiburg. In being challenged by Müntzer to interpret the significance of the monstrous birth, Luther denies any prophetic knowledge. Luther's own denial of interpretive prophetic knowledge seems, however, to do little damage to the positing of Luther's prophetic role. Later on in his career, Luther comfortably interpreted signs and portents. Second, with a broadened definition of what makes a prophet, failure to interpret signs would not disqualify one.

15 Abraham Friesen, *Thomas Müntzer, a Destroyer of the Godless; the Making of a Sixteenth-Century Revolutionary* (Los Angeles, 1990), 126, 127.

16 Thomas Müntzer, *The Collected Works of Thomas Müntzer*, ed. and trans. Peter Matheson (Edinburgh, 1988), 324.

17 Ibid., 329.

18 "All I have done to the wily black crow released by Noah from the ark is this: like an innocent dove I have flapped my wings" . . . "It serves you right, you Esau, that Jacob has pushed you aside." Ibid., 333, 346.

19 "Although Goliath would put his trust in his armour and his shield, David would teach him a lesson. Saul too, began by doing some good, but it was David, who after lengthy wanderings, had to bring it to fruition." Ibid., 349.

20 Ibid., 333.

21 Ibid., 336.

22 Ibid., 344.

23 Ibid.

24 Barnes, *Prophecy and Gnosis*, 13.

25 Ibid., 14.

26 Johann Gerhard, *Loci Theologici* 6, ed. Eduard Preuss (Berlin, 1869); quoted in Scott Murray, "What Did It Mean to Be Lutheran among the Orthodox Lutheran Fathers?," in John A. Maxfield, ed., *The Pieper Lectures Volume 4: What Does It Mean to Be Lutheran?* (St. Louis, 2000).

27 *AC* V.

28 *AC* V.

29 *AC* XIV.

30 Gerhard, *Loci*, in Murray, "What Did It Mean," 33.

31 Ibid., 37.

32 Ibid., 34.

33 It is almost certain that this ideal would not be always upheld. Barnes's work has established how many orthodox Lutherans preached a prophetic apocalypticism that was foreign to the confessions. Similarly, Jürgen Beyer, "A Lübeck Prophet in Local and Lutheran Context," in Bob Scribner and Trevor Johnson, eds., *Popular Religion in Germany and Central Europe* (London, 1996), 166–182 has established prophetic practice among the laity that went beyond what was established in the confessions. However, for establishing that Arndt attempted to submit to confessional ideals the actual practice is less relevant.

34 Heiko Oberman, "Preface," in Johann Arndt, *True Christianity*, trans. Peter C. Erb (New York, 1979), xvi.

35 The major difficulty in dealing with Weigel is the scarce availability of his works. While a modern critical edition of his works and correspondence is being undertaken, the two most recent and thorough examinations have been that of Andrew Weeks, *Valentin Weigel (1533–1588): German Religious Dissenter, Speculative Theorist, and Advocate of Tolerance* (Albany, 2000), and Steven Ozment, *Mysticism and Dissent* (New Haven, 1973), chapter 8.

36 Arndt was familiar with Weigel's works, and his knowledge of them became an issue, initially, in the Danzig controversy of 1618. Arndt would acknowledge his reading of Weigel, and later critical studies of *True Christianity* would show Arndt's dependence on Weigel in chapter 34.

37 Ozment, *Mysticism*, 211.

38 Ibid., 224.

39 Ibid., 225.

40 Ibid., 230.

41 Letter to Petrus Piscator, January 14, 1607, *WC*, 28.

42 "Dass ich deswegen aus meinem Vaterlande, dem Fürstentum Anhalt, vertrieben worden, weil ich denen, so in Glaubenslehren mit uns streitig sind, nicht beipflichten konnte." Letter to Balthasar Mentzer, October 29, 1620, *WC*, 42.

43 "Mit Undancke lohnete, weil ich im Exilio, da ich aus dem Fürstenthum Anhalt von Calvinisten vertrieben." Letter to the Braunschweig Council, June 26, 1599, *Rambach*, 600.

44 "Harte Verfolgung und Verstossung aus meinem lieben Vaterland, dem Fürstenthum Anhalt." Letter to Statius Kahlen, November 1, 1608, *Rambach*, 608.

45 "Ach … sollte man nicht eifern wider die Bosheit, die nun so gross ist, dass sie in den Himmel steiget und schreiet, darauf entweder eine blutige und giftige Sündfluth, oder das Feuer zu Sodom, oder der Hunger zu Samaria und Jerusalem gehöret?" Letter to Wolfgang Frantzius, March 29, 1620, *Fr. Arndt*, 159.

46 "Dass sich die Welt wider solche eifrige Schriften heftig gesperret und aufgelehnt, sonderliche solche junge Leute, die nicht durch Gewohnheit haben geübte Sinnen zum Unterschiede des Guten und des Bösen, Erb. 5, 14. Weil ich aber . . . auch eine treu eifrige Absicht, nämlich der grossen beharrlichen Unbussfertigkeit und Gottlosigkeit der Welt durch solche meine Büchlein zu widersprechen." Ibid., 158.

47 "Die entsetzliche Bosheit dieser unserer verderbten Zeit" and "die angeborene Verderbnis des Herzens." Letter to Petrus Piscator, January 14, 1607, WC, 27.

48 "Die Welt wird gar zu heilloss." Letter to Johann Gerhard, August 3, 1607, Rambach, 606.

49 Postmillennialism, the belief that the world would eventually be converted and that peace would reign on earth before Christ's coming, was not a standard theological tenant until the later seventeenth century. Those who did see a better time coming in the sixteenth century generally believed that it would only be on account of Christ returning and abolishing all wickedness.

50 Letter to Balthasar Mentzer, October 29, 1620, WC, 40–42.

51 Bodo Nischan, "The Exorcism and Baptism Controversies in the Late Reformation," Sixteenth Century Journal 18 (1987): 50.

52 "Dass Gott sei in dem Wort und durch das Wort wirke." Ibid., 42.

53 "Und zwar durch das geoffenbarte Wort Gottes, durch Christi Verdienst und Exempel, durch die Wirkung des Heiligen Geistes, durch den vorleuchtenden Glauben und die Rechtfertigung." Ibid., 41.

54 "Dass ich von meiner Jugend an bis in das graue Alter . . . keinem einzigen Irrtum, der wider die augsburgische Konfession und die Konkordienformel laufen, oder dem Wort Gottes zugegen sein sollte, zugetan gewesen." Ibid., 42.

55 Letter to Wolfgang Frantzius, March 29, 1620, Fr. Arndt, 158–161.

56 ADB, 319.

57 Ibid.

58 "Habe ich in deutscher Sprache . . . antworten wollen, damit jedermann diese meine Entschuldigung lessen koenne." Letter to Wolfgang Frantzius, March 29, 1620, Fr. Arndt, 158.

59 "Die herrlichen Mittel . . . das Wort Gottes." Ibid.

60 "So habe ich viel solcher Ungewitter darüber ausgestanden und in grosser Geduld vorüber gehen lassen." Ibid., 160.

61 "Der alten Schlange dadurch auf den kopf getreten ist." Ibid.

62 Josef Eskhult, "Latin Bible Versions in the Age of Reformation and Post Reformation: On the development of new Latin versions of the Old Testament in Hebrew and on the Vulgate as revised and evaluated among the Protestants," in Anders Jarlert, ed., Kyrkohistorick Aarsskrift 2006 (Lund,

2006), 35. Eskhult writes that the Lutherans consistently edited the Vulgate that the Genesis account would read *semen* of the woman, which was believed to be a prophecy of Christ.

63 "Sind den die Propheten und Apostel Enthusiasten gewesn, da sie voll Gottes und voll Geistes worden sind . . . ?" Letter to Wolfgang Frantzius, March 29, 1620, *Fr. Arndt*, 158.

64 "Wo ist das zerbrochene herz? Wo sind die heissen Thränen? Wo ist das einsame Vögelein auf dem Dache, das da wachet und seufzet? Wo ist jemand, der wider den Riss stände, und sich zur Mauer machte wider den Zorn Gottes?" Ibid.

65 "Man wolle doch um Gottes willen die Prinzipien und Grundlehren meiner Büchlein vom wahren Christenthum, nämlich, den unergründlichen Sündenfall, das verlorne Bild Gottes, Busse und Glauben, die neue Creatur, das Leben Christi in den Gläubigen, den Streit des Fleisches und des Geistes, das zerbrochene Herz, die Nachfolge des Exempels Christi." Ibid., 161.

66 Letter to Petrus Piscator, January 14, 1607, *WC*, 26–29.

67 Piscator does not appear in either the *Neue Deutsche Biographie* or the *Allgemeine Duetsche Biographie*.

68 See Robert Preus, *The Theology of Post-Reformation Lutheranism* 1 (St. Louis, 1970), 53–56.

69 Piscator's small number of printed works include *Disputatio De aeterna Praedestinatione Salvandorum, sive Electione aeterna Filiorum Dei ad salutem* (Frankfurt, 1608), *Commentarius in Formulam Concordiae* (Gotha, 1610), and *Disputatio De Deo Uno in Essentia, et Trino in Personis* (Jena, 1610).

70 "Ich kann Luther zum Zeugen anführen, der anders redet, wenn er disputiert, anders, wenn er die Laster straft. Es stehen einige Örter in der Kirchenpostille von den guten Werken und von der Gnadenwahl, die er gebraucht, die Busse und Lebensbesserung einzuschärfen." Letter to Petrus Piscator, January 14, 1607, *WC*, 28.

71 "Und ich schreibe nicht sowohl denen, die noch stehen in dem Stande vor der Bekehrung, als denen, welche Christum schon durch den Glauben erkannt haben und doch hiednisch leben." Ibid., 28.

72 Letter to Johann Gerhard, August 3, 1607, *Rambach*, 606.

73 Edmund Weber, Johann Arndts Vier Bücher vom wahren Christentum als Beitrag zur protestantischen Irenik des 17. Jahrhunderts (Marburg, 1969), 102.

74 "Das ich alles, was ich geschrieben, nach unsern Symbolischen Glaubens-Büchern wolte verstanden wissen." Letter to Johann Gerhard, August 3, 1607, *Rambach*, 605.

75 "Will ich Friede haben, wann ich keinen andern Beruff bekomme, etwa an einem Ort hinbegeben, vielleicht nach Eisleben und ein Privatleben anfangen." Ibid., 605.

76 Ibid., 606.

77 "Habe seit ihr vor 2. Jahren bey mir gewesen, keinen guten Tag gehabt."
Ibid., 606.

78 "Zeige nur die Art und Weise, die Praxin und den Process oder Lauff der
Bekehrung, und schreibe alles der göttlichen Gnade in Christo Jesu zu."
Ibid., 606.

79 "Ich hätte es nimmer gemeinet, dass unter den Theologen so gifftige böse
Leute wären." Ibid., 606.

80 The most recent account of the Danzig controversy is found in Martin Brecht,
"Das Aufkommen der neuen Frömmigkeitsbewegung in Deutschland," in
Martin Brecht, ed., *Geschichte des Pietismus* 1 (Göttingen, 1993), 142–145.

81 The major work, Lucas Osiander's *Theologisches Bedencken*, set off a chain
of works alternately criticizing and defending Arndt. See chapter 1.

82 "Dass aber diese hohen Geister sich dawider aufblähen, muss ein böser
wind sein, der sie angewehet hat, und tröste mich damit, dass ich lauter
allein das wahre Christentum." Letter to Daniel Dilger, May 4, 1620, in
WC, 38.

83 "Der bleibe in seiner Blindheit." Ibid., 39.

84 "Ist mein Werk aus Menschen, so wird es nicht bestehen; ist es aber aus
Gott, so warden sie es nicht dämpfen konnen." Ibid., 37.

85 "Ich muss aber auch erfahren, was des Satans engel sei, der die mit Fäusten
schläget." Ibid., 39.

86 "Es stehet das Reich Gottes nicht in Worter, sondern in Kraft." Ibid., 38.

87 "Eine wirkliche, lebendige, kräftige Gabe und Erleuchtung." Ibid.

88 "Bewegung Herzens . . . das innerliche Zeugnis des Heiligen Geistes."
Ibid.

89 "Selbsterkenntnis und innerlichen Herzenbuße und Besserung." Ibid., 37.

90 Letters to Duke August, January 28, 1621, *Rambach*, 616, and January 29,
1621, *Rambach*, 616–618. The full text of the letter from January 29 can
be found in appendix C.

91 Daniel Cramer, *Apocalypsis, oder Offenbarung S. Johannis* (Stettin, 1619).

92 This has been put forth by Bodo Nischan in much of his work. See especially "Germany after 1550" in Andrew Pettegree, ed., *The Reformation
World* (London, 2000), 399.

93 "Zurück ziehen von der gar zu disputir- und streitsüchtigen Theologie,
daraus fast wieder eine Theologia Scholastica ist." Letter to Duke August,
January 29, 1621, *Rambach*, 616.

94 "Dass viele grosse Theologi weniger von Christo haben, als man vermeynet, dass sie haben." Ibid., 618.

95 "Man wird Christum eh ergreifen, wenn man ihm nachfolget," Ibid., 616.

96 "Und wird noch einmal die Zeit kommen, da man über die Akadamien in
deutschland klagen wird." Ibid., 616.

97 "Denn es bestehet ja das Wahre Christentum zwei Stücken: 1. in der Lehre Reinigkeit; 2. in des Lebens Heiligkeit." Ibid., 617.

98 Ibid.

99 Ibid., 616.

100 The biographical section on Arndt's move from Anhalt to Quedlinburg and his move to Braunschweig are based on Brecht, *Geschichte des Pietismus*, 132, and Eric Lund, *Johann Arndt and the Development of a Lutheran Spiritual Tradition* (unpublished PhD dissertation, Yale University, 1979), 99–106.

101 Johann Arndt, *Zehen Lehr-und Geistreiche Predigten: von den Zehen grausamen und schröcklichen Egyptischen Plagen* (Frankfurt am Main, 1657).

102 Lund, *Johann Arndt*, 100.

103 "Habe ich den Beruff . . . Diesem Gezeugen habe ich, Da ich . . . eine ehrliche Vocation gehabt." Letter to the ministerium at Quedlinburg, July 7, 1599, 600.

104 "Weiss mich der klage Gottes uber die falschen Propheten unschuldig." Ibid., 601.

105 "Und erfahre nun auch, was der Prophet Jeremias spricht: Herr! Ich weiss, dass Menschen thun stehet nicht in seinen Hand . . . Im 32 Psalm spricht der heilig Geist: Ich will dich unterweisen und dir den Weg zeigen." Ibid., 601.

106 "(Gott) beruffet zu seinen Amt und zu seinen Creuz." Ibid.

107 "Der Unehrlichen Schimpffung meines Namens . . . mit so grosser Schmach und Lästerung." Ibid.

108 Ibid.

109 Lund, *Johann Arndt*, 105.

110 "Das Sie aus liebe zur Wahrheit und zur Ehre des heiligen Predigt-Amtes." Letter to the ministerium at Quedlinburg, July 7, 1599, 602.

111 "Solcher Danck solte einem getreuen Lehrer nicht allein des Predigt-Amtes, sondern auch der Welt und seines Lebens müde machen." Letter to the Braunschweig Council, June 26, 1599, *Rambach*, 599.

112 Ibid.

113 Ibid.

114 "Mit Undancke lohnete, weil ich im Exilio, da ich aus dem Fürstenthum Anhalt von Calvinisten vertrieben." Ibid., 600.

115 Little is known of Statius Kahlen beyond his status as burgomaster. Kahlen is not referenced in either the *Allgemeine Deutsche Biographie* or the *Neue Deutsche Biographie*.

116 "Weil mir gestern zuwissen worden, welcher gestalt mein herr College mich hart verfolget wegen meiner Entschuldigung . . . mich für einen Schwarmer ausgeruffen." Letter to Statius Kahlen, November 1, 1605, *Rambach*, 602.

117 "Dass ich bey so viele hundert Leuten solte in solchen Verdacht kommen ... einen zum Ketzer machen." Ibid., 603.
118 Letter to Statius Kahlen, November 1, 1608, *Rambach*, 608–609.
119 "Mich folgends zu einen Pastoren derselben Kirchen nach Gottes willen zu bestellen." Ibid., 608.
120 "Dass mir niemals meine öffentlich harte Verfolgung und Verstossung aus meinem lieben Vaterland, dem Fürstenthum Anhalt, so wehe gethan als diese." Ibid., 608.
121 "Wenn mich nicht mein gut Gewissen und das exempel meines Herrn Jesu Christi, und seiner werthen Apostel geströset, so wäre ich des todes gewest." Ibid., 609.

Conclusion

1 Quoted in Carter Lindberg, "Introduction," in Carter Lindberg, ed., *The Pietist Theologians* (Oxford, 2002), 3.
2 Valentin Ernst Löscher, *The Complete Timotheus Verinus*, trans. James L. Langebartels (Milwaukee, 1998), 11, 12, 51, 52, 64.
3 Heinrich Schmid, *Die Geschichte des Pietismus* (Nördlingen, 1863), 3.
4 Albrecht Ritschl, *Geschichte des Pietismus* 2 (Bonn, 1880), 52.
5 Johannes Wallmann, "Die Anfange des Pietismus," in *Pietismus und Neuzeit* 4 (1977): 11–53.
6 Wilhelm Koepp, *Mystik im Luthertum* (Berlin, 1912), and Eric Lund, *Johann Arndt and the Development of a Lutheran Spiritual Tradition* (unpublished PhD Dissertation, Yale University, 1979).

Daniel van Voorhis earned a PhD in history from the University of St. Andrews, Scotland. He served as assistant dean in the School of Arts and Sciences at Concordia University, Irvine, where he was associate professor of history and assistant dean. His book *Monsters: Addiction, Hope, Ex-Girlfriends, and Other Dangerous Things* was released in 2017. Dan continues in his role as cohost of the *Virtue in the Wasteland* podcast and recently stepped away from the world of academia to pursue his vocation as a speaker and full time writer with the 1517 Legacy Project.